John Milton's Epic Invocations

Renaissance and Baroque Studies and Texts

Eckhard Bernstein
General Editor

Vol. 26

PETER LANG
New York • Washington, D.C./Baltimore • Boston • Bern
Frankfurt am Main • Berlin • Brussels • Vienna • Oxford

Philip Edward Phillips

John Milton's Epic Invocations

Converting the Muse

PETER LANG
New York • Washington, D.C./Baltimore • Boston • Bern
Frankfurt am Main • Berlin • Brussels • Vienna • Oxford

Library of Congress Cataloging-in-Publication Data

Phillips, Philip Edward.
John Milton's epic invocations: converting the muse / Philip Edward Phillips.
p. cm. — (Renaissance and Baroque: studies and texts; v. 26)
Includes bibliographical references and index.
1. Milton, John, 1608–1674—Religion. 2. Christianity and literature—England—History—17th century. 3. Christian poetry, English—History and criticism.
4. Epic poetry, English—History and criticism. 5. English poetry—Classical influences.
6. Muses (Greek deities) in literature. 7. Invocation in literature. 8. Paganism in literature.
I. Title. II. Series: Renaissance and Baroque: studies and texts; vol. 26.
PR3592.R4P47 821'.4—dc21 98-20805
ISBN 0-8204-4119-8
ISSN 0897-7836

Die Deutsche Bibliothek-CIP-Einheitsaufnahme

Phillips, Philip Edward:
John Milton's epic invocations: converting the muse / Philip Edward Phillips.
–New York; Washington, D.C./Baltimore; Boston; Bern;
Frankfurt am Main; Berlin; Brussels; Vienna; Oxford: Lang.
(Renaissance and baroque; Vol. 26)
ISBN 0-8204-4119-8

The paper in this book meets the guidelines for permanence and durability
of the Committee on Production Guidelines for Book Longevity
of the Council of Library Resources.

Printed in the United States of America

To my father—

At tibi, care pater, postquam non aequa merenti
Posse referre datur, nec dona rependere factis,
Sit memorasse satis, repetitaque munera grato
Percensere animo, fidaeque reponere menti.

Milton, *Ad patrem* (1637)

Table of Contents

Illustrations

Acknowledgments

It gives me great pleasure to thank those who have contributed so much to the successful completion of this book, which began as a doctoral dissertation at Vanderbilt University. Professor Laurence Lerner encouraged me to pursue my interest in poetic invocations to the Muse and to explore the problem of paganism for Christian poets of the Renaissance. Even after his retirement, Professor Lerner continued to offer his insightful and prompt criticism of my work by post from England. I am equally grateful to Professor Leonard Nathanson for his continued interest in my research and his watchful guidance in seeing this study to its completion. I also wish to thank Professor Margaret Anne Doody for offering valuable comments upon my manuscript and subsequently for encouraging me to pursue publication.

I have profited greatly from the generous advice of many readers. I am particularly indebted to Professor A. D. Nuttall, New College, Oxford, for commenting upon early versions of this work and sharing ideas on epic openings with me in conversation. Professor Nuttall's study on literary beginnings, *Openings: Narrative Beginnings from the Epic to the Novel* (1992), influenced my critical approach to examining epic invocations and continues to enhance my reading of Vergil, Dante, and Milton. Furthermore, I wish to thank the following readers for their advice and support: William H. Race, William Engel, John Plummer, and Noel Harold Kaylor, Jr. I also wish to thank Heidi Burns, Benjamin Hallman, and Jeff Galas at Peter Lang Publishers for their help and advice.

This study has been greatly enhanced by generous research grants from the Graduate School and the Department of English, Vanderbilt University, and from the Center for Renaissance Studies, Newberry Library, Chicago. A Dissertation Enhancement Grant from Vanderbilt (1996) allowed me to conduct research at the British and Bodleian Libraries as well as to consult with Professor Lerner in England. Two Center for Renaissance Studies Consortium Grants (1995 and 1996) enabled me to travel to Chicago to examine first-hand many of the sixteenth- and seventeenth-century works discussed in this study as well as to attend the Milton Seminar held in May of 1996. Some of my most productive hours were spent pouring over ancient texts in the Newberry, and I am grateful for the opportunity to read and work there.

I am very much obliged to many librarians, including those in the Bodleian Library, the British Library, the Jean and Alexander Heard Library, and the Newberry Library. I am thankful for the efficiency of the MS Students' Reading Room staff in the British Library, who provided me speedy access to the Egerton MS Collection. I am especially grateful to the Reading Room staff at the Newberry Library, particularly Margaret Kulis, Reference Librarian, Special Collections, and to Darlyne Pryds, Assistant Director of the Center for Renaissance Studies, for all their kind assistance. I am also grateful to the Photoduplication Department at the Newberry Library for permission to reproduce the first page of Abraham Cowley's *A Poem on the Late Civil War* (1697) and the frontispiece to John Milton's *Poems* (1645).

I am grateful to the organizers of the Conference on John Milton at Middle Tennessee State University for the opportunity in 1995 and 1997, respectively, to present my essays, "'The Inspired Gift of God': The Generic Genius of Milton's *Hymn to Holy Light*" and "From Clio to Urania: Epic Invocations in *The History of Britain*." The helpful comments that I received from conference participants enabled me to develop both papers into sections of my concluding chapter.

I am indebted to Kirsten Anderson, Larry Mapp, Matt Callihan, Larry Kamm, and Chris Flack for sharing their computer expertise with me and to Jonathan Rogers and Amanda Kinard for proofreading early versions of the manuscript. I am also grateful to Carolyn Levinson, Angie Saylor, Janis May, Lisa Callum, and Dori Mikus for seeing that early drafts of this work made their way to the appropriate readers.

My greatest debt, of course, belongs to those who have encouraged and sustained me throughout my life and academic career—my family and friends. I particularly wish to thank my father, Carl Phillips, for believing in me and supporting my aspirations, and my wife, Elaine Phillips, whose keen criticism of my work and whose love and support have enabled me to complete this project.

Philip Edward Phillips
Nashville, Tennessee
October 1999

Introduction

Quando vidi costui nel gran diserto,
   'Miserere di me' gridai a lui
   'qual che tu sii, od ombra od omo certo!'
Rispuosemi: 'Non omo, già fui,
   e li parenti miei furon lombardi,
   mantovani per patrïa ambedui.
Naqui *sub Julio*, ancor che fosse tardi,
   e vissi a Roma sotto 'l buono Augusto
   al tempo delli dei falsi e bugiardi.
Poeta fui, e cantai di quel giusto
   figliuol d'Anchise che venne da Troia,
   poi che 'l superbo Ilïòn fu combusto.
Ma tu, perchè ritorni a tanta noia?
   Perchè non sali il dilettoso monte
   ch' è principio e cagion di tutta gioia?'

(Dante, *Inferno* 1.64-78)[1]

Lost in the dark woods and nearly driven to despair by the frightening figure of the she-wolf, Dante's Pilgrim calls out to the dim, human shape in the distance for aid. Vergil,[2] who once sang of the Fall of Troy and the journeys of Aeneas, hears the Pilgrim's cry and responds to his distress. Acknowledged by the Pilgrim as the "fountain which pours forth so rich a stream of human speech," Vergil replies that he hymned the "false and lying" pagan gods, and for that he must dwell forever in Limbo. Although Vergil cannot earn himself a place in Paradise, he can nevertheless fulfill his divine mission—to lead the Pilgrim safely through Hell and Purgatory—and bring his charge within sight of the Heavenly light. Vergil becomes the Pilgrim's guide and Muse; what he himself could not attain he can provide to Dante, leading the Italian poet to the mountain which leads up to the source and principle of the Good.

This episode from the first canto of the *Inferno* illustrates several things significant to our discussion of epic invocations and the problem of invoking a pagan Muse to inspire Christian works. First, finding himself lost in the dark woods, the Pilgrim requires a guide—just as a poet needs the inspiration of the Muse—in order to find his way to regions beyond his ability to attain. Second, Vergil essentially becomes synonymous with the pagan Muse; indeed, as the "fountain" (*fonte*) of eloquent human speech whose "beautiful style" (*bello stilo*) had influenced and directed Dante's own career, Vergil was literally Dante's source of inspiration. However, having descended into the world of shades and having witnessed God's truth, Vergil, with clear vision, can now lead the Pilgrim on his journey. Finally, though Vergil's gods had been false, in the Middle Ages the Roman poet had been seen as a pre-Christian Christian by many, and his *Eclogue* IV, commonly called the *Messianic Eclogue*, had been interpreted as prophetic of the birth of Christ.[3] Dante likely did not subscribe to the view that Vergil understood the true meaning of his "prophetic" words but he nevertheless granted him an authority in his poem second only to that of the Scriptures, even referring to Vergil's words as divinely inspired.[4] Vergil, as Dante's guide through Hell and Purgatory, represents the natural light of Reason, which suffices Dante—with the assistance of Grace—until his arrival at the edge of Paradise; however, it is Beatrice, the representative of divine Wisdom, or *Sapientia*, who leads the Pilgrim to his final destination. Nevertheless, Dante employs Vergil as his Pilgrim's Muse in the *Commedia* to lead him from darkness to eternal light; although a pagan figure, Vergil serves as an agent of God capable of leading Dante toward divine knowledge.

Christian poets from Late Antiquity to the Renaissance repeatedly faced the difficulty of naming their Muse, especially when she was one of the classical nine Muses and not the Holy Spirit of God. English and French writers well into the seventeenth century continued to debate whether or not invoking the classical Muse was appropriate in an explicitly Christian poem. Despite this heated debate over the use of pagan conventions in divine poetry, the pagan gods remained strong throughout the Middle Ages and the Renaissance, even into the Enlightenment to some degree. According to Jean Seznec, the pagan gods survived during the Middle Ages by virtue of interpretations of their origin and nature propounded by antiquity itself. Indeed, the pagan gods and Muses were not "restored" in the Renaissance because they had never really disappeared from collective memory or imagination. Rather, through *syncretic* readings of ancient texts—reading the pagan gods allegorically as Christian types—the pagan gods were able to survive through the Middle Ages, preserved from oblivion and attacks from their enemies, and contribute significantly to the art and thought of the Renaissance.[5]

This persistent tradition of syncretism, however, became a contested issue for Christian poets of the sixteenth and seventeenth centuries. According to Laurence Lerner, the quarrel between the dominant "syncretist" tradition and the "Puritan" tradition—which rejected Christian readings of pagan figures—centered upon the issue of the Fall of Man:

> The quarrel goes back to the early Fathers, and was re-animated by the Reformation. Ultimately, it hinges on how seriously you take the Fall of Man. If man is depraved in all his faculties, as Calvin held; if the light of Nature was extinguished by the Fall, so that the wisdom of unredeemed man is devilish counsel at best, then the Christian must have no truck with the wisdom of antiquity. Pan is not the emblem of Christ, but his enemy.[6]

In the seventeenth century the battle lines between the pagan and Christian in religious literature became more clearly drawn, and in no other poet can we see the conflict so painfully enacted than in John Milton. Lerner reminds us that, while it is a commonplace for us to regard Milton as both a Puritan and a Humanist, "for him it was no commonplace but a long struggle between the deepest elements of his being" (164). The contradictions which resulted from Milton's struggle—such as reading Pan as Christ while rejecting the pagan gods, or calling simultaneously upon the Heav'nly Muse and the pagan goddess of astronomy for inspiration—as well as the great poetry that resulted, is the central concern of this study of invocations to the Muse.

Milton, however, was not the first to struggle with such issues, though his invocations in *Paradise Lost* are the most famous in the English tradition. The French poet Guillaume Du Bartas (1544–1590), in fact, had previously confronted this issue with a stern "Puritan" rejection, calling particular attention to the improper use of the Muses in his *La Semaine* and *L'Uranie*. Du Bartas's conversion of Urania to the Heavenly Muse exerted considerable influence upon poets from France and England. In Joshua Sylvester's translation of *Urania, Or, The Heavenly Muse*, Du Bartas the speaker at first meditates upon his "desire t'immortalize [his] Name," leading to a consideration of "my Countries Storie," "Th' un-worthy Prince," and "wanton *Venus*" as subjects for his Muse. However, in the fourteenth stanza Urania enters into the poem, and in her own voice identifies herself and reproves the poet's misguided ambitions to write of the earthly court:

> I am URANIA (then aloud, said shee)
> Who humane-kinde above the *Poles* transport,
> Teaching their hands to touch, and eyes to see
> All th' enter-course of the Celestiall Court.[7]

Urania tells her chosen poet that her inspiration will enable him to soar above the confines of this world, to tell of things greater than national themes, princes, and erotic love. Urania, whose seat is the "Celestiall Court," presents herself as the Heavenly Muse, superior to her classical, and pagan, sisters (stanzas 16-17):

> I grant, My learned Sister warble fine,
> And ravish millions with their *Madrigals*:
> Yet all, no lesse inferiour unto mine,
> Then Pies to Syrens, Gesse to Nightengals.
> Then take Mee (BARTAS) to conduct thy Pen,
> Sour up to Heav'n; Sing me th' Almighties' praise:
> And tuning now the *Jessean* Harp again,
> Gaine thee the *Garland* of eternall *Bayes*.

Du Bartas's Urania clearly rejects the pagan Muses, comparing their songs to playful *Madrigalls* and hers to the *Jessean* Harp, and assures her bard that her heavenly inspiration will guide his pen to write of greater things. Like Hesiod, Du Bartas finds himself chosen by the Muse to be her instrument on earth; for his efforts he will be rewarded with more than staff and voice—he will receive "eternall *Bayes*." Towards the end of the poem, Urania pronounces to her bard and to all aspiring poets, "Hence-forth no more profane the *Sacred Muses*" (stanza 74), by which she means not the Muses of Olympus but the Heavenly Muses. Thus, with the aid of Sylvester, Du Bartas announces the end of the pagan Muses as a legitimate source of divine inspiration in seventeenth-century English poetry.

While the Muses had maintained their vitality during the Middle Ages through syncretic readings of pagan mythology, by the time of Thomas Carew's *An Elegy upon the Death of the Dean of Paul's, Dr. John Donne* (1633), the Muses had come to be regarded by many poets as *clichés*. To writers such as Du Bartas and Abraham Cowley, his English disciple, the Muses had become pagan *lies*. Religious poetry written by both Du Bartas and Cowley explicitly asserts that invocations to the Muses either need to reject the pagan past or to convert the Muse to Christianity. It was Cowley, not Milton, who aspired to write the first neo-classical epic in English; however, Cowley soon realized from his own study of the classics as well as from Renaissance commentaries upon epic poetry that he must invoke the Muse to *begin*. Cowley's solution, which recalls Du Bartas's, was to turn the pagan Muse into a Christian Muse. He attempts to do this in the *Davideis* (1656) by invoking Christ as Muse and then by offering his Muse *to* Christ as a Magdalene, a redeemed whore, to his service. Besides his hostility toward the pagan gods, Cowley's presentation of his Christian Muse as redeemed whore suggests his discomfort with the Muse's feminine attributes; Cowley adopts a "Puritan" position here, insisting that the Muse can either be a disciple of Christ or a whore. Cowley fails to complete the epic, however, as he fails to complete his historical epic, *A Poem on the Late Civil War* (1679). In a sense, Cowley's personal war upon the pagan Muse takes precedence over his own ability to tap into the Muse's traditional powers of creativity and inspiration.

From his early poetry to *Paradise Lost*, Milton confronts the same questions about the Muse that Du Bartas and Cowley faced: How does one invoke a pagan *convention* in the service of a *Christian* theme? Does calling upon a pagan Muse necessarily mean rejecting Christianity? Milton's early poetry reveals a balance between the poet's "Puritanism," on the one hand, and his "syncretism," on the other, in confronting these questions. In Milton's *Nativity Ode* (1629), the infant Christ banishes the pagan gods, but the image nevertheless recalls Pindar's account of the infant Herakles overcoming the serpents sent to kill him and his twin brother. In *Lycidas* (1638) and *Epitaphium Damonis* (1640), Milton laments the deaths of Edward King and Charles Diodati within the conventional context of the pastoral elegy; however, both poems convey the author's deep sense of personal loss as well as his anxiety over the future, and both end with a vision of Christian consolation. Indeed, Milton's early pattern of invocations, from his verse translations of the Psalms to his Latin elegy to Diodati, reveals the poet's comfortable blending of pagan and Christian elements.

In *Paradise Lost*, however, Milton must confront the "meaning" and the "name" of his Muse. While Milton never fully rejects the Muse's pagan past, his four proems (*PL* I, III, VII, and IX) increasingly emphasize his Muse's Christian "meaning" (associated alternately with Father, Son, and Holy Spirit) over the "name," presented by Milton as the "Heav'nly Muse" and "Urania," the same used by Du Bartas. Milton's Muse is alternately male and female: when addressed as an attribute of the Trinity, the Muse may be regarded as "male," but when invoked as Divine Wisdom, the Muse resembles Sophia. While Milton's Muse can be seen as a function of the Holy Spirit, she may also personify the feminine Greek goddesses invoked by Hesiod and Homer. In the end, Milton's Muse seems to balance all of these attributes, but not always comfortably. By the opening of Book IX, Milton's Celestial Patroness no longer requires the poet's invocation. But while her pagan origins remain a vital part of her identity, the Muse comes to represent divine inspiration and the source of *all* creation. Her gifts, when requested by God's chosen *vates*, or poet-prophet, are granted to the poet with "upright heart and pure." The Muse's *real* identity, even when her "nightly visitations" come "unimplor'd," remains ambiguous. It is through his re-establishment of the Muse's ambiguity and his creative use of classical forms that Milton brings the Muse back to life. In order to understand the transformations of the Muse in seventeenth-century England, we must examine this "crisis" of the pagan Muse in its proper context by examining Milton's invocations alongside those of Cowley.

During the English Civil War, Commonwealth, and Restoration, a religious crisis becomes a political and military crisis: What is the relationship between a Christian nation and its classical and pagan past? The Royalists establish a Christian nation that is connected to a classical past, while the Puritans reject that idea of a classical and pagan past as they attempt to work God's purpose out in the world. Although the Royalist Cowley and the Puritan Milton were opposed in their political views and their religious affiliations, they both struggled with the same questions: How can one make a pagan Muse viable in Christian literature? How will the English Civil War redefine what it means to be "English" or to be "Christian"? Both poets attempt to answer these questions by turning to a public genre concerned with national origin and definition—the classical epic. Both initially decide to use the epic to articulate a particular version of England's origins and religious and civic virtues. The fact that both poets did not write that particular epic—Cowley failed, while Milton chose instead to write a universal Christian epic—reveals some anxiety about being immersed in the present. Being in the midst of history, not outside it, neither poet was able to address the question of England's origin because neither knew what England was in the process of becoming.

When Abraham Cowley and John Milton use and transform the classical epic in seventeenth-century England, they also confront the tradition of invoking the Muses' powers of music, inspiration, and divine wisdom to begin their epics, assess their own sense of vocation within the lineage of epic poets, and define what will be a new strain of epic in English. Both poets invoke the Muse for assistance in telling the "story" and in defining England's national origin and self-definition. In sixteenth- and seventeenth-century England, epic poetry was viewed both as the highest poetic genre and the proper medium for the expression of a culture's virtues, and any poet serious about his or her vocation aspired to compose the great national epic. And yet, such potential epic poets faced what W. Jackson Bate later calls "the burden of the past"; each poet had to confront and use a heritage, with a full knowledge of it and with so much admiration for it, and at the same time try to be himself, or to assert his own identity.[8] Cowley and Milton (and later Dryden and Pope) felt strongly this burden and the challenges of the traditional career of the poet, derived from the sequence of Vergil's major works and the achievements of the poets who followed; it was their task, then, to institute a new tradition with new models in England, and each poet, in his own way, contributed to the rebirth and/or transformation of the classical epic by taking up the mantle of *vates* and by attempting to establish a difference within the tradition.

In order to explore the complex relationship between poetic form and political crisis, my methodology combines rhetorical and philological analysis and new historicist theory. By placing Milton's invocations within the context of other English and French attempts to "convert" the Muse in the Renaissance, I hope offer a fresh approach to the subject and to provide a foundation for further new historicist discussions of origins and invocations as well as feminist approaches to the identity of the Muse. It is necessary for Renaissance scholars to remember and to understand the importance of the original classical literature that Milton and his contemporaries knew and consciously used. My intention in pursuing a philological approach to Milton's work is not to reprimand, but to remind post-structuralist Renaissance scholars of the classical basis of English poet's education and work. My contribution to current critical discourse, I hope, will be to provide a useful analysis of an ancient literary convention's use and transformation during a moment of great cultural crisis. Just as some recent studies have focused upon the "critical moment" of colonization in Renaissance culture and literature, so does this study focus upon the "critical moment" when Christian writers must reconcile their religious beliefs with their classical education.

Philosophically, my exploration of what it means to begin an epic is especially indebted to A. D. Nuttall's work on openings from the epic to the novel,[9] which provides a useful theoretical approach for "natural" and "interventionist" beginnings as well as a way of examining the poet's presence in the work or the poet's difficulty in establishing a voice within a form that is both personal and literary. The Bible, Nuttall suggests, provides most people's example of "*the* natural beginning, the Genesis of the world," while Homer's *Iliad* provides an example of an interventionist opening, beginning as it does in the middle of the Trojan War and presenting a narrative unity—Achilles' wrath—that presumably did not exist prior to the poem (204). These competing opening formulae become most interesting, though, when we consider an epic poet, like Vergil, who begins his poem *in medias res* but reveals a nostalgia for a "natural" beginning. As Nuttall observes in his discussion of the *Aeneid*, even Aeneas himself "strains with a sort of famished desire for something better than this mess of shadows, spectral cities, Greek images—for a Roman home that is an origin" (205). Milton and Cowley, like Vergil, both desire to invoke a Muse from the source of all things and to ground their epics in a *true* beginning. While Cowley becomes caught up in the problem of using a pagan generic form as a vehicle for his Christian invocation, Milton exploits the power of the invocation to access a Muse both Hellenic and Christian. Both poets begin their epics with "interventionist" invocations, but those invocations become the *loci* for debating or questioning sources in terms of the Muse.

On a literary level, then, this study concerns the convention of beginning a poem by first invoking the Muse and the conflict that emerges between her pagan and Christian characteristics. On a philosophical and historical level, this study concerns the search for origins in epic poetry. In both cases, the questions raised are the same: Where does one begin when one wishes to write a poem, specifically an epic poem? Where does one find the grounding or authority for what one is attempting to write? What is the nature of inspiration to these poets? To what extent is the notion of inspiration an external force or an internal force summoned by the poet? What is the relationship between the epic poet's invocation of the Muse, whether classical, Christian, a combination of the two, and the epic form's concern with the recovery of origins? Who is the Muse? Can the classical Muse properly be called upon to relate a Christian theme? By exploring and answering these questions, I hope to provide a fresh consideration of the use of invocations and the Christianization of the Muse in seventeenth-century England.

The classical Muses—Calliope, Clio, Erato, Euterpe, Melpomene, Polyhymnia, Terpsichore, Thalia, and Urania—served respectively as the deities of epic poetry, history, love poetry, lyric poetry, tragedy, songs of praise to the gods, dancing, comedy, and astronomy, and were generally recognized as the daughters of Zeus and Mnemosyne (or Memory). In Antiquity, both the prevailing conception of the Muses and their canonical number of nine come from the *Theogony*, in which the Muses approach the poet on Mount Helicon. Hesiod's narrator recounts, "they gave me a branch of springing bay to pluck for a staff, a handsome one, and they breathed into me wondrous voice, so that I should celebrate things of the future and things that were aforetime."[10] Besides the traditional tokens of the office of poet and the inspiration to sing, the Muses give their chosen bard insights into the past and the future. In the *Theogony*, the poet Hesiod is called upon "to sing of the family of blessed ones who are forever, and first and last to sing of themselves [Zeus's daughters]."[11] At first, the Muses were associated with particular locations—Mount Helicon, Mount Olympia, and the sacred fountains Aganippe and Hippocrene—and were usually considered feminine—invoked by poets as "Nymphs," "Virgins," "Goddesses," and "Daughters of Memory." The Sicilian poets associated the Muses with their own countryside; Milton, following the example of Moschus and Vergil, transplanted the "Sicilian Muses" into his own *English* pastoral landscape in *Lycidas*. It was not until late Roman times, however, that poets begin to distinguish between the various intellectual functions of the different Muses[12] and to call upon their particular attributes in epic and lyric poetry.

The epic tradition of the *invocatio*, literally *to call upon* or *to invoke*,[13] is as old as the Muses themselves and begins with Homer's Olympian Muses, who function both to inspire the poet with song and to recall epic catalogues (see *Il*.2.484ff.). The word itself, *invocare*, places emphasis upon the poet's voice, or *vox*, which calls upon a presence, the "other than I" known as the Muse. The father of didactic poetry, Hesiod, also calls upon the Muses. Having been given the gift of song from the Muses, Hesiod seeks their assistance in relating the origin and genealogy of the Olympian gods: "Tell me this from the beginning, Muses who dwell in Olympus, and say, what thing among them came first."[14] For Hesiod, Homer, Vergil, and Milton, the invocation of the Muse is more than a ceremony required before beginning an epic poem; to call upon the Muse is to make a beginning. Indeed, the Muse *is* the beginning.

The formal *invocatio*, customarily used to open an epic poem, consists of two parts, the *invocation* and the *request*; in form, it bears a natural similarity to the classical hymn and the biblical prayer, which also name the addressee and make a general or a specific petition. In a sense, an invocation is an admission of need and incompleteness. The poet invokes the Muse to receive a "voice" outside of himself, a voice that fills the lungs or moves the pen to write inspired poetry. The invocation also establishes a relationship between poet and Muse. Indeed, both Hesiod and Pindar invoke the Muses in order to prove their own pedagogical vocation. In *Fasti*, Book VI, Ovid confirms this sacred function of the invocation, asserting the poet's divine inspiration because he sings of divine things:

> est deus in nobis; agitante caelescimus illo:
> impetus hic sacrae semina mentis habet.
> fas mihi praecipue voltus vidisse deorum,
> vel quia sum vates, vel quia sacra cano. (5–8)[15]

Indeed, the same may be said of Milton, whose divine Muse validates and supports his role as *vates*. Milton echoes Ovid's conception of the *vates* as sacred to the gods and receptive to their divine inspiration in *Elegy VI*, where he writes: "Dis etenim sacer est vates, divumque sacerdos, / spirat et occultum pectus et ora Jovem" (ll. 77–78).[16] Both Milton and Cowley, as *vates*, appeal to their Muses in their invocations, suggesting both a connection to the ancient tradition as well as a current desire to be their country's poet.

The Muse's function in epic poetry expands considerably from Homer to Vergil. Homer's invocation of the Muse in the *Iliad*, Book 1, 1–2, reads "Sing, goddess, the anger of Peleus' son Achilleus and its devastation"[17]; Vergil's invocation stresses the Muse's ability to sing the causes of Juno's wrath ("Musa, mihi causas memora").[18] Like Homer, who invoked the Muse(s) on several occasions in the *Iliad*, Vergil invokes the Muse to demarcate different stages in the *Aeneid* as well as to recall historical personages, battles, and catalogues of ships ("Nunc age . . . Erato").[19] Knowing that he would only write one epic, Vergil resolved to combine Homer's *Iliad* and *Odyssey* in the first line of the *Aeneid*: "arma" (arms) "virumque" (and the man). His opening contains not one, but two beginnings: Vergil the poet sings (*cano*) the theme of the epic and then invokes the Muse for inspiration. After Vergil, the invocation of the Muse becomes conventional in epic poetry and, indeed, essential, despite the inevitable clash that pagan invocations will later have with Christianity in the Middle Ages. Dante invokes the Muses, in accordance with classical practice, at every important turning point in his *Commedia*, calling attention to its consciously divided parts and emphasizing the spontaneity of his verse. In these things, Milton follows Dante's example, also indicating that his epic derives from a carefully structured plan while at the same time asserting that his verse is inspired by the "Heav'nly Muse," just as Dante's was inspired by "Love."[20] In later writers, though, the feminine identity of the Muse could pose a problem for poets who would substitute Christ as the source of poetic inspiration. Nevertheless, the Muse retains her feminine identity in nearly all iconographical representations produced in the Renaissance.

Vergil does not simply call upon the Muse for memory but more importantly to highlight transitions in the narrative. At the beginning of the *Aeneid*, Vergil confidently announces his theme: "Arma virumque cano, . . . " (1.1). His invocation to the Muse, "Musa, mihi causas memora" (1.8), seeks the cause of Juno's wrath against Aeneas and the Trojan race: "Tantaene animis caelestibus irae?" (1.11) In Book VII, however, Vergil does re-invoke the Muse in the manner of Homer, "Nunc age, . . . Erato," that she might relate information concerning Latium and catalogues of troops (41-43):

> tu vatem, tu, diva, mone. dicam horrida bella,
> dicam acies actosque animis in funera reges,
> Tyrrhenamque manum, totamque sub arma coactum
> Hesperiam.[21]

E. R. Curtius correctly observes that "the epic invocation of the Muses, which could be repeated before particularly important or particularly 'difficult' passages, serves in Virgil and his followers to decorate narrative and to emphasize its high points."[22] While Vergil uses multiple invocations less frequently than Homer—calling upon the Muse in the *Aeneid* Books 1, 7, 9, and 11—he more clearly reinforces his epic's intentional structural design. This modification of the tradition by Vergil later benefits Milton, who employs four invocations in *Paradise Lost* for similar purposes. Milton, however, pushes the convention to the limit, fully integrating his invocations into the epic narrative itself and establishing the ancient tradition of the epic poet's sacred role as bard.

With the advent of Christianity and the decline of paganism, Christian writers become increasingly critical of the Muses. In fact, the rejection of the Muses in Christian poetry becomes a *topos* in itself from the fourth to the seventeenth century; during this time, many religious poets invoke the Holy Spirit, Christ, or God (235). Perhaps the most famous example of the rejection of the Muses comes in the work of Boethius (c. 480–524 AD). In *De Consolatione Philosophiae*, 1 prose 1, Lady Philosophy banishes the strumpet (*meretriculas*) Muses of poetry, claiming that their songs "choke the rich harvest of the fruits of reason with the barren thorns of passion" and "accustom a man's mind to his ills, not rid him of them."[23] She calls upon the Muses only to denounce them and to assert her *own* remedy for Boethius' despairing narrator: "Sed abite potius Sirenes usque in exitium dulces meisque eum Musis curandum sanandumque relinquite."[24] According to Lady Philosophy, her patient requires a cure (*mediciniae*, 1 p 2, 1) not a complaint (*querelae*, 1 m 2, 2); the Muses' *songs*, she maintains, cannot provide the true remedy offered by the *reason* of philosophy. As Lady Philosophy will argue in 3 p 9, perfect happiness, or the *summum bonum*, can only be found by invoking the Father of all things (*rerum omnium patrem*, 103); poetry's gifts are partial, she suggests, while philosophy's are eternal, leading to the *summum bonum*.[25]

Nevertheless, the Muses remain connected with the epic form, and literary critics of the Renaissance continue to affirm the importance of beginning epic poems with an invocation to the Muse or to some celestial power to guide the poet in his writing.[26] As late as his *Traité du Poëme Epique* (1675), Le Bossu argues for the necessity of including the invocation of the Muse and the proposition, whether mixed or separated, at the beginning of the epic poem. According to Le Bossu, "the Poet cannot omit the *Invocation*," for without it "he speaks of things which he would know nothing of, unless some God or other had reveal'd them to him."[27] Indeed, Le Bossu affirms the importance of calling upon the Muse or some source of poetic inspiration before undertaking the work, or even an important section of the work.[28] These ideas found their way from France to England through timely English translations of these critical works. Poets writing about history or origins in a public form such as the epic accepted the practice—even the *need*—of invoking an "authority" for their version of historical events, and that authority outside history was the Muse.

This study of epic invocations participates in an ongoing critical dialogue on origin and poetic authority in seventeenth-century England. In the chapters to come, I explore the distinctions that A. D. Nuttall establishes between literary beginnings that are "devoutly natural" or "proudly artificial,"[29] and consider for

Cowley and Milton the conditions that produce an epic as well as the sources of inspiration that are invoked and ideally replaced by the poet's voice. The poet, who is always within Time and unable to begin at the beginning as did God—Who, *in principio*, said, *fiat lux*—must therefore *necessarily* intervene in the larger historical narrative. Indeed, epic poets customarily follow Horace's notion of the *in medias res* opening and plunge into the midst of things, as did Homer, rather than begin a work on the fall of Troy *ab ovo* with the birth of Helen.[30] According to Horace, the poet is foolish who attempts to begin at the *very* beginning; instead, the poet should hurry his audience to the issue, blending facts with fiction, so that "primo ne medium, medio ne discrepet imum."[31] Indeed, on a cosmic scale, there is a limit to which one can reach back to find a beginning, and Horace, like others who follow him, recognizes that limit. Yet, while the epic form itself cannot encompass the full scope of history, it nevertheless strives for encyclopedic scope and relies metaphorically upon a "divine" source of inspiration. Acknowledging that there is a difference between an epic's beginning and its formal opening—usually in the form of an invocation to the Muse—I demonstrate the extent to which invocations resemble the classical, and later Christian, hymn, and examine literary invocations in the epics of Cowley and Milton. Furthermore, I explore a pattern of invocation or prayer that reflects these poets' epic intentions and growing sense of poetic vocation within a venerable literary tradition and the ways in which they engage in the pagan/Christian crisis in English poetry.

Alvin Snider's recent work on the discourse of origins in seventeenth-century England informs my discussion of invocations and the vocation of the epic poet. According to Snider, Francis Bacon, Milton, and Samuel Butler believed that the truth of an idea could be determined by inquiry into its genesis, and looked for authority in rudimentary and untainted principles. Snider rightly sees epic unity as a function of recovering an "absolute historical starting-point"; he argues that "the difficulty of writing an epic poem in the seventeenth century, even a Christian religious epic with a new type of hero, was compounded by the difficulty of situating experience in an utterly past world," a problem faced by both Cowley and Milton in their epics.[32] Snider correctly links the concerns of epic and philosophical discourse, since both seek to establish themselves in relationship to a primal truth. While Snider focuses on Milton's quest for origins in *Paradise Lost* in terms of what he terms the "metaphor" of mirroring as knowledge and knowledge as the process of representation and reduplication, I explore Milton's and Cowley's complex relationship with their Muses and their singular concern with the connection between the historical present with the mythical past.

David Quint's recent discussion of generic form and politics intersects with my treatment of the ideological purpose of epic and the epic poet's moral or religious position as expressed in his invocation(s) and his choice of Muse.[33] Quint establishes two opposing traditions in epic: the linear, teleological narrative belonging to the imperial conquerors (Vergil's *Aeneid*) and the episodic and open-ended narrative identified with romance, the story told of and by the defeated (Lucan's *De Bello Civili*). Quint situates *Paradise Lost* and *Paradise Regained* within these rival traditions, associating Adam's and Eve's story with Lucan's, Eden with the Romance tradition, and *Paradise Lost* with the larger movement of the seventeenth century in the direction of the romance tradition. Although I share Quint's interest in the inter-relationship between ideology and literary form and agree, in part, with his division of epic legacy into traditions of the "winners" and "losers," I shall argue that each tradition is capable of considerable flexibility and growth. I shall suggest that Cowley's epics fit much better into the Lucanian tradition than does Milton's *Paradise Lost*, which draws more upon the strength of Vergil's Augustan epic to assert "Eternal Providence" over martial prowess than it does upon the episodic and open-ended narrative design of Lucan's *De Bello Civili*. Vergil's *Aeneid* can be used and refashioned by Milton (and even by Pope during the Enlightenment) to undercut classical values and to assert modern ones: the epic of empire can serve as the voice of the Christian poet and the satirist.

Finally, Margaret Anne Doody's discussion of the early Restoration's fascination with space and changing locations in Cowley's *Davideis* and Milton's *Paradise Lost*[34] informs my cultural and literary discussion of form and generic experimentation in seventeenth-century epic poetry. Doody convincingly argues that "Post-Civil War poets have an urgent desire to tell a whole story, to discourse at length about the whole course of political and moral conflict" (62). She argues that many seventeenth-century poets are daunted by the prospect of writing "lengthy retrospective accounts of major conflicts," and, aside from Milton, no poet of the period in England produces a "finished and effective" epic (63). I would suggest that such failure owes something to seventeenth-century poets' attempted participation in the tradition of the "losers," a tradition not suited to a heroic narrative that requires unity.

Indeed, Milton both incorporates and redefines the conventions and themes of former epics, from Antiquity through the Renaissance: *Paradise Lost*, according to Doody, "consumes epic styles, devices, and narrative formulae, to the point that they become unstable in any other poem . . . we are meant to discard them, and with them all epics save this one alone" (64). Consequently, Doody asserts that Milton is one of the first Augustan poets of the Restoration period, that he "participates in the Restoration-Augustan project of exploding genres," and that his epic "exhibits the typical Augustan desire for complexity and inclusiveness" (64). While I share Doody's understanding of the epic as an exhaustive form that attempts to displace previous examples in the tradition, I question the possibility of "exploding" genres so that no further attempts in the form are possible. When one epic poet asserts himself against his predecessors, a struggle ensues in which the epic form undergoes a necessary metamorphosis; I concentrate on the ways English epic poets define themselves as such based upon their invocations to the Muse and their ongoing search for origins and authority.

In order to address the seventeenth-century issues of "converting" the pagan Muse and "beginning" an epic with an invocation, I divide my study into four sections, the first setting the context for the three that follow. I begin with Abraham Cowley's epics, the *Davideis* (1656) and *A Poem on the Late Civil War* (1679), as well as his perspective upon the epic career as established in his poetry. I then proceed to a comprehensive study of Milton's works, from the *Nativity Ode* to *Lycidas* and *Epitaphium Damonis* and finally to *Paradise Lost* (1667). By recognizing the close relationship between the invocation and the classical/Christian hymn, I argue that the pattern of invoking the Muse is an integral component of the epic poet's unfolding sense of his vocation, and that both invocations and the epics that they introduce seek origins, whether poetic, historical, or divine.

Chapter I, "Rejecting the Pagan Gods: Abraham Cowley and the Christian Muse," focuses upon Abraham Cowley and his multiple contributions to the promotion of classical forms in English poetry, especially his invocations to the Muse and statements affirming his vocation of poet, found both in his occasional poetry and in his two epic poems. Having introduced Pindar into English (his *Pindarique Odes* also participate in the tradition of the invocation), Cowley is also the first to compose a Biblical epic in English. Yet while Cowley would begin an epic "on the sorrows of King David" and later attempt a royalist epic, *A Poem on the Late Civil War* (1679), his efforts would not produce a finished epic. In certain ways, his failure to complete his epic task parallels Lucan's difficulty in presenting a clear set of heroic values in his *De Bello Civili*; both poets respectively address the issue of current or recent civil war within a narrative form that is both historical and mythological, while at the same time they discard the traditional apparatus of divine intervention. Cowley sees himself writing in the tradition of Vergil, and his notes to the *Davideis* as well as his Latin translation of the first book further support his vision of epic scope. However, Cowley, who demonstrates a pattern of invocations in his shorter verse and who attempts to Christianize the Muse in his epic verse, ultimately fails to redefine the epic tradition successfully.

In order to investigate the question of poetic invocations, this chapter examines Cowley's early relationship to the Muse and to the epic career in his poem, *On the Death of Mr. Crashaw*; his engagement with the pagan/Christian Muse "crisis" in the *Davideis*, Book I; and his transformation of the Muse's tasks in his unfinished epic, *A Poem on the Late Civil War*. A survey of these poems, along with a brief consideration of Richard Crashaw, will reveal that the issue of "Christianizing" the Muse is a central one in the literature of the seventeenth century and important for an understanding of Milton.

Chapter II, "Milton's Early Invocations: From the Psalms to *Comus*," examines Milton's early verse, including his paraphrases of the Psalms, *On the Morning of Christ's Nativity*, *L'Allegro*, *Il Penseroso*, and *Comus*, tracing Milton's repeated use of invocations and his progressing interest writing his Christian epic. Primarily, this chapter examines closely the issues raised when one considers the function and meaning of an invocation, especially when an impersonal and pagan form must be adapted to a Christian situation, as is the case in the *Nativity Ode*. Milton sees the birth of Christ as banishing the pagan gods, and yet it is here that he calls upon the "Heav'nly Muse" for the first time. I argue that Milton's whole career, in fact, can be seen as an attempt to unpack the meaning of this expression—"Heav'nly Muse"—from the *Nativity Ode* to *Paradise Lost*.

Chapter III, "But now my Oat Proceeds: Pastoral Legacy and Epic Beginnings in *Lycidas* and *Epitaphium Damonis*," explores the use of poetic conventions and their relation to personal feelings, a point central to my discussion of invocations since they are such a striking convention. It is interesting to observe that Milton wrote the elegy to his close friend Diodati in Latin while he wrote an elegy in memory of King—a person he knew less well—in English, suggesting that Milton thought the distancing strategy was necessary precisely because the grief was stronger. Milton's invocation of the Muse in both poems also raises the question: Does the introduction of a pagan figure involve a rejection of Christianity? No, if you are a syncretist, as was the early Milton. Yes, if you are a "Puritan." Both elegies conclude with the traditional *consolatio* in apotheosis, permitting the poet to feel some confidence in heavenly rewards for the dead. By the end of *Lycidas*, however, Milton leaves us with a carefully wrought blend of the Christian and pagan, and, like the end of *Comus*, the poem offers a picture of Heaven that is still very much like Elysium.

In Chapter IV, "From Clio to Urania: Milton's Epic Invocations in *The History of Britain* and *Paradise Lost*," I argue that, like Cowley, Milton demonstrates an awareness of his vocation as epic poet early in his career, beginning while a student at Cambridge and extending throughout his life. In support of this argument, I explore the pattern of invocations in Milton's works and assess Milton's growing concern with divine origins and poetical calling, seen first in his projected but eventually aborted *Arthuriad*. A brief exploration of *The History of Britain* reveals Milton's conflicting desire to represent history accurately while amplifying the heroic and mythological origins of the British people in figures such as Brutus, Arthur, and Alfred. My discussion of Milton's *History of Britain* underscores the work's epic qualities, especially evident in its epic-like invocation and its heroic portraits.

Finally, my study culminates in a discussion of *Paradise Lost*, the fullest expression of epic form and scope in the tradition. Rather than serving as a national epic for England, however, Milton's poem serves as a Christian epic that calls each individual to make his "solitary way" in the world (*PL* 12.649). Although Milton subverts Roman *pietas* in *Paradise Lost*, replacing it with the Christian values of humility and love, he must reconcile its pagan form with its Christian theme. Unlike the poetry of the early Milton, *Paradise Lost* fights a battle between its explicit "Puritanism" and its vestigial "syncretist" spirit. By invoking "the Meaning, not the Name," Milton seemingly rejects the Muse's pagan associations while asserting her Christian identity; however, Milton's

"Heav'nly Muse"—which recalls Du Bartas's Muse of the same name—remains ambiguous. It is this ambiguity of the Muse's identity that gives strength and new life to Urania. Milton's Muse, ultimately, is both the "Heav'nly Muse" and the Muse of Hesiod, Homer, and Vergil.

Chapter I

Rejecting the Pagan Gods: Abraham Cowley and the Christian Muse

> Does not the passage of Moses and the Israelites into the Holy Land, yield incomparably more Poetical variety, than the voyages of Ulysses or Æneas? Are the obsolete thread-bare tales of Thebes and Troy, half so stored with great, heroical and supernatural actions (since Verse will needs find or make such) as the wars of Joshua, of the Judges, of David, and divers others? Can all the transformations of the Gods give such copious hints to flourish and expiate on, as the true Miracles of Christ, or of his Prophets, and Apostles?
>
> Cowley, Preface to his *Works*, 1656

Abraham Cowley firmly believed that biblical, not classical, themes were the most admirable and most worthy material for poetry. Rejecting the mythology contained in Ovid's *Metamorphoses*, a favorite source book for poets of the Renaissance, Cowley maintains that the miracles of Christ and the actions of Old Testament prophets and heroes provide a far nobler tradition for the religious poet to draw upon when composing verse than the heroic deeds sung by Statius and Vergil. Although Cowley, like Spenser, saw himself as an inheritor of the epic tradition of Homer and Vergil and consciously attempted to pursue a similar career path, he waged a lifelong struggle against paganism in English devotional poetry. While Cowley continued to employ classical forms and to venerate the notion of poetic inheritance, he simultaneously eschewed the invocation of the pagan Muses in lyric and epic poetry and fought diligently to replace the literary influence of classical mythology with Christian truth in his works. While Cowley's poetic efforts may not have lived up to their author's expectations (or readers' for that matter), they brought the issue of paganism in Christian poetry to the literary forefront and made a lasting impression upon Milton, whose "answerable style" would successfully carry the task of writing a Christian epic to fruition.

Cowley asserts in his Preface of 1656 that the originary narratives of Moses and David should be esteemed more highly by a Christian audience than the adventures of Homer's Ulysses or Vergil's Aeneas. For Cowley, Ovid's *Metamorphoses* was a fine work of mythology, capable of exciting the imagination of the poet, but the recorded words and deeds of Christ, Elijah, Peter, and Paul expressed the highest kind of poetry: divine truth. At the same time, however, Cowley recognized that the task of writing sacred poetry is not as easy as "only turning a story of the Scripture . . . or some other godly matter . . . into Rhyme; He is so far from elevating of Poesie, that he only abases Divinity." Cowley further asserts the dangers and difficulties inherent in such a task: "In brief, he who can write a profane Poem well, may write a Divine one better; but he who can do that but ill, will do this much worse." Cowley refers to himself both as "the Muse's Hannibal"[1] and as "th' Apostle,"[2] indicating his self-confidence in his role as God's own poet-priest, or *vates*, in a world too much enamored of the pagan gods. In his major poems, from his elegy to Crashaw to his neo-classical epics on David and the English Civil War, Cowley confronts the problem of adapting and transforming classical literary forms and conventions to serve modern Christian purposes.

Therefore, a study of poetic invocations to the Muse and the nature of poetic inspiration in seventeenth-century England properly begins with Abraham Cowley, himself a poet of many "beginnings" and most importantly the first to introduce the *Odes* of Pindar[3] and the biblical epic into English verse. As Samuel Johnson notes, Abraham Cowley "was in his own time considered as of unrivalled excellence . . . and Milton is said to have declared that the three greatest English poets were Spenser, Shakespeare, and Cowley."[4] Upon his death, Charles II is said to have remarked "that Mr. Cowley had not left a better man behind him in England"; the poet was subsequently buried next to Chaucer in Westminster Abbey.[5] Having praised Cowley for his "early-ripe and lasting" Wit, his close friendship with Lord Falkland, "contracted by the agreement of their Learning and Manners," and his twelve-year service to the royal household in France during and after the Civil War, Thomas Sprat goes on to characterize Cowley's commitment to divine poetry: "he only dedicated it to the service of his Maker, to describe the great images of Religion and Virtue wherewith his mind abounded. And he employed his Musick to no other use, than his own David did towards Saul, by singing the Praises of God and Nature, to drive the evil Spirit out of mens minds."[6] From Sprat's assessment of Cowley one can better understand the poet's seriousness of purpose in promoting the truth of the Christian faith and his personal dedication to making poetry serve the purpose of divine praise, just as David's Psalms magnified his God.

Jean Seznec argues that in the Renaissance preference was given to myths "rediscovered" in their "primal purity" over those handed down and thereby preserved from late antiquity through the Middle Ages.[7] Writers of the Renaissance, including Du Bartas and his English follower Cowley, felt the need to rehabilitate the pagan gods, bringing the newly professed "pagan cult of life" into line with the spiritual values of Christianity (320). Seznec writes that, at first, humanism and art seem able to reconcile the two worlds; however, by the end of the sixteenth century and the beginning of the seventeenth century many poets must avow the "disaccord" hiding beneath the surface. "From being objects of love," Seznec argues, "the gods are transformed into a subject of study" (321). Unlike early Milton, Cowley has difficulty accepting and applying syncretic readings of texts; his *Davideis* and the elaborate collection of notes that accompany the poem demonstrate his need to Christianize the epic form. Thus during the Renaissance, as Seznec observes, the pagan gods become increasingly more erudite on the one hand (especially in Milton) and less alive on the other (in Cowley). What remains particularly interesting about Cowley, however, is that while rejecting the pagan gods he continues to use classical/pagan forms in his poetry. Cowley's poetry fails to inspire the reader, perhaps, because the poet remains too self-conscious about rejecting the pagan tradition, spending more time pioneering than writing inspired verse.

In Cowley, and later in Milton, one can see this tension between classical form and Christian argument most clearly in the invocations to the Muse. It is in such epic invocations that we find the theme of the poem (or the epic in miniature) presented in a traditional form descended from Homer and Vergil as well as the identification of the poet's source of inspiration. The "original" source of the poem, though, can be the Muse alone, the Muse speaking through or with the poet, or the poet alone, with some cursory nod toward an external source. Identifying this "original" source is important because in doing so one may more clearly define the poet's place in the epic tradition, establish the degree to which he is redefining or reshaping the tradition, and pinpoint the author's "theory" of the nature of poetic inspiration.

In order to explore the question of invocations—who is being invoked to do what, how the invocations relate to the design of the poem, what poetic devices are appropriate to an invocation, what choices the poet has to make, where the invocation comes, and what it tells us about the poet's beliefs about poetic inspiration—I shall examine Cowley's early relationship to the Muse and to the epic profession in his poem *On the Death of Mr. Crashaw*, his engagement with the pagan/Christian Muse controversy in the *Davideis*, Book 1, and his transformation of the Muse's tasks in his uncompleted *A Poem on the Late Civil War*. Such a survey will reveal that the issue of "converting" the Muse is a central one in Cowley's verse, an examination of which is necessary for an understanding of Milton's more complex invocations to the Muse in *Paradise Lost*, written in some degree against the backdrop of Cowley's precedent.

Cowley's attitudes toward epic poetry, and indeed poetry in general, show some debt to the mixture of Aristotelian and Christian views held by Torquato Tasso:

> We should at least grant that the end of poetry is not just any unworthy of a good poet to give the pleasure of reading about base and dishonest deeds, but proper to give the pleasure of learning together with virtue.[8]

Writing in defense of the style of his own epic poem, *Gerusalemne Liberata*, Tasso takes great pains to meet every objection that had been raised against it and to assert his own agreement with Aristotelian principles. However, given Tasso's concern with Christian ideals of virtue, this passage demonstrates a desire to redefine values of heroism and a belief in poetry as the vehicle for presenting those values. Tasso could do so within the scope of epic and romance and with the blending of pagan and Christian conventions. For Cowley, though, classical or pagan conventions were unacceptable in divine poetry. The pagan Muse simply had to be Christianized if the poet really wanted to present poetic truth as divine truth.

Cowley was not original, however, in his efforts to convert the pagan Muse to Christianity. Like Sidney and Spenser before him, and later Milton, Cowley took Guillaume Du Bartas's Muse in *La Semaine* and *L'Uranie* as models for his Christian Muse in the *Davideis*. Cowley's position against pagan elements in Christian poetry in his occasional pieces also owes a debt to Joshua Sylvester's English translation of Du Bartas's *Divine Weekes and Workes* (1605). Applying Tasso's observation—"while it is necessary to invoke divine aid at all times and places, writers generally do so at the beginning of their work"[9]—to his own poetry, Du Bartas piously begins his *Divine Weekes and Workes* with an invocation to God:

> Thou glorious Guide of Heav'ns star-glistring motion,
> Thou, thou (true Neptune) Tamer of the Ocean,
> Thou Earth's drad Shaker (at whose only Word,
> Th' Eölian Scouts are quickly still'd and stirr'd)
> Lift up my soule, my drousie spirits refine,
> With learned Art enrich This Worke of mine . . . (1.1–6)[10]

Sylvester's marginalia to the invocation—"The poet imploreth the gracious assistance of the true God of Heauen, Earth, Aire, and Sea, that he may happily finish the worke he takes in hand"—further reinforces Du Bartas's commitment to generic form and religious faith. Du Bartas substitutes the true God for the traditional Muse. To emphasize this point, the poet displaces the pagan god, calling upon the Christian God (who created the sea and the land) the "True Neptune." But note the resonant ambiguity of such a locution: it could be "syncretist"—the truest way to state what the figure of Neptune represents—or it could be "Puritan"—suggesting that whereas Neptune is a false idol, this is the true God. A slight shift in emphasis, then, changes the implied theological context. For Du Bartas, and his English translator, God is figured as the source of poetic strength (who alone can "Lift up my soule") and the humanistic arts ("with learned Art enrich . . ."). Du Bartas's Heavenly Muse, God, does not simply represent poetic inspiration; he is creativity itself. But so is the Muse, if one believes in her. The point is, then, that for Du Bartas God is the true source of creativity falsely attributed to the Muse.

Perhaps even more striking, perhaps, is Du Bartas's reversal of the invocation and the proposition.[11] Having first invoked God's aid, the poet encloses his proposition within his petitions, thereby making the poem's argument a gift of God:

O Father, grant I sweetly warble forth
Vnto our seed the WORLD'S renowned BIRTH:
Grant (gracious God) that I record in Verse
The rarest Beauties of this VNIVERSE;
And grant, therein Thy Power I may discern:
That, teaching others, I my self may learn. (1.7–12)

Du Bartas's theme is the creation of the world and his source of inspiration the Creator himself. His invocation and petitions clearly reveal that the poet looks outward and upward for the truth—here, toward the Divine Logos—which he aspires to express. Such truth cannot be received from a pagan, and therefore a make-believe, Muse. In addition, following the example of the French poet, Sylvester the translator adds his own invocation to God, in which he acknowledges his own insufficiency for a task so great and asks God for the inspiration to teach "dum Infants thy drad Praise to speak" (l.18). Abraham Cowley, sharing Du Bartas's didactic mission, simultaneously remained committed to his epic career (modeled upon the lives and works of Vergil and Spenser) and to his religious rejection of invocations to the pagan Muse. An examination of this tension in his epic attempts and in selected occasional poetry will offer an interesting perspective upon the status of the Muse in during the seventeenth century and set the stage for a more detailed analysis of Milton's life-long dedication to a simultaneously Christian and humanistic Muse.

From "Muse's Hannibal" to Poet Militant

While Cowley's youthful poem *The Motto* announces the poet's early decision to become the "Muses Hannibal" and climb the "Alpes" of poetry to "make the Age to come my own," his more mature elegy *On the Death of Mr. Crashaw* powerfully prefigures Cowley's ongoing concern with the tension between pagan and Christian elements in his own poetry and in seventeenth-century religious poetry in general. For Cowley, the real source of inspiration must be the Christian Godhead, or else the poetry is profane. Nevertheless, Cowley's elegy to his close friend and sometimes poetic model abounds in pagan conventions while the poet meanwhile eschews them. As Milton will later do in *Lycidas* and *Epitaphium Damonis*, Cowley participates in the ritual of mourning through writing his elegy to his close friend; from this personal and literary experience Cowley can emerge as the new Christian *vates*.

The poem begins with an invocation to the poet's departed friend, which focuses upon the two aspects most worthy of praise, his earthly vocation of poet and his heavenly status as saint:

Poet and Saint! to Thee alone are given
The two most sacred Names of Earth and Heaven.

The hard and rarest Union which can be
Next that of Godhead with Humanitie.
Long did the Muses banisht Slaves abide,
And built vain Pyramids to mortal pride;
Like Moses Thou (thou Spells and Charms withstand)
Hath brought them nobly home back to their Holy Land. (1-8)[12]

The poem begins with an apostrophe to Crashaw, whom the poet credits with combining the best of mortal and immortal qualities. As poet, Crashaw is presented as a new Moses: Cowley suggests that just as the biblical Moses freed God's chosen people, the Israelites, from their bondage in Egypt, so Crashaw has freed the Muses from enslavement to pagan pride, symbolized here by the grand scale of the pyramids. For this accomplishment, Cowley would elevate his departed friend to a position next only to the Godhead itself. Crashaw is a modern poet-prophet, a Moses-figure, whose invocations, now cleansed of pagan "spells and charms," recall the Muses to their true home, their "Holy Land," God.

Cowley continues in his efforts to place Crashaw's source of inspiration back to the true, original source. Since Crashaw's songs were holy, Cowley writes, "Thou need'st not write new Songs, but say the Old." Creativity and divine inspiration, then, are not things made fresh and new by the poet; they are old things, granted to the *vates*. By affirming the Sacred Muse through divine poetry, Crashaw needs nothing more. The "Old" songs are the truest songs. Cowley wishes to return us to our proper origin in the Christian Godhead, but the task is not so simple: "Still the old Heathen Gods in Numbers dwell, / The Heav'enliest thing on Earth still keeps up Hell." Cowley's meaning in the first line seems to be two-fold: the "Heathen Gods," which likely mean pagan gods and Muses, dwell in "Numbers"—that is, they remain numerous in quantity and remain entrenched in poetry. From Cowley's perspective, the "Heav'enliest thing on Earth," or poetry, should ideally serve to glorify God and his Heaven, not keep up Hell.

Thomas Carew, in *An Elegy Upon the Death of the Dean of Paul's, Dr. John Donne* (1633), makes a similar point. Carew also wants the old heathen gods banished, but for aesthetic rather than theological reasons. Indeed, Carew praises Donne for clearing out England's poetic garden and planting new wit and invention in the place of outworn classical conventions:

The Muses' garden, with pedantic weeds
O'erspread, was purged by thee; the lazy seeds
Of servile imitation thrown away,
And fresh invention planted. (25–28)[13]

In the epitaph which concludes the poem, Carew interestingly refers to Donne as "Apollo's first, at last the true God's priest" (98), calling attention to the dual aspects of his poetic career within the context of the "two flamens," (97) or priests of the Roman religion. But Donne mastered paganism only to replace it with Christianity, leaving "strict laws . . . Too hard for libertines in poetry": "They will repeal the goodly exiled train / Of gods and goddesses, which in thy just reign / Were banished nobler poems" (61–65). As he praises Donne for exiling the trains of pagan gods and goddesses from poetry, Carew also announces that they will soon enough be recalled from banishment by lesser poets. Soon English verse, "refined by thee [Donne] in this last age," will "[t]urn ballad-rhyme" and "those old idols" will be "[a]dored again with new apostasy" (68–70). While Carew may have some misgivings about the theological problems associated with using pagan forms for Christian poetry, his main objection to the pagan gods is that they have become clichés in English poetry.

Cowley's elegy to Crashaw, however, condemns pagan conventions and themes because they are *lies*, distortions of divine truth. In doing so, Cowley clearly wishes to promote his own programmatic purposes, which are both poetic and theological. Heathen Muses, for Cowley, are nothing better than false idols, unjustly elevated to divine status. In the following passage, Cowley makes an interesting comparison (based upon stereotypes) between fallen Muses and fallen, or less than perfect women: "What different faults corrupt our Muses thus? / Wanton as Girles, as old Wives, Fabulous!" Here, Cowley negatively associates the pagan—and therefore corrupted—Muses with the feminine. The pagan Muses are "wanton" and immature on the one hand and insubstantial or "fabulous" on the other. But Crashaw's Muse brings hope for redemption: "Thy spotless Muse, like Mary, did contain / The Boundless Godhead, / A fruitful Mother, and a Virgin too." Here, Cowley recalls the "spotless" tradition expressed so well by the Pearl Poet. Cowley's medieval image of purity is connected to Mary, the mother of God, and the brides of Christ. Cowley praises Crashaw for elevating poetry from its pagan depths to new Christian heights. Crashaw's Muse, which "contained the Godhead," also expresses religious truth. Literally, if the Muse equates to Mary, then Crashaw's poetic achievements brought to term and delivered God/Christ into the world as Mary brought Jesus into the world. Cowley plays upon the paradox of the Virgin mother, applying the significance of her role to the role of the poet. In this manner, Cowley successfully contrasts this positive view of the feminine with the negative one presented earlier in order to elevate the status of religious poetry and its practitioners.

However, Cowley, a faithful Anglican, still must reconcile Crashaw's Catholicism with his own faith before completing his *encomium*. Discussing Crashaw's faith, Cowley writes:

His Faith perhaps in some nice Tenents might
Be wrong; his Life, I'm sure, was in the right.
And I my self a Catholick will be,
So far at least, great Saint, to Pray to thee.

Downplaying the letter of the law—"in some nice Tenents [he] might be wrong"—and instead drawing attention to his friend's life allows Cowley to Christianize the conventional apotheosis and take liberties with the Catholic practice of praying to the Saints. Indeed, Cowley's basic strategy is to take material that is normally used for aesthetic reasons and insist on measuring it by theological standards. Here, however, it is most striking that he is aestheticizing doctrine. Cowley can pray to Crashaw, who now dwells among the blessed in heaven. It is fine to pray to a saint, Cowley suggests, if you do it as a way of recognizing his poetic contribution. Cowley's elegy/prayer, then, appropriately takes the form of a literary hymn and begins in the grand-style: "Hail, Bard Triumphant! and some care bestow / On us, the Poets Militant Below!" Cowley's epithet, "Bard Triumphant," treats Crashaw, for a moment, as if he were the Muse. Now among the heavenly saints, Crashaw has the power to assist those below who continue the fight on behalf of heaven. Crashaw is both "Bard"—suggesting his place in the lineage of Homer and Hesiod—as well as "Triumphant"—a designation often reserved for Christ's victory over death and sin. As in Milton's *Lycidas*, the emphasis shifts from a meditation upon the death of a friend to the current vocational aspirations of the surviving poet. Cowley recognizes and accepts the necessity of taking up the poetic mantle left behind by Crashaw. Seeing himself as a Christian soldier, whose sword is the pen, Cowley simply asks in his first petition[14] for "some care" from his departed friend to assist him (the poet militant) and the church on earth (the church militant) in fighting "our Old Enemy." As Crashaw has "triumphed" over death, so Cowley would wish to triumph over the pagan gods in English poetry.

Next, recalling his friend's imagined ascension into heaven, Cowley identifies Crashaw with the Old Testament prophets: "Thou from low earth in nobler Flames didst rise, / And like Elijah, mount Alive the skies." Here Cowley defines Crashaw's victory over death and his status as biblical prophet; Crashaw's upward movement is associated not only with the biblical account[15] but also with the notion of poetic inspiration and the light of divinely-inspired truth. Cowley wishes to ascend the heavens—that is, to blaze a new path for religious poetry—with the grace of God and the blessing of his new patron saint, Crashaw, now his Muse:

> Elisha-like (but with a wish much less,
> More fit thy Greatness, and my Littleness)
> Lo here I beg (I whom thou once didst prove
> So humble to Esteem, so Good to Love)
> Not that thy Spirit might on me Doubled be,
> I ask but Half thy mighty Spirit for Me.

Cowley, Elisha-like, follows the tradition of the Old Testament prophets.[16] In the biblical account, though, Elisha asks for and receives a double portion of Elijah's spirit. Here then, it seems that the poet comments upon the abundance of spirit in Crashaw. At least rhetorically, Cowley acknowledges Crashaw's superiority, owing either to his fully realized status in heaven or to his memory as a poet and servant of God. Certainly Cowley is being sincere, but his ego will nevertheless assert itself more in the invocation to the *Davideis*. In his second petition ("Lo I beg . . ."), beginning with *hypomnesis* that recalls past esteem and shared love between the speaker and the departed friend-turned-Muse, Cowley requests not more but half of Crashaw's creative spirit. Thus the poem concludes with the desire for poetic inspiration and the poet's promise to his departed friend: "And when my Muse soars with so strong a Wing, / 'Twill learn of things Divine, and first of Thee to sing." While Cowley pays the highest tribute to Crashaw by acknowledging the strength of his influence and the worthiness of his poetry, this closing passage reveals something significant about Cowley's relationship to the Muse. The Muse metamorphoses from the addressee, Crashaw, to Cowley's personal Muse ("my Muse") who will sing "of Thee" (that is, of Crashaw). With these lines Cowley completes the ritual of transferring the poetic mantle from Crashaw to himself; now with the blessing of God and his new patron saint, Crashaw, Cowley's poetry will hopefully gain strength and soar on its own to sing of things Divine.

As Theocritus and Vergil before him, and Milton, Shelley, Tennyson, and Whitman after him, Cowley draws upon the elegy's formal powers of lament and consolation for strength and assurance in his newly won vocation. Thus, the work of mourning becomes the orphic task of transcending loss and replacing it with a ritualized poetic utterance. As Celeste Marguerite Schenck writes, "the orphic task, as understood by the poets, is the search for a literary rebirth by means of an initiatory descent. The subsequent recovery (and continuance) of voice is a guarantee of literary immortality."[17] Like other elegists before him, Cowley offers his elegy to Crashaw as a memorial not only to the memory of his friend but also as a statement announcing the beginning of his own literary career. By singing of the dead and building upon his literary and religious accomplishments, Cowley aspires to take on the role of *vates* and gain "Sacred Fame" for himself and his cause.

"In These Untrodden Paths to Sacred Fame": Cowley and Biblical Epic

Cowley began his epic, *Davideis, a Sacred Poem of the Troubles of David* (1656), at Trinity College, Cambridge in about 1638 (when Milton was beginning to think of his *Arthuriad*), and expanded it in later years, without completing more than four of the projected twelve books.[18] In his 1656 Preface, Cowley takes the "Puritan" position of condemning mythological fables and urging the claims of biblical history: "Amongst all holy and consecrated things which the Devil ever stole [and] alienated from the service of the Deity; as

Altars, Temples, Sacrifices, Prayers, and the like; there is none that he so universally, and so long usurpt, as Poetry" (12). Arguing that literary and architectural forms of praise have impiously been perverted from their proper object of worship, namely God, Cowley calls for immediate action: "It is time to recover ["Poetry"] out of the Tyrants hands, and to restore it to the Kingdom of God, who is the Father of it" (12). From Cowley's perspective, epic poetry, which traditionally elevates the values and accomplishments of a nation in the person of the hero (as in the *Aeneid*), should maintain its formal structure—its integrity as a temple or altar—but offer itself in the service of the source of all that is good and true: God the Father.

Cowley's zeal for purging poetry of pagan corruption reveals itself most strongly in the poet's choice of Muse for his epic while his learned notes to the *Davideis* attest to his concern for heroic precedent and propriety in technique and style, as well as his desire to rewrite the tradition and its sources of inspiration by converting the pagan Muse. According to Douglas Bush, "Cowley's exaltation of sacred themes, as his elegy on Crashaw also shows, was mainly based on sincere religious feeling, but it included two other motives, a poet's desire for fresh material and what he emphasized in his praise of *Gondibert*, the realistic standards of truth and human life held by a modern rational mind."[19] But Cowley's achievement also owed a debt to Sylvester and Tasso, and Milton's esteem for Cowley was likely built upon on his reading of the *Davideis*, the first neoclassical religious epic in English and the first in heroic couplets which Milton so vehemently criticized.[20]

According to A. H. Nethercott, Cowley's *Davideis* was "lavishly overpraised in its own day, and lavishly overridiculed by the heavy-handed Dr. Johnson later."[21] In fact, Cowley did begin his epic with great enthusiasm. As for the whole project, he intended to immortalize all the troubles of David in an heroic poem of twelve books after the pattern of Vergil, and, according to his Preface of 1656, to conclude "with that most poetical and excellent elegy of David's on the Death of Saul and Jonathan." Cowley's commitment to the tradition of literary imitation was so great, in fact, that he translated book one of the *Davideis* into Latin, and likely intended to produce a separate Latin version in twelve books, after the scheme of Vergil. As David Trotter justly observes, Vergilian epic represented to Cowley "a pattern into which the history of the Jews could be fitted . . . [and] . . . provided a context for events whose significance was not immediately apparent."[22] In short, Trotter argues, the epic genre offered Cowley "an assurance of resolution" necessary in an heroic narrative (100).

An assurance of resolution was particularly necessary for the unity of Cowley's epic. Without it, the *Davideis* would raise more questions than it answered and would thereby compromise Cowley's religious aims. Even worse, Cowley's Muse, explicitly addressed in the invocation as God, or the "Eternal Word," might be rendered false or unreliable. While the history of King David had sufficient historicity for an epic, its religious content and significance in the

Christian faith would provide Cowley with other challenges—issues of accuracy and faith—which could be addressed by Cowley only by invoking the proper Muse.

So who is Cowley's Muse? To what extent does Cowley's Muse help him restore poetry to "the Kingdom of God"? Does Cowley successfully convert the Muse from paganism to Christianity? Can a Muse ever really be Christian? To answer these questions we must first turn to the invocation to Book I and Cowley's notes upon the poem and his choice of names. In the manner of Vergil, Cowley begins with a proposition wherein the plot of the epic is set forth:

> I Sing the Man who Judahs Scepter bore
> In that right hand which held the Crook before;
> Who from best Poet, best of Kings did grow;
> The two chief gifts Heav'n could on Man bestow.
> Much danger first, much toil did he sustain,
> Whilst Saul and Hell crost his strong fate in vain.
> Nor did his Crown less painful work afford;
> Less exercise his Patience, or his Sword;
> So long her Conque'ror Fortunes spright pursu'd;
> Till with unwearied Virtue he subdu'd;
> All homebred Malice, and all forreign boasts;
> Their strength was Armies, his the Lord of Hosts. (1.1–12)

Cowley opens his epic in the Vergilian manner with an assertive *cano*, or "I sing," before calling upon any kind of divine aid to help him narrate the plot or to provide him with the poem itself, as in Homer's *Iliad.* Cowley focuses upon his hero's authority and origins: David, once a shepherd (symbolized by the "Crook") became God's divinely anointed king (symbolized by the "Sceptre"). Moreover, Cowley calls attention to David's outstanding achievement (his Renaissance *virtù* or Hellenic *areté*) as "best Poet"[23] and as the "best of Kings, / The two chief gifts Heav'n could on Man bestow." Although presented as the "gifts" of God, David's excellence in both vocations reflects the Homeric and Aristotelian ideal of a man who is a "very God among men."[24] Though not literally a God among men, Cowley's David possesses "unwearied Virtue" given to him by God to fight against God's enemies, "Saul and Hell." Like Aeneas, David must face "much toil" before subduing his enemies and (re)establishing his people and their God in Judah. Cowley's proposition, which looks ahead to David's struggles and to his eventual triumph, concludes fittingly by contrasting false with true sources of inspiration and power: "Their strength [Saul's and Satan's] was Armies, his [David's] the Lord of Hosts." Thus, before calling upon his heavenly Muse, Cowley assures us that David's God is the true God, and the source of all power.

Having laid out his epic plan in the proposition, a fairly straightforward affair, Cowley next invokes the Muse, a more radical and certainly more problematic undertaking. Following the formal classical precedent, Cowley uses direct address to invoke the Muse. However, this Muse differs considerably from Erato and Calliope; Cowley addresses him both as the Father, progenitor of Abraham and David,[25] and as the Son of God, who died upon the cross the salvation of humanity. In doing so, Cowley ascribes all creative and redemptive powers to God. The body of the invocation, from epithets to specific petitions, reveals Cowley's conscious transformation of the pagan Muse from classical convention to Christian logos. The following section, lines 13–24, presents a consistent view of the Muse as the Christian Godhead, culminating in a strikingly visual and iconographic depiction of Christ's passion:

> Thou, who didst Davids royal stem adorn,
> And gav'st him birth from whom thy self wast born.
> Who didst in Triumph at Deaths Court appear,
> And slew'st him with thy Nails, thy Cross and Spear,
> Whilst Hells black Tyrant trembled to behold,
> The glorious light he forfeited of old,
> Who Heav'ns glad burden now, and justest pride,
> Sit'st high enthron'd next thy great Fathers side,
> (Where hallowed Flames help to adorn that Head
> Which once the blushing Thorns environed,
> Till crimson drops of precious blood hung down
> Like Rubies to enrich thine humble Crown.)

Rather than addressing one of the sacred daughters of Memory, Cowley calls upon God, the Father of David's line, the Creator of the universe, and the Son, who with his sacrifice conquered death and sin. In all forms, Cowley's Christian Muse is male, not female. The poet appeals directly to the source for the inspiration to write his biblical epic—no subtle transformations of Urania or Erato, but simply a substitution of the true Muse for the false Muse. In this invocation, as it begins at least, Cowley remains true to his desire to "Baptize" poetry in the water of the "Jordan," for it will never become clean by bathing in the Water of Damascus."[26] In providing the reader with David's genealogy, Cowley retraces humanity's origin in God, showing us the path to salvation and eternal peace. Cowley's catalogue of God's powers and *sedes* culminates in the poet's vision of Christ on the cross—for humanity, a beginning in itself—marking the end of Old Testament law and the beginning of Christ's new commandments. Cowley's Baroque meditation upon the wounds of Christ recalls the visual and sensual imagery of Richard Crashaw's *Steps to the Temple* (1646), *Delights of the Muses* (1646), or *Carmen Deo Nostro* (1652). *In Saint Mary Magdalene or The Weeper*, Crashaw meditates upon the tears which Mary Magdalene shed and used to anoint the feet of Jesus in a way similar to Cowley's meditation upon Christ's blood as rubies. Crashaw begins the poem with a question—"Loe where a WOVNDED HEART with Bleeding EYES conspire, /

Is she a FLAMING Fountain, or a Weeping fire?"[27]—which creates a vivid visual impression upon the reader. In stanza 14, Crashaw seems to develop the image of Mary's eyes to Baroque excess:

> And now where'er he strayes,
> Among the Galilean mountaines,
> Or more vnwellcome wayes,
> He's follow'd by two faithfull fountaines;
> Two walking baths; two weeping motions;
> Portable, & compendious oceans.

By transforming Mary's tear-filled eyes into fountains, then baths, and finally oceans, Crashaw dwells upon the physical in sensuous—even grotesque—detail and excess in an attempt to lead the reader from the icon to a higher understanding of the true object of meditation, Christ. As Robert T. Peterson observes, the immediate sensation of Crashaw's poetry may be visual, but "the direct visual experience of printed words on a page is little more than the vastly larger indirect experience that follows."[28] For Crashaw and Bernini (and Cowley in his iconographic depiction of Christ's passion), the Baroque imagery "embraces total reality, reconciles its opposing forces, and sees the life of man as passing, as becoming, as always flowing into the future" (121). But Cowley's image may provide more resonance through its allusion to the poetry of Crashaw than through any sustained development of the dramatic situation of Christ's crucifixion. For Cowley quickly and abruptly shifts from Muse as icon to Muse as poetic inspiration, as figured in David's lyre, and alternately as a pillar of cloud and pillar of fire,[29] leading the poet to his personal Promised Land—a career as God's sacred poet. At this point, Cowley's Muse turns from God himself, then religious icon, to a more conventional feminine identity blended with Old and New Testament imagery:

> Ev'en Thou my breast with such blest rage inspire,
> As mov'd the tuneful strings of Davids Lyre,
> Guid my bold steps with thine old trav'elling Flame,
> In these untrodden paths to Sacred Fame;
> Lo, with pure hands thy heav'enly Fires to take,
> My well-changed Muse I a chast Vestal make!
> From earths vain joys, and loves soft witchcraft free,
> I consecrate my Magdalene to Thee!
> Lo, this great work, a Temple to thy praise,
> On polisht Pillars of strong Verse I raise!
> A Temple, where if Thou vouchsafe to dwell,
> It Solomons, and Herods shall excel.
> Too long the Muses-Land have Heathen bin;
> Their Gods too long were Dev'ils, and Vertues Sin;

But Thou, Eternal Word, hast call'd forth Me
Th' Apostle, to convert that World to Thee;
T' unbind the charms that in slight Fables lie,
And teach that Truth is truest Poesie. (1.25–42)

Cowley's initial image of God—the Muse—as a pillar of fire leading his chosen people out of the wilderness seems consistent with the poet's desire to Christianize his poetry, as does his own desire "with pure hands thy heaven'ly Fires to take." However, having first invoked the Muse as Christ in line 13, he then dedicates his Muse (not Christ?) to Christ: "From earths vain joys, and loves soft witchcraft free, / I consecrates my Magdalene to Thee!"[30] Suddenly, Cowley's Muse changes from Christ to Magdalene, from male to female Muse. As Magdalene, Cowley's Muse embodies the poet's programmatic purpose: to redeem the classical Muse (a whore to paganism) by converting her to Christianity (now a follower of Christ). Indeed, Cowley presents his Muse as a convert, and thus as an image for the Christianizing of the Muse. But the invocation does not work as an invocation. Indeed, Cowley shows considerable uncertainty about the nature of his poetic inspiration. Perhaps Sacred Fame is a problem for Cowley: on the one hand he wants to acknowledge God as the fountain of all creation (thereby replacing the pagan Muses) but on the other he wants to be God's apostle and single-handedly convert the Muse. He wants to present his "well-changed Muse" to God as a "chast Vestal." And that would be Cowley's work, not the work of God or the Holy Spirit.

So, is God Cowley's Muse or not? Suddenly the Muse is female again, and closer to the conventional model, but dressed up in biblical clothing. By shifting from Christ to Magdalene as Muse, though, Cowley transfers the origin of the poem from God to poet. No longer divinely inspired, the *Davideis* becomes the poet's gift to God. Nuttall is correct when he argues that "no real Muse is present" in Cowley's invocation and that "the deity invoked is unequivocally external to the poem." Moreover, Nuttall correctly adds that the Muse, when she appears, is wholly metaphorical, representing nothing more than poetry.[31]

As we can see, Cowley is clearly concerned with refining the sullied Muse. As a classical guide, Cowley suggests, she was a whore, but in her Christian form she is a now a "chaste Vestal." But the power to create is uncertain here: where is the source of inspiration now, in God or in Cowley? Cowley seems to assert that he has made the Muse pure for God; she is now a Magdalene, a whore turned into a faithful disciple of Christ. Cowley views his poetic creation, the *Davideis*, as a "great work" by virtue of its purer source in God's "heaven'ly Fires." Following Herbert's lead, Cowley's *Davideis* (and its weighty critical apparatus in the Notes) will be a Temple to God; in keeping with its epic scale, Cowley exclaims, the poem will be a Temple greater and more worthy even than Solomon's or Herod's. According to Cowley's vision for the project, the epic will shine forth with its own excellence (*virtù* or *aretê*) and exceed all previous attempts.

The final lines of the invocation to the "well-changed Muse" embody Cowley's poetic theory concerning pagan elements in Christian poetry. Here, Cowley replaces classical with Christian values and distinguishes between the true and false. Furthermore, Cowley asserts his own relationship to God, calling himself an Apostle, as well as clearly defining his didactic purpose: "To unbind the charms that in slight Fables lie, / And teach that Truth is truest Poesie." The same movement between a pagan Muse and Christianity also appears in the poetry of Crashaw, whose blending of holy and worldly imagery influenced the poetry of Cowley.

In his hymn, *To the Name Above Every Name, the Name of Jesus*,[32] Crashaw calls upon the name of Jesus to descend from "the Bright / Regions of peacefull Light" (115), an invocation that resembles that of the Attendant Spirit in Comus. Throughout the poem, Crashaw invokes the Name of Jesus in very much the same way that poets invoke the Muse—"Come, louely NAME; life of our hope!" (125). Therefore, this poem serves as an excellent example of the successful transfer of pagan strategies to Christian subject matter. Crashaw begins with the Vergilian *cano*, "I sing the Name which none can say / But touch't with An interior Ray" (1–2), but immediately focuses upon the attributes of the Son of God: Jesus is "the Name of our new Peace; our Good; / Our Blisse: & Supernaturall Blood" (3–4). Calling upon the name of Jesus, in fact, raises the level of poetry (line 43) even as the poet embellishes his verse with an abundance of worldly and sensual imagery (especially lines 158–191). The Name of Jesus becomes the source of human fertility and poetic creativity:

> WELCOME to our dark world, Thou
>   WOMB of Day!
> Vnfold thy fair Conceptions; and display
> The Birth of our Bright Ioyes. (161–164)

And later the Name transforms into the Christ-child's gifts brought from the Orient, magnifying them a thousand-fold and culminating in a rapturous taste of Paradise:

> SWEET NAME, in Thy each Syllable
> A thousand Blest ARABIAS dwell;
> A Thousand Hills of Frankincense;
> Mountains of myrrh, & Beds of spices,
> And ten Thousand PARADISES
> The soul that tasts thee takes from thence. (183–188)

Crashaw repeatedly invokes the "SWEET NAME" of Jesus as if performing variations upon a musical theme in order to heighten the meditative potential of the poem, and the name—Jesus—that is at its center. Almost always excessive in sensuous details, Crashaw's devotional poetry nevertheless transcends its seeming self-indulgence by focusing upon a Christian image or name. Cowley, who admired Crashaw, employed similar pagan strategies for Christian purposes—though not as grotesque—when calling upon his Muse in the *Davideis* and elsewhere for inspiration and confirmation in his vocation.

On the whole, I agree with Nuttall's assessment that, for Cowley, the Muse simply becomes synonymous with poetry.[33] As Cowley states in his fifth note to the *Davideis*, Book I, he desires "to be made an Apostle for the conversion of Poetry to Christianity, as S. Paul was for the conversion of the Gentiles; which was done not only by the Word, as Christ was the Eternal Word of his Father; but by his becoming a Particular Word or Call to him."[34] Cowley further suggests that his meaning will be "more fully explained in the Latin Translation," where he makes the connection between his poetic calling and Paul's religious conversion more explicit.[35] Cowley certainly takes his own vocation seriously, as well as his dedication to Christianizing poetry. However, as much as Cowley attempts to explain his invocation to the Muse in his Notes, he nevertheless fails to convince the reader that the Muse has accepted the call to become "baptized in the Jordan" or that one can ever really convert the pagan Muse into an instrument of God by divorcing her from her classical heritage. Ignoring syncretic possibilities, Cowley both employs and rejects classical epic conventions without admitting that he is doing so. Perhaps that is why the Muse ceases to sing to him.

But Cowley does invoke the Muse again in the *Davideis*, Book I,[36] to begin his digression upon Musick:

> Tell me, oh Muse (for Thou, or none canst tell
> The mystick pow'ers that in blest Numbers dwell,
> Thou their great Nature know'st, not is it fit
> This noblest Gem of thine own Crown t' omit)
> Tell me from thence these heav'nly charms arise;
> Teach the dull world t' admire what they despise.

Cowley admits in his own Note 33, however, that the invocation to the Muse, though appropriate for the introduction of the subject of "Musick," is purely conventional. He writes, "I chuse here upon this new occasion, by the by to make a new short Invocation of the Muse, and that which follows, As first a various unform'd, is to be understood as from the person of the Muse: For this second Invocation upon a particular matter, I have the authority of Homer and Virgil." Citing classical precedents for his invocation and informing the reader as to which part is the poet's and which the Muse's part of the poem, Cowley seemingly gives up all pretensions to divine inspiration. However, the verse paragraph that follows reveals a striking parallel between Creation and creation. God creating the universe is behaving like a poet, and the World is God's Poem:

> As first a various unform'd Hint we find,

Rise in some god-like Poets fertile Mind,
Till all the parts and words their places take,
And with just marches verse and musick make;
Such was Gods Poem, this Worlds new Essay.

Cowley compares the rhetorical canon of invention to God's creation of the world: "In the beginning was the Word." Where there was once chaos and darkness, now there is a "Hint" which grows into an harmonious creation. While Cowley implies that he is unworthy of so great a task and still dependent upon the Heav'nly Muse for inspiration, his parallel between the mind of the poet and the mind of God is strikingly arrogant. However, unlike the first invocation in which Cowley attempted to convert the Muse to Christianity, the second merely demarcates a transition in the text of the poem from the proper narrative to a learned digression.

As Cowley admits in his Preface, "I am far from assuming to my self to have fulfilled the duty of this weighty undertaking: But sure I am, that there is nothing yet in our Language (nor perhaps in any) that is any degree answerable to the Idea that I conceive of it."[37] Concerning the worthiness of the task and the significance of its message, Sprat agreed with Cowley, remarking that the *Davideis*, "is a better instance and beginning of a Divine Poem, than I ever yet saw in any Language . . .The subject was truly Divine, even according to Gods own heart . . . in all there is an admirable mixture of humane Virtues and Passions, with religious raptures."[38] In spite of his support and admiration of Cowley, though, Sprat's language reveals some significant, and unfortunate, truths about the *Davideis*. Indeed, the *Davideis* was a fine "beginning," blending "humane Virtues and Passions, with religious Raptures," as Sprat says. But it was only a beginning, not a finished epic. And yet these very qualities underscore Cowley's role as innovator above that of "inspired" poet. Cowley concludes his Preface with an admission that while he had not been up to the task of writing the great Christian epic in English perhaps someone else of greater talents would in the future: "And I shall be ambitious of no other fruit from this weak and imperfect attempt of mine, but the opening of a way to the courage and industry of some other persons, who may be better able to perform it thoroughly and successfully."[39] Though he did not know it at the time, Milton's *Paradise Lost* would soon do more than inaugurate the Classical epic tradition in England—it would embody and define it for generations to come.

From Christian to Martial Muse: Cowley's *A Poem on the Late Civil War*

Abraham Cowley's *A Poem on the Late Civil War*, published posthumously in 1679,[40] was probably written during the author's period of residence at Oxford, the King's Headquarters, to which he had moved from Cambridge upon the outbreak of the Civil War. According to Allan Pritchard, Cowley likely began writing his poem "in the summer or early autumn of 1643," and gave up work on the poem "in the unfortunate period for the Royalist cause which followed the first Battle of Newbury."[41] Cowley's heroic narrative poem is important for our discussion because of what it reveals about Cowley as epic poet, its singular use of poetic invocations, and its attempt to present contemporary events within an epic framework. Indeed, Cowley is less able to identify the Muse; here, she becomes more conventional and less pivotal in the creative process than in the *Davideis*.

A Poem on the Late Civil War begins with a brief preface entitled, "The Publisher to the Reader," in which the publisher traces the history of the poem and comments upon its merits as well as those of its author. His language reveals both an admiration for the genius of the writer and an acknowledgment of the inspiration necessary for a work of such scope:

> Meeting accidentally with this Poem in Manuscript, and being informed that it was a Piece of the incomparable Mr. A. C.'s, I thought it unjust to hide such a Treasure from the World. I remember'd that our Author in his Preface to his Works, makes mention of some Poems written by him on the late Civil War, of which the following copy is questionably a part. In his most imperfect and unfinish'd Pieces, you will discover the Hand of so great a Master. And (whatever his own Modesty might have advised to the contrary) there is not one careless stroke of his but what should be kept sacred to Posterity. He could write nothing that was not worth preserving; being habitually a Poet and Always Inspired. In this Piece the Judicious Reader will find the Turn of the Verse to be his; the same Copious and Lively Imagery of Fancy, the same Warmth of Passion and Delicacy of Wit that sparkles in all his Writings. And certainly no Labours of a Genius so Rich in its self, and so Cultivated with Learning and Manners, can prove an unwelcome Present to the World.[42]

From the perspective of the publisher, any production of Abraham Cowley's should be preserved; as a poet by vocation, Cowley is "always inspired," and the source of that inspiration is divine. Not only does the publisher's admiration for the powers of the poet and his almost divine calling to compose great poetry capture popular conceptions of the poet, but it also makes a good marketing pitch to potential readers of the work.

Cowley's *Civil War* attempts to place the contemporary events of the struggle between the Parliamentarians and the Royalists into an epic narrative which directly participates in the historical events it relates. According to Gerald M. MacLean, Cowley's text "manipulates heroic conventions to analyze the war as a problem of historical causation. In this account, the present degenerates from a glorious past because of an infernally generated reformist zeal threatening the fabric of traditional social behavior and political relations."[43] From the first line of the poem it is clear that the scope is heroic; Cowley's language is in the grand-style and his subject is war. Although the lines of good and evil are clearly drawn, the outcome is not. Herein echoes of Lucan abound, in its theme of civil war announced in the poem's first line ("What Rage does England from itself divide . . ."), its language of strife and bloodshed, and its collection of heroic portraits, or *encomia* to the King's faithful military commanders. In a recent article, D. M. Rosenberg offers some useful insights into Cowley's use of panegyric in the *Civil War*. Noting that both Cowley and Milton, deeply read in classical epic and aware of its generic comprehensiveness, included in their heroic narratives poetry of praise, satire, and elegies, Rosenberg writes that "Cowley's panegyric passages place great emphasis upon the courtly and chivalric values of Cavalier heroism. He emphasizes the theme of heroic *virtù* in his miniature epic portraits of Royalist military heroes. These panegyrics combine the aristocratic ideals of the soldier, the courtier, and the man of learning."[44] Rosenberg contrasts these passages of praise with Milton's hymns praising God in *Paradise Lost*.[45] Both poets, he argues, employ the elegiac mode when confronting the tragic loss brought about by epic warfare:

> Milton's entire poem is an elegy on the loss of innocence, the inevitability of war and death, "and all our woe" (1.3–4), but it is also a hymn of praise and a poem of consolation that are integral parts of his theodicy. In the *Civil War*, Cowley's many elegies on the deaths of great Royalist soldiers, of course, resemble the epic laments for dead heroes in the *Iliad* and *Aeneid*.[46]

I mention Cowley's and Milton's use of the elegiac mode at this length because it is central to an understanding of their respective uses of poetic invocations, or lack of invocations, in their epics. Both epics concern loss and offer consolation, but Cowley, because he situates his narrative in present history—an epic that he cannot control from beginning to end—he must make his poetic resources, even his very Muse, serve unforeseen purposes.

Both Cowley and Milton wished to follow Tasso's injunction to "give the pleasure of learning together with virtue."[47] However, while Milton's *Paradise Lost* would have sufficient historicity to succeed as an epic of origins and as an epic speaking to its own time (and of its own time), Cowley's lacked that historicity and therefore could not teach of the rightness of the Royalist cause if the Royalists were losing the war. Perhaps his *Civil War* seemed to be an opportunity greater than his *Davideis* to present that which was historically and divinely true (not to say that the biblical account of David lacked those things to a seventeenth-century audience) without the classical/pagan ornamentation discussed at such great length in his commentary upon the *Davideis*. Given the course of history and the fate of Charles I, however, Cowley's epic upon those events was likely subject to the same failure.

Even though Milton's Adam and Eve must leave the Garden at the end of *Paradise Lost*, still they have the possibility of redemption through the exercise of their free-will: "The world was all before them, where to choose / Their place of rest, and Providence thir guide" (*PL* 12.646–647). Just as the Greek and Roman authors knew the scope of their epics before writing them, so too did Milton. His proposition in Book 1 of *Paradise Lost*, therefore, could present his epic's theme; his invocations could lead the poet through the stages of the plot. Milton could gain in strength and self-reflexivity, allowing him to offer his readers a keener insight into the ongoing process of inspiration and to present his justified claim to divine calling. Invocations to the Muse in the *Civil War*, however, present a different view of poetic inspiration—for Cowley, the Muse, whether Christian or pagan, is needed elsewhere besides the customary place at the beginning of the poem. Cowley's Muse is needed in the war effort itself, both as an agent of force supporting the King and as a source of inspiration in the poet's *encomia* to Royal leaders. Supporting the King and his military commanders amounts to supporting the Divine Right authority of the Crown. However, while Cowley's Muse remains steadfastly loyal to the King and his institutions, her identity, whether pagan or Christian, remains uncertain.

Unlike Homer, Vergil, and Lucan, Cowley opens the *Civil War* without invoking the Muse. Instead of beginning with an invocation to the Muse, Cowley's lengthy proem to the work begins with a series of rhetorical questions which serve to underscore the tragic nature of the war and to connect it to the tradition of loss embodied in Lucan. Looking at the 1679 edition of the poem, one notices that even the engraver calls attention to the elegiac quality of the poem by including a winged cherub within the factotum, giving the first page of the poem the appearance of a commemorative effigy. (See fig. 1.) The ornamentation used by the publisher reveals an interesting commentary upon the themes of Cowley's poem—civil discord, defeat, and death.[48] Cowley properly begins the poem by stating the epic's major themes:

> What Rage does England from itself divide,
> More than the Seas from all the World beside.

These first two lines essentially comprise the epic's proposition (though Cowley will later elaborate upon this Rage and the nature of England's division at greater length) and should be examined in some detail. The passage is a direct address appeal to an unidentified addressee, likely the reader. "What Rage . . ." is a rhetorical question that takes us into the midst of the nation's troubles; these troubles are internal and self-destructive, and more divisive than geographical boundaries like the English channel. MacLean writes that "in Cowley's version of history, England's natural and historical order, the true conditions of its claims to civilization, are represented by the Elizabethan model of successful war abroad and peace at home under just monarchs."[49]

(1)

A

POEM

On the late

CIVIL WAR.

Hat Rage does *England* from it ſelf divide,
More than the Seas from all the World beſide.
From every part the roaring Cannons play,
From every part Blood roars as loud as they.
What *English* Ground but ſtill ſome Moiſture bears,
Of Young Mens Blood,and more of Mothers Tears!
What Airs unthickened with the Sighs of Wives,
Tho' more of Maids for their dear Lovers Lives.

B Alas,

Figure 1. First page of Abraham Cowley's *A Poem on the Late Civil War* (1697), with a factotum containing a winged cherub. (Courtesy of the Newberry Library, Chicago)

Suggesting that Cowley professes to solve the problem of civil war by presenting the troubles as "an interlude—of tragic and heroic proportions—in the continuing epic of England's glorious monarchy," MacLean argues that "the poem postulates an eventual future that will be made even more glorious by the victory of the Stuarts over the self-divisive rage currently fracturing what is supposed to be a united nation."[50] By addressing geographical matters, Cowley underscores Britain's unique and self-sufficient position as an island cut off (in a sense) from Europe and focuses the reader's attention upon this unique body of land as if it were a human agent turned against itself. This "Rage" becomes an irrational and harmful disease that threatens the health of all.[51]

In the place of the expected invocation to the Muse for inspiration and memory,[52] Cowley follows his proposition with an extended lament for England. Relying upon his own memory, not that of the Muse's, he searches back to England's more golden periods of history when such shameful rebellions did not occur. While on the one hand Cowley compares contemporary England to a diseased body and the Parliamentarians or "Rebels" with darkness, on the other he equates Charles I and the Royalists with health and light. Perhaps because this is a poem of loss Cowley does not ask the Muse to inspire his verse. Indeed, Cowley never names his Muse. But Homer and Vergil treated similar themes of war and defeat; Vergil asked his Muse, "tantaene animis caelestibus irae,"[53] in order to understand the nature of Juno's wrath toward the defeated and now homeless Trojans. In the Augustan epic, gods and goddesses may have it in for certain mortals, yet other deities may lend aid to them. Vergil could sing of "arms and the man," but he could also see into his hero's future and know that Aeneas would someday found a new Troy in Latium. Cowley could not see into the future, nor could he call upon Clio to do it for him.

Perhaps a better parallel to Cowley's emphasis upon the sheer destruction and carnage brought about by war would be Lucan's *De Bello Civili*, which narrates the battle at Pharsalia and its consequences. Like Cowley, Lucan provides occasional portraits, as it were, of individuals of note. Lucan begins his epic with a proposition (1.1-7) stating the poem's epic theme—war, and the worst kind of war, civil war:

> Bella per Emathios plus quam civilia campos,
> Iusque datum sceleri canimus, populumque potentem
> In sua victrici conversum viscera dextra,
> Cognatasque acies, et rupto foedere regni
> Certatum totis concussi viribus orbis
> In commune nefas, infestisque obvia signis
> Signa, pares aquilas et pila minantia pilis.[54]

The thematic parallels between Lucan and Cowley are clear: "Bella" and "What Rage" amount to the same idea for the two poets. Both conflicts are presented as criminal and infectious activities, undermining national identity and unnaturally pitting brother against brother. Moreover, neither proposition is followed by the customary invocation to the Muse. The focus here is on the "I" and his perception of the diseased body of Rome or England, respectively.

Rather than following his proposition with an invocation to the Muse, Lucan continues to lament the state of affairs in Italy in the aftermath of the epic struggle between Caesar and Pompeius. Significantly, both Lucan and Cowley focus upon the here-and-now of the poem—war—and upon its bloody nature. For Lucan, such destruction and loss of life amounts to madness: "Quis furor, o cives, quae tanta licentia ferra?"[55] But Lucan never invokes the Muse at the opening of his epic; instead, he builds up to a panegyric to Nero, which can easily be taken as praise as well as condemnation of the Emperor. Yet in spite of Lucan's dislike of Julius Caesar and the Caesarean values represented in the person of Nero, Lucan cannot not help admiring Caesar's greatness as a leader in his epic (though one also has sympathy for Pompeius' patriotism and admiration for Cato's stoicism). Cowley, familiar with Lucan's *De Bello Civili*, likely modeled the opening section of his own *Civil War*—as well as the abundant gore throughout—upon this classical precedent. But whereas Lucan used his invocation-turned-*encomium* against its object of "praise"—the Emperor Nero[56]—Cowley eschewed a formal invocation to Clio or Erato in favor of a series of sincere royal *encomia*, which extol the virtues of the King's loyal servants.

After his opening proposition, Cowley's proem continues, developing ideas of self-alienation, conflict, and loss of life:

From every part the roaring Cannons play,
From every part Blood roars as load as they.
What English Ground but still some Moisture bears,
Of Young Mens Blood, and more of Mothers Tears!

We note Cowley's use of anaphora ("From . . . From") and repetition ("every part . . . every part") linking the contemporary weapon of war—the cannon—to the loss of blood. This repetition magnifies and multiplies the loss of life on the battlefield and suggests the repeated firing of cannons. We also observe the unfortunate metaphor of the "blood roaring," careless and unsuccessful hyperbole. Cowley also develops water imagery more here in the moist English soil. As an island, England is perpetually green and fertile; now the land is corrupted by war. The soil is drenched with "Young Mens Blood," young men cut off before their time (as Cowley himself might be), and drenched with the tears of Mothers, who like the soil are life-bearing but now barren.

Cowley's depiction of "Mothers tears" begins a pathetic appeal that is further amplified by extension to Wives and Maids: "What Air unthickened with the Sighs of Wives, / Tho' more of Maids for their dear Lovers Lives." Just as the soil is full of tears, so the air is filled with sounds of grief and sadness—the moans of wives and maids who have lost someone to the "Rage" of war. We recognize here a movement from Mother England to mothers of soldiers, from wives, who have experienced the marriage bed, to maids, who have only longed for it (I'm assuming a well-bred seventeenth-century audience here). The poignancy of the pathos builds upon the movement from old to young and out of the despair felt when confronted with the prospect of dying in the flower of youth. Cowley, clearly moved by the devastation of the war and perhaps mindful of its potential to have cut short his own poetic career, approaches the "What boots it?" topos when, with authentic feeling, he concludes: "Alas, what Triumphs can this Victory shew, / That dies us Red in Blood and Blushes too!" This rhetorical question is only the first of many posed by the poet to make sense of the war and its consequences for England. Because the people of England are turning against each other, England is in a poor state: "But now alas we strive, / Our own, our own good Soveraign to Captive!" Cowley's use of repetition here marks the poet's disbelief at England's present course.

He next recalls—without the aid of the Muse—a short catalogue of English heroes and better times (situated in the past). First, he recalls Henry V: "It was not so when Agincourt was won, / Under great Henry served the rain and sun." Next Elizabeth I: "It was not so when that vast fleet of Spain, / Lay torn and scatter'd on the English Main, / Through the proud World, a Virgin terror strook." Again, Cowley's use of anaphora ("It was not so . . . It was not so . . .") negatively contrasts the present troubles with the glories of the past. Cowley taps into the collective memory of the nation, and not into the infinite memory of the Muse, to recount two monarchs who properly focused England's "Rage" outward rather than inward to win glory. Cowley's conclusion to the section underscores the futility and folly of England's present course of self-destruction: "Thus our Fore-Fathers Fought, Thus bravely bled, / Thus still they live, whil'st we alive are dead."[57] And after recalling the golden days of James and Charles as if in a pastoral Arcadia, Cowley asks: "How could a war so sad and barbarous please, / But first by slandering those blest days of peace?" Here, Cowley accuses opponents of the King of bringing in the "Plague" to drive out the "diseases" of the state (p. 7), an idea that he amplifies with religious imagery: "Fond men! who knew not that they were to keep / For God, and not for sacrifice, their sheep" (p. 8). If written before King Charles' execution, these lines give an eerie foreshadowing of things to come. More importantly, however, Cowley wishes to play upon both the pastoral tradition of Theocritus and Vergil and the biblical tradition of Christ as good shepherd. By accusing the soldiers of neglecting their charge—the sheep, or the King—Cowley reveals them as bad pastors. Moreover, Cowley might also be suggesting that the country is reverting to Old Testament practices of animal sacrifices, superseded by Christ's new commandments in the New Testament.

Next comes the conflict over the Prayer Book, which leads to further calls for blood and a digression upon the death of Orpheus. So how then does Cowley confront this despair? He invokes images of Royalist heroism and calls upon his Muse to lend a hand to the Royalist cause and to inspire him as he attempts to record heroic actions and character in verse. When the war begins within the poem, so do the heroic portraits of Worster, Rupert, Stafford, Charles, Lindsey and Aubigny, Stephen, and finally Bainford (pp. 11–19).

However, it is not until the first Royalist victory that Cowley makes a reference to the Muses, who serve a symbolic rather than inspirational purpose: "To Oxford next Great Charles in Triumph came, / Oxford the British Muses second Fame" (p. 20). Cowley eschews the Muses' classical associations in favor of more martial and nationalistic ones; indeed, Cowley attempts to modernize the Muses by transferring either their honorable associations or their symbolic significance to contemporary Royalist heroes. On the other hand, Cowley, throughout the poem, compares the Rebels to Lucifer's fallen comrades, whose actions are synonymous with Chaos, while reaching back to England's originary myths of Brutus and Uther, as well as Arthur, to validate and strengthen the position of Charles and his supporters.

Cowley writes a scathing, allegorical satire upon the Rebels, who are anti-civilization, anti-learning, and anti-church, whose actions threaten the rightful order of things maintained, for now, at Charles' court in Oxford:

> Here Learning with some State and Reverence looks,
> And dwells in Buildings lasting as her Books,
> Both now Eternal, but they had Ashes been,
> Had these Religious Vandals once got in.
> Not Bodley's Noble Work their Rage would spare,
> For Books they know the chief Malignants are.
> . . .
> Beggary and Scorn into the Church they'd bring,
> And make God Glorious, as they made the King. (pp. 20–21)

In contrast to the Rebels' destructive zeal, Charles and his royal seat are presented as the locus of learning, history, and order. Oxford embodies a combination of humanistic study and Christian piety, the same values which Cowley's Muse possesses in the *Davideis*. The Rebels, who threaten the King from without, threaten civilization itself as did the Vandals who sacked Rome under Gaiseric in 455 A.D., marking the beginning of the end of the Western Empire.

In their religious zeal and rage, Cowley's Rebels seek to "glorify" God by destroying his greatest gifts to humanity—human reason and divinely-ordained government. But Cowley counters this picture of destruction with a call for British valor, derived from Arthurian heritage:

> Ye noble Brittains, who so oft with Blood
> Of Pagan Hosts, have died old Tamar's Flood,
> If any drop of mighty Uther still,
> Or Uther's mighty'r Son your Veins does fill.

Shew then that spirit, till all men think by you
The doubtful Tales of your Great Arthur true. (pp. 23–24)

Invoking the legends and tales of Brutus and Arthur, Cowley (Muse-like) hopes to inspire his countrymen to reclaim their noble past. Cowley follows this appeal with an *encomium* to Hopton: "Miraculous Man! how would I sing thy praise, / Had any Muse crowned me with half the Bays / Conquest hath given to thee" (p. 25). At last, Cowley returns to his Muse. But again, the poet transfers the honors due the poet to the military commander; Cowley does not feel worthy to sing of one whose accomplishments carry so much more weight than his own in this momentous period of English history. His use of the inexpressibility topos here resembles that assumed by the epic poet who calls upon the Muse for her memory and wisdom. The expression, "half the Bays," recalls as well Cowley's tribute to Crashaw, discussed earlier. Clearly, the Muse as a real creative force is not present in the poem; Cowley can only call upon the name of the Muse to magnify further his heroic portrait of this "Miraculous Man."

After his brief *encomium* to Hopton, Cowley continues to mention in a *paralepsis* others whose services to the King are worthy of praise,[58] but soon breaks off with a display of emotion: "But Tears break off my Verse" (p. 25). Finally, Cowley invokes Greenvil—"Hail mighty Ghost!"—in the elevated or grand style, whose spirit has now infused and strengthened those who still remain and "Cavendish whom every Grace and every Muse, Kiss'd at his Birth."[59] Once again, Cowley reserves the services of the Muses for those men fighting for their King.[60]

Cowley's final reference to the Muse occurs near the end of the poem, when the poet commemorates the bravery and chivalric values of Cavendish:

With much of state brave Cavendish led them forth,
As swift and fierce as tempest from the North.
Cavendish whom every Grace and every Muse,
Kiss'd at his Birth; and for their own did chuse:
So good a Wit they meant not should excel
In Arms, but now they see't and like it well . . .
. . .
Scarce did the Power Divine in fewer days,
A peaceful World out of Chaos raise. (pp. 29–30)

This epic portrait of the Royalist Cavendish calls attention to the ideal qualities of courtly and chivalric values which he possesses. Moreover, Cavendish's vocation, first as Wit and then as soldier, has been chosen for him at birth by the Graces and the Muses, a fact acknowledged by the poet Cowley, for whom such divine calling at so early an age should not seem unnatural. Indeed, the Graces' and Muses' approval of Cavendish's wit is something that Cowley shares, reflecting as much upon the poet here as upon his object of praise. But there is more to this *encomium*: Cavendish has even exceeded all expectations, and his excellence in Arms meets with divine approval.

Cowley then shifts from pagan forms of praise to Christian in his hyperbolic description comparing Cavendish's ability to create "a peaceful World out of Chaos" with God's creation of the world in Genesis. Divine inspiration is present here, but it is approvingly channeled into acts of war which would restore order and harmony to the world of England's civil war.

Despite the optimism of these heroic portraits, though, Cowley's historical epic resonates more fully with the tone of sustained lamentation. After a series of rhetorical questions which cast blame upon the Rebels for causing this Chaos, Cowley's narrative breaks off after the final comma:

> . . . What then mean your Lies
> Your Sacriledges and Pulpit Blasphemies,
> Why are all Sect's let loose, that ere had Birth,
> Since Luther's noise wak'd the Lethargick Earth, . . .

At this point, the publisher adds: "The author went no further" (p. 32).[61] For Cowley's seventeenth-century audience, such an ending would perhaps make sense; for someone writing in praise of the Royalist cause during the war, the tide of history—presently in favor of the Puritans—could be too much even for a poet chosen early by the Muses to sing of wars and kings.[62]

A careful reading of *A Poem on the Late Civil War* reveals that Cowley is thoroughly caught up in the actions of the war itself. While epics are generally forceful and positive, asserting the superiority of a nation or people and projecting future glories, they are also usually written after the fact. Cowley's *Civil War*, at times, seems like an extended lament, at others like a search for better days. He does not invoke the Muse in the conventional manner of Homer or Vergil for poetic inspiration or memory: Cowley's epic, instead, is literally before the poet's eyes and its heroes are struggling to keep up the fight. Epic values and myths, therefore, are not fixed but in a constant state of flux. Though Cowley's presentation of the good and the dark forces reflects his conviction concerning the legitimacy of royal prerogative and hierarchy, his verses of praise for Charles' defenders almost take the form of prayers. Cowley cannot invoke his Muse for poetic inspiration because she is already busy "inspiring" the leaders of Charles' army. If she is not doing her job well enough, Cowley is afraid to be the first to say so.

In a sense, both the *Davideis* and *The Civil War* present a pattern of lament and consolation found in most epics, from the *Iliad* to *Paradise Lost*. The success of Cowley's epics, like that of other epic poets', depends upon the success and magnitude of the cure. The Muse, invoked by the poet, is instrumental and reflective of the poet's achievement. The result is a new beginning, sufficient for the culture with all its values and tradition. Cowley's epics, however, do not provide us with such a beginning. Cowley's *Davideis*, though more promising and complex than his other poetic works, remained unfinished and its Muse uncertain. Indeed, much of Cowley's argument of the poem is to be found not in the poem itself but in its Notes. Cowley's *Civil War*, on the other hand, remained too much grounded in current history (and not enough in the mythical past or in Eternity), and his Muse conventional and undefined. In both cases, Cowley provides no stable grounding to ensure the continuation of national values or identity. After the Civil War and the Restoration, Cowley would retire to the country, where his life and literary productions would reflect the reversal of the epic career pattern. Cowley's *Plantarum in Six Books*,[63] even with its digression upon the Late Troubles, shows the author's concern with the past and little vision for the future.

Chapter II

Milton's Early Invocations: From the Psalms to *Comus*

John Milton's poetry reveals a pattern of invocations, from his early verse through his epic, *Paradise Lost*. These invocations are strongly influenced by the Psalms and by the *Odes* of Pindar, and an understanding of their use by Milton is essential for an understanding of the poet's sense of poetic calling. Early in his poetic career, Milton demonstrated a clear awareness of his vocation as *vates*, or poet-priest.[1] For Milton, the vocation of poet was both an artistic and a religious calling. An examination of his early verse will reveal the theme of the search for origins, both as poetic convention and as a concept central to his being. More importantly, the early poetry will open the door to a larger discussion of the poet's personal involvement in an apparently impersonal genre, whether an ode, a lyric, or an epic. Just as the epic genre concerns the origins of a people or race, devout Christians should constantly turn to God, their maker and source of strength, for inward illumination. But when the poet calls upon his "Heav'nly Muse," who or what is really being invoked? The tradition of invocation is a pagan one, but Milton adapts it to a specifically Christian situation and, in most cases, within the context of an explicitly Christian poem. My discussion of Milton's early poetry, therefore, will explore how these two elements—pagan and Christian—are held in relation to each other as Milton seeks to define himself as poet-prophet.

To validate to his poetic authority as *vates* (a pagan office converted to a Christian calling) Milton grounds his source of inspiration either in the mythical past—for example, in the Trojan Brutus in *Comus* or in God's chosen people in David's Psalms—or in the literary tradition of invoking the Muse. Milton's early poetry, therefore, serves to prepare him for his higher themes of divine inspiration, freedom and its responsibilities, and divine origins in *Paradise Lost*. From his first invocation to the "Heav'nly Muse" in the *Nativity Ode*, Milton's very career as poet becomes an attempt to uncover the meaning of this expression.

Preparations for an Epic Career

Invocations to the Muse can be found in Milton's earliest attempts at verse—his translations of the Psalms of David—and in his later works before the prose treatises and *Paradise Lost*, *Lycidas* and *Epitaphium Damonis*. Well read in classics and a devoted Puritan, Milton turned both to the Muses and the Holy Spirit for inspiration, and his early poetry reveals an ongoing tension between the poet's syncretist inclinations and his sincere devotion to God. By tracing the recurring invocations we can form a clearer picture of how Milton regarded himself as a poet and how these invocations reflect his growing sense of self-awareness as *vates*—a designation constantly shifting between its pagan and Christian significance.

Milton's interest in the Psalms is first visible in 1624 when, at the age of fifteen, he paraphrased Psalm 114, first in English, then Greek, and translated Psalm 136 into English. These first attempts, like his later translations of 1648 and 1654, were strongly influenced by the prosody of the Sternhold and Hopkins version (c. 1547), widely used in congregational singing, the Latin paraphrases of the Psalms by George Buchanan, Ovid's use of learnedly allusive geographical names, and the often exaggerated language of Du Bartas's *Divine Weeks*.[2] They also reveal the poet's real and early interest in issues of faith and devotion to God, as well as his concern for beginnings or origins—the topics of these two psalms. Milton's selection of Psalms 114 and 136 suggests an inclination toward finding the proper voice with which to address God and a growing sense of the reciprocity between God's bountiful gifts to his chosen people and the duty or faith required of his servants. Even at the age of fifteen, Milton felt a sense of divine calling and sought to ground his faith in the God of Israel.

Psalm 114 begins appropriately, for our discussion, with the issues of inheritance and service to God:

> When the blest seed of *Terah's* faithful son,
> After long toil their liberty had won,
> And past from *Pharian* fields to *Canaan* Land,
> Led by the strength of the Almighty's hand,
> *Jehovah's* wonders were in *Israel* shown,
> His praise and glory was in *Israel* known. (ll. 1–7)

The I-Thou relationship established here between "the blest seed of *Terah's* faithful son," or Abraham, resembles the relationship between the faithful Christian and his God, and also that between the poet and his Muse. In either case, the psalmist recognizes the providence of God, both in the lineage of the human agent and the necessity of His strength in order to bring about the establishment of His chosen people. Merritt Y. Hughes notes that Milton changed his reading of the original Psalm, which calls the Israelites the "house of Jacob," in order to make the allusion to Abraham. Although his father, Terah, was an idolater, Abraham "by faith . . . when he was called to go out into a place which he should after receive for an inheritance, obeyed" (Heb. 9.8).

The message is clear: God commands and his faithful servant, Abraham, obeys. But Abraham, like the faithful poet, must simultaneously work out God's purpose in the world and realize his own place in God's historical pattern. Abraham goes into the promised land, with his joint heirs Isaac and Jacob, as St. Paul says, looking for "a city which hath foundations, whose builder and maker *is* God" (Heb. 9.9). Besides treating the theme of inheritance, Psalm 114 concerns the founding of a people, a nation, in the promised land of Israel—all epic themes. Throughout his poetic career, Milton will return to these issues of divine calling and servitude to God in his poems of praise and his invocations to the Muse or the Holy Spirit.

Likewise, Milton's translation of Psalm 136 concerns the psalmist's duty to praise the Lord for his kindness and mercy, common themes found in the Psalms of David:

> Let us with a gladsome mind
> Praise the Lord, for he is kind,
> For his mercies aye endure,
> Ever faithful, ever sure.
> Let us blaze his Name abroad,
> For of gods he is the God. (ll. 1–6)

This translation, more ambitious than the other because of its verse form, is interesting in its similar emphasis upon God's role as creator of heaven and earth, conqueror of the Egyptians, and founder of Israel. God is worthy to be praised by the psalmist, above all, because "to his servant *Israel*, / He gave their Land therein to dwell" (ll. 73–74), and will continue to watch over His people. From his early *Nativity Ode* to his later epic, *Paradise Lost*, Milton's narrator continually acknowledges the omnipotence of God and explores the reciprocal relationship between the inspirer and the inspired. The poet's voice becomes the voice of God, and the Muse's or Holy Spirit's inspired gift of song the poet's inspired gift to God.

Milton's Poetic Nativity: *On the Morning of Christ's Nativity*

While the paraphrases and translations reveal Milton's early interest in notions of inheritance and faith, it is not until *On the Morning of Christ's Nativity* (1629) that the poet comes out into the world as a poet with his own voice. This personal poetic voice, however, is not without the support of classical and Christian forms of address. Abraham Cowley had gone to great pains in his biblical epic, the *Davideis*, to adhere to the precedent set by Vergil regarding the necessary invocation of the Muse only to reject her pagan aspects in favor of Christian ones. Indeed, Cowley went so far as to present his converted Muse to Christ as a reformed Magdalene. Milton, on the other hand, accepts the pagan convention of invoking the Muse, building upon it within the framework of his *Nativity Ode*, but also rejects those same pagan traditions, seeing the birth of Christ as banishing the pagan gods. Indeed, Milton's invocations to the Muse, beginning with the *Nativity Ode*, reveal the poet's debt to Vergil's epic *exordium*, consisting of the statement of the theme followed by the direct address to the Muse. This patterning of verse is combined with Milton's own knowledge of biblical forms of prayer. Through Milton's continuing use of invocations, from the *Nativity Ode* to *Paradise Regained*, we can discern a pattern of the *vates* simultaneously seeking and asserting a poetic voice—and a Christian voice at that—capable of epic utterance.

The placement of the *Nativity Ode* as the first selection in the 1645 and 1673 editions of his poetry certainly indicates Milton's high estimation of the poem. Milton's theme is the triumph of Christ over the gods of paganism. It is here that Milton first invokes, but does not specifically name, the "Heav'nly Muse." Indeed, the *Nativity Ode* marks a turning point in Milton's life; just having turned twenty-one on December 9th, the poet wishes to offer a gift both reflective of his talents and pleasing to the infant God. In the *Nativity Ode* and *Elegia Sexta*, which serves in some ways as its gloss, we can observe the poet securing his place within the epic tradition, building upon pagan notions of inspiration before arriving, finally, at a Christian voice.

Elegia Sexta, written in the same month as the *Nativity Ode* to Charles Diodati when he was visiting in the country, offers particular insights into Milton's purposes for writing the *Nativity Ode* and his developing views concerning the "serious" poet. *Elegia Sexta* begins with a playful use of the classical Muses and progresses to a more serious consideration of the character and dedication required by the aspiring epic poet. While critical opinion about the seriousness of Milton's self-dedication as epic poet varies, both the themes and poetic forms used in these two works confirms Milton's early engagement with the issue of poetic calling.

At the beginning of *Elegia Sexta* we learn that Diodati's "Muse" has called upon Milton's "Muse" to respond to his previous letter. Milton responds to Diodati's assertion that "poetry is a fugitive from wine and feasting" (l. 13), by claiming that "Carmen amat Bacchum, Carmina Bacchus amat" (l. 14). Indeed, Milton, in an Ovidian humor, refuses to separate poetry from wine because wine often inspires creativity. Milton connects Diodati's feasts of December to the religious feasts honoring the birth of Christ (ll. 9–12). Milton approves of this festivity and refuses to separate Bacchus from song, or wine from poetry (ll. 13–14). He offers multiple examples of those inspired by Bacchus: Apollo (l. 15), who "was not ashamed to wear the green garland of ivy and to prefer its leaves to his own laurel" (l. 16); the Nine Muses who have "often mingled with the rout of Thyoneus" (ll. 17–18), or Bacchus, whose other name, Lycaeus, means "releaser" of genius and high spirits; Ovid; Anacreon; and even Pindar, whose "every page is redolent of consumed wine" (ll. 23–24) and Horace. Finally, the list ends with Diodati himself, in whom Milton claims "the favor of Bacchus, Apollo, and Ceres is united" (l. 34).

According to the poet, Diodati should not believe that the Muses have left him; indeed, Milton reassures Diodati that once the festive music begins, he will distinctly feel the surge of creativity within him:

> Crede mihi, dum psallit ebur, comitataque plectrum
> Implet odoratos festa chorea tholos,
> Percipies tacitum per pectora serpere Phoebum,
> Quale repentinus permeat ossa calor;
> Perque puellares oculos digitumque sonantem
> Irruet in totos lapsa Thalia sinus. (ll. 43–48)[3]

Even now, Milton supports traditional holidays, as he will later do in *A Mask*[4]; so, he suggests, do the gods.

Indeed, Milton argues, poets whose themes are comic, erotic, or lyrical, should partake heartily of wine and eat their fill at grand banquets. However, the poets, who aspire to write of grander things—"wars in heaven under Jupiter in his prime, and pious heroes and chieftains half-divine"—or those who wish to sing "now of the sacred counsels of the gods on high, and now of the infernal realms where the fierce dogs howl" (ll. 55–58)—in other words, those poets who wish to take up epic themes—should live sparingly, eat herbs, and drink "sober draughts from the pure spring" (l. 62). But this is not all. Milton writes that beyond this,

> scelerisque vacans et castra iuventus,
> Et rigidi mores, et sine labe manus.
> Qualis veste nitens sacra, et lustralibus undis,
> Surgis ad infensos augur iture Deos. (ll. 64–66)[5]

While Milton's prior advice to Diodati contained truth disguised by some degree of levity, this advice to the epic poet seems more serious, and clearly more pertinent to his own life. The epic poet's youth must be innocent and chaste, and his hands spotless; his character should be like that of the sacred priest who walks in the presence of the angry gods. Indeed, Milton says in conclusion before progressing to his summary of his *Nativity Ode*, "Diis etenim sacer est vates, divumque sacerdos, / Spirat et occultum pectus et ora Iovem" (ll. 77–78). Like Tieresias, Calchas, Orpheus, and Homer before him, Milton acknowledges the sacred function of the *vates*, or poet-priest, and identifies himself in that position: the bard serves the gods as a priest, and both his heart and his mouth "breathes out Jove." While the concept is pagan, the real desire for inspiration is Christian. Milton, the Puritan poet, desires to be infused with the Word of God and to demonstrate his devotion by living a godly life. Just as the poet receives inspiration ("in"-"spiro," Lat.) from the Muses, who breathe their song into him, he likewise gives expression to (or "breathes out") their song in his poetry. As this idea works itself out in pagan literature, so it functions in Christian poetry.

While Milton the poet and scholar could read, absorb, and improve upon what he had inherited from the great poets who had gone before him, he soon realized that the creation of great art ultimately comes from "outside" of the poet. Whether from God or from the Muse, the gift of creativity is something that cannot necessarily be summoned at will. This is one of the lessons taught by the *Nativity Ode*, and one that Milton himself learned in the process of writing it. Milton had just turned twenty-one on December 9th, 1629, and this poem reflects his coming-of-age as a poet. Since he had not yet been "church-outed" by the Prelates, Milton saw his poetry as a kind of ministry and blended his artistic skills with the oratorical skills of the pulpit. Milton's desire to write devotional poetry here coincides with his belief in himself as *vates*.

Unlike other poems of the period that treat the birth of Christ, focusing upon the event itself,[6] Milton's *Nativity Ode* explores the larger consequences of the event, from prelapsarian life to the Fall of Man, and to the prospect of Humanity's ultimate redemption. Moreover, the *Nativity Ode* is indebted to Pindar's formal and public odes, which celebrated specific events with a view towards their universal significance,[7] as well as to the Psalms of David and the Renaissance ode tradition. Indeed, Milton's comments in *The Reason of Church Government* (1642) confirm that Milton had studied the Greek models and planned to "imitate those magnific odes and hymns wherein Pindarus and Callimachus are in most things worthy."[8] Adapting the Pindaric ode form to his own uses, Milton introduces a specific event—here, the birth of Christ—and establishes its larger significance, ultimately celebrating "in glorious and lofty hymns the throne and equipage of God's almightiness."[9]

It is commonplace for Miltonists to recognize that the opening four stanzas of *On the Morning of Christ's Nativity* are meant to function as the formal introduction to "The Hymn" that follows. These four stanzas may then be divided into two sections: while stanzas I and II constitute the *exordium*, stanzas III and IV constitute the invocation. This pattern accords with that established in Vergil's *Aeneid*. In the *exordium*, Milton announces his theme:

I

This is the Month, and this the happy morn
Wherein the Son of Heav'n's eternal King,
Of wedded Maid, and Virgin Mother born,
Our great redemption from above did bring;
For so the holy sages once did sing,
That he our deadly forfeit should release,
And with his Father work us a perpetual peace.

II

That glorious Form, that Light unsufferable,

And that far-beaming blaze of Majesty,
Wherewith he wont at Heav'n's high Council-Table,
To sit the midst of Trinal Unity,
He laid aside; and here with us to be,
Forsook the Courts of everlasting Day,
And chose with us a darksome House of mortal Clay. (ll. 1–14)

Like the epic *exordium*, stanzas I and II give an abstract of the poem that is to follow. However, unlike Vergil's opening to the *Aeneid*, Book 1, "arma virumque cano," in which the epic poet "sings" his theme in the first-person singular ("cano") before invoking his Muse, Milton never uses the first-person. Instead, he simply and matter-of-factly presents us with the time and circumstances of the divine birth. He begins with the Virgin Mary and the "holy sages," or prophets, who had foretold in the Old Testament the coming of the Son of God.

Yet, this physical scene is quickly overshadowed by the significance of "Our great redemption from above" which will eventually free humanity from death and, "with his Father work us a perpetual peace" (ll. 4–6). The heavenly realm presented here closely resembles the Platonic world of Forms; indeed, Christ, "that glorious Form, that Light unsufferable" (l. 8), lays aside his abstract / divine form to offer himself as a sacrifice for humanity. His descent from the "Courts of everlasting Day" to our "darksome House of mortal clay" (ll. 13–14) parallels Plato's journey of the soul from its spiritual existence prior to its journey into the material world and thereby suggests the importance of recognizing, or remembering, the "light" and truth of the Christ-child.

Stanzas III and IV, which constitute the formal invocation of the "Heav'nly Muse," follow:

III

Say Heav'nly Muse, shall not thy sacred vein
Afford a present to the Infant God?
Hast thou no verse, no hymn, or solemn strain,
To welcome him to this his new abode,
Now while the Heav'n by the Sun's team untrod,
Hath took no print of the approaching light,
And all the spangled host keep watch in squadrons bright?

IV

See how from far upon the Eastern road
The Star-led Wizards haste with odors sweet:
O run, prevent them with thy humble ode,
And lay it lowly at his blessed feet;
Have thou the honor first, thy Lord to greet,
And join thy voice unto the Angel Choir,

From out his secret Altar toucht with hallow'd fire. (ll. 15–28)

Here, Milton invokes the "Heav'nly Muse" for the first time in his career and in a manner that prefigures his invocation of Urania—Muse of astronomy and metaphor for the Holy Spirit—in *Paradise Lost.* This invocation marks the beginning of Milton's lifelong struggle to come to terms with the identity of his Muse, whose meaning and name remain ambiguous until *Paradise Lost*. Here, the naming of the Muse comes within the context of rejecting the pagan gods (and presumably pagan traditions)—a seemingly contradictory move on Milton's part. But does the rejection of the pagan gods necessarily involve the rejection of the Muse? Not for the early Milton, who besides being a firm believer was also a humanist and a syncretist. He seems comfortable with the ambiguity of the Muse's identity: she can be for the poet both the Homeric Muse, who supplies the epic poet with song, as well as a metaphor for the Holy Spirit of God. She can also be a hybrid Muse, blending elements pagan and Christian but "meaning" the same thing: divine inspiration. After all, Du Bartas had recently "Christianized" Urania and transformed her into the "Heavenly Muse." Milton was certainly familiar with Du Bartas and Sylvester's translation of *His Divine Weekes and Workes*, and he likely modeled his own "Heav'nly Muse" upon the French poet's example. In any case, the opening of the *Nativity Ode* marks an important stage in Milton's career as a poet devoted to his Christian Muse but still very much a devoted student of the classics.

Having described the scene of Christ's birth and stated its cosmological significance, Milton asks his Muse for a gift appropriate for the "Infant God" (l. 16). The only appropriate gift would be a verse, a hymn, or a solemn strain, in accordance with the classical hierarchy of genres.[10] Interestingly, though, the poet urges the Muse not to delay; in fact, she needs to provide this poetic gift *before* the arrival of the wise men! He says, "prevent them with thy humble ode, / And lay it lowly at his blessed feet" (ll. 24–25), suggesting that her song should both "blow before and ahead" ("pre-vent") of the wise men as well as stop them from getting there first. Even more striking, perhaps, is the fact that Milton attempts to insert himself into the situation—into the very fabric of the poetic narrative—as if his status writing *about* the biblical story were somehow the same as the Wise Men's status of offering gifts *within* it. Although Milton clearly values the plain, or humble gift, he nevertheless seems intent upon *primacy* when he seeks the "honor first" (26). Furthermore, Milton suggests that the poet's gift of an ode or verse takes rank over the material gift of the Wise Men—another important aspect of the Christian *vates* as God's chosen poet.

So whose gift is it now? The Muse's or Milton's? "Thy voice" seems to become Milton's voice, or our voice (that is, Milton's *and* the Muse's), when the poet depicts the Muse's voice joining "the Angel Choir, / From out his secret Altar toucht with hallow'd fire" (ll. 27–28). Through the Muse, then, Milton can imagine having access to the *secret Altar* and the inspiration enjoyed by the prophets. However, Milton's inclusion of himself with gift of song in the poem suggests his confidence in his vocation and perhaps a hint of arrogance.

Just as the proem has two parts—the *exordium* and the invocation—the poem as a whole has two parts. These two parts of the poem may be characterized as the poet's request and the Muse's reply, or "The Hymn." In a sense, then, the *Nativity Ode* explicitly functions as a dialogue between the poet and the Muse, and suggests that poetry comes from that source outside oneself that we call the Muse or inspiration. It is that which makes the poem. But we know that the process is more complicated than that. Clearly, Milton is writing the poem, both the exordium and "The Hymn." Or is he? George Herbert engages in a similar, explicit exchange between the poet / speaker and his source of inspiration, God, in his poem *Dialogue*.[11] In this poem, Herbert's speaker asks his "Sweetest Saviour . . . What delight or hope remains?" in the first stanza; in the second, Jesus responds. The pattern continues in the next two stanzas, the speaker's words in regular type and Jesus' words in italics. A. D. Nuttall, contrasting possible seventeenth- and twentieth-century responses to Herbert's poem, suggests that God would likely be pleased with his creature Herbert's gratitude and submission; however, the poem continues to pose an interesting problem between "Revelation and tradition"—or rather, between inspiration and convention. Nuttall writes,

> The humility of the first stanza is of course deliberately presented by the poet as wrong-headed. Accordingly, it invites a loving correction from God. But before God can, so to speak, clear his throat to answer, lo, the creature Herbert is scribbling away at the second stanza and God's part is there, written out neatly for him. Herbert in the poem does not simply submit himself to the will of God; he personally supplies the divine correction.[12]

On the one hand, the poet Herbert is presumably receiving *some* inspiration from God as he writes the poem. On the other hand, though, Herbert writes God's lines for him. But how can it be any other way? Milton faces a similar dilemma here in the *Nativity Ode*—where the poet, Milton, would place himself in the poem as well as outside it—and in the invocations in *Paradise Lost*. While we can say that Milton *literally* wrote his words on the page, we cannot say for certain that he did not have some divine help. Indeed, Milton took his God and himself *very* seriously. Even if it cannot be established that God's or the Muse's lines are not *really* their own—divinely dictated to the poet—one can say that Milton, like Herbert, believed himself to be "modifying and re-phrasing impulses vouchsafed to him by God," as Nuttall suggests.[13]

By the end of the *Nativity Ode*, Milton, or the Muse, has compressed the whole of human history into a moment, coming full circle and concluding where the poem began—in the stable, reflecting upon the miraculous birth of the infant God. Paradoxically, the Word made flesh,[14] but here a speechless babe, has controlled the "damned crew" and his light has blinded the pagan gods. Like the God of *Paradise Lost,* the Infant God does not need to speak or act; he merely brings things to be. There is power in divine stasis:

XXVII

But see! the Virgin blest,
Hath laid her Babe to rest.
Time is our tedious Song should here have ending:
Heav'n's youngest-teemed Star
Hath fixt her polisht Car,
Her sleeping Lord with Handmaid Lamp attending:
And all about the Courtly Stable,
Bright-harness'd Angels sit in order serviceable. (ll. 237–244)

Almost as from a Celestial vision the poet returns to the simple scene before him: the mother Mary and her child, the Son of God. And so, Milton suggests, the end of the poem is our beginning; all attend the Saviour in this "Courtly Stable," where "Bright-harness'd Angels sit in order serviceable" (ll. 243–244). Having established this relationship with the "Heav'nly Muse" and beheld a vision of God's mercy in the birth of his Son, Milton awaits his own calling to serve.

In the *Nativity Ode*, Milton's invocation of the Muse and his use of the Pindaric tradition underscores his own commitment to the vocation of *vates.*[15] Indeed, Milton successfully adapts the Pindaric tradition of celebrating athletic victories to his vision of the triumph of Christ.[16] In *Nemean* 1, Pindar celebrates Hieron's powerful and wealthy general, Chromios, for winning a chariot race, an accomplishment that ultimately has its beginnings in the gods and the divine abilities that they grant to men:

The beginnings have been laid by the gods
with that man's divine abilities,
but in success is
the summit of absolute glory, and the Muse
loves to recall great contests. (ll. 8–12)

Comparing Chromio's career with Herakles' life, Pindar recounts how the infant Herakles thwarted Hera's plans by strangling the two snakes that she had sent to kill him and his twin brother in their crib (ll. 43–47). By comparing Chromios to Herakles, Pindar heightens the general's achievements and implies that the same fame won by Herakles will also be won by him. In Medieval and Renaissance syncretism, Herakles was often seen as a type of Christ, and was surely seen as such by the early Milton. In the *Nativity Ode*, Milton suggests the same kind of syncretic reading of Christ, who in his infancy banishes the pagan gods and who in the future will bring peace and salvation to the world. By calling his *Nativity*

Ode both an "humble ode" and a "Hymn," Milton confirms his awareness of the close relationship between these forms. By the end of the poem, Milton aspires to achieve the victorious associations of the Pindaric tradition and the inspired mood of David's Psalms in his "gift" to the Infant God.

L'Allegro and *Il Penseroso*: Dueling Muses

Written late during Milton's years at Christ College, Cambridge, and before going to Horton, *L'Allegro* and *Il Penseroso* reflect and build upon Milton's university training in rhetoric and debate. Structurally and thematically similar to his *Prolusions*, each poem argues for a mutually exclusive position—one for Mirth, the other Melancholy—or together present complementary perspectives of equal goods. However, another way of looking at the companion poems involves a closer analysis of the invocations of Mirth and Melancholy which follow the opening diatribe of each poem. Walter Schindler has argued convincingly that these invocations—one to Euphrosyne, or Mirth, and the other to Melancholy—along with the closing statements from each poem, in which the poet "chooses" to live either with Mirth or with Melancholy,[17] reveal the poet's concern about his vocation. Schindler maintains that "from beginning to end, each poem is an invocation intent on imagining the vocational results of choosing a particular source of inspiration,"[18] but since the poet reaches no "final choice" in the end, "invocation becomes an open-ended experiment in identity."[19] While this search for self-identity through deliberate association with these seemingly opposite Muses is not the central point of the companion poems, it is certainly an important aspect to explore in relation to Milton's public and private self-presentation as poet, divinely inspired by the Muse.

Unlike Cowley, whose epic *Davideis* abounds in elaborate self-commentary on the poet's choice of a clearly Christian Muse, Milton is not concerned in *L'Allegro* and *Il Penseroso* with the issue of classical versus pagan in his search for a Muse. Rather, Milton begins and ends the poems with frame invocations, balancing Mirth and Melancholy as equally appealing alternatives. However, rather than calling upon Mirth and Melancholy to come *from* somewhere (as would be customary in an proper invocation), Milton's contemptuous invocations banish them *to* somewhere. Perhaps this strategy is connected to Milton's desire to keep the ideals at a distance, to balance them, as it were, for contemplation and further reflection. Both Mirth and Melancholy offer ideally complete and self-sufficient pleasure, yet both remain ideals and therefore not viable alternatives for a poet who wishes to dedicate himself to the Muse. Although Milton eventually may seem to favor melancholy, or the contemplative life, for its inward illumination, he makes no clear *choice* at the end.

Milton begins *L'Allegro* with a diatribe against Melancholy, in which the disease, or humor, is banished by the youthful spirit of Mirth. The picture that

Milton presents is one of darkness, death, and horror. The opening invocation *dismisses* Melancholy:

> Hence loathed Melancholy
> Of *Cerberus* and blackest midnight born,
> In *Stygian* cave forlorn
> 'Mongst horrid shapes, and shrieks, and sights unholy,
> Find out some uncouth cell,
> Where brooding darkness spreads his jealous wings,
> And the night-Raven sings;
> There under *Ebon* shades, and low-brow'd Rocks,
> As ragged as thy Locks,
> In dark *Cimmerian* desert ever dwell. (ll. 1–10)

Similar to the section of Robert Burton's *Abstract of Melancholy* from his *Anatomy of Melancholy*, in which pleasure is offered as a cure for the dangerous melancholy that ends in insanity, Milton's opening presents only the negative attributes of melancholy. Milton's depiction of Melancholy in the opening of *L'Allegro* is grotesque: Melancholy is a product of the classical underworld, removed from light and knowledge by virtue of its birth to Cerberus and "blackest midnight." Melancholy exists alone, removed from the intercourse of human activity and exchange, in a "Stygian cave forlorn." Far from a creative attribute, Melancholy is forgetful, forgotten, and relegated to the barren "dark *Cimmerian* desert." Moreover, Melancholy is a dark—and even "unholy"—humor, and as such seems removed from the light of heaven.

After such a defamatory depiction of Melancholy the poet follows with an invocation to Mirth in an effort to save us from the fatal attraction of Melancholy's potential dangers. The invocation begins:

> But come thou Goddess fair and free,
> In Heav'n yclep'd *Euphrosyne*,
> And by men, heart-easing Mirth,
> Whom lovely *Venus* at a birth
> With two sister Graces more
> To Ivy-crowned *Bacchus* bore. (ll. 11–16)

Instead of invoking a Goddess whose devotees would be expected to dwell in darkness and solitude, the poet here calls upon Euphrosyne, giving alternate genealogies: she is either the daughter of Venus and Bacchus, who pleases the senses and liberates the mind, or "(as some Sager sing)," the daughter of Zephyr and Aurora, "so buxom, blithe, and debonaire."[20] Following the hymn tradition, Milton gives the Goddess's various names, both those used by the gods and by men, and thereby defines her natural attributes which are closely linked to the fertility of spring.

Almost anticipating the temptation to wallow in the joys of springtime and the pleasures of mirth, Milton once again invokes the goddess, who he fears may steal away: "Haste thee nymph, and bring with thee / Jest and youthful Jollity . . . / Come, and trip it as ye go, On the light fantastic toe, / And in thy right hand lead with thee, / The mountain nymph, sweet Liberty."[21] Mirth's association with the spring makes her a more serious deity, who fits within the natural hierarchy of virtues; Milton expands upon this notion to assert that through Mirth's power one enters into a direct sensuous and aesthetic response to the world. He therefore asks for "Sport that wrinkled Care derides" and "Laughter holding both his sides" (ll. 31–32). The result is one's liberation from everyday cares.

Milton concludes his conventional invocation of Mirth, though, with a direct appeal to the deity to listen and respond to his petitions according to his merits as her follower:

And if I give thee honor due,
Mirth, admit me of thy crew
To live with her, and live with thee,
In unreproved pleasures free. (ll. 37–40)

In this section, the poet establishes a conditional relationship between himself and the goddess in a way common to classical Greek Homeric hymns to Apollo. In a sense, the speaker is also pledging his loyalty and talents to his goddess as well as rejecting the life of contemplation for the life of leisure, variety, and liberty. To live in "unreproved pleasures free" with Mirth *and* Liberty, then, suggests living a life of polygamy and free love; the life of Mirth, then, promises variety and freedom. Thus, by the end of the poem, the speaker can say eagerly, "These delights if thou cans't give, / Mirth, with thee I mean to live" (ll. 151–152), hoping and indeed praying that the goddess will respond favorably to his petition. However, some doubt still remains.

Il Penseroso presents the opposite view, arguing for the positive qualities of Melancholy as one would do in a formal debate; it stands in opposition to the real and imagined merits of Mirth in *L'Allegro*. Like its companion piece, *Il Penseroso* begins with a forceful diatribe that calls Mirth's pleasures into question, implying that her gifts are, at best, transitory and unworthy of a serious and mature mind. Once again, the poet would banish the ideal *to* somewhere:

Hence vain deluding joys,
The brood of folly without father bred,
How little you bested,
Or fill the fixed mind with all your toys;
Dwell in some idle brain,
And fancies fond with gaudy shapes possess,
As thick and numberless
As the gay motes that people the Sunbeams,

Or likest hovering dreams,
The fickle Pensioners of Morpheus' train. (ll. 1–10)

Here, Milton rejects the Horatian ideal of retired leisure, his defamatory opening adeptly taking into account the charges brought against it in order to refute them as one would do in a debate. Calling Mirth "[t]he brood of folly without father bred" suggests again the theme of liberty, figured negatively as promiscuity and questionable parentage or origin. Those pleasures presented in *L'Allegro* are now seen as childish "toys" possessing "gaudy shapes"; the gifts of Mirth, like 'hov'ring dreams," lack substance and permanence. Mirth, according to the argument presented in *Il Penseroso*, dwells in "some idle Brain" (l. 5), recalling Milton's argument in favor of Learning over Ignorance in *Prolusion VII*.[22] Milton presents a clear tension between the attractions of Mirth and the necessary austerity of the aspiring *vates*. Mirth is good in its place, and Milton is attracted to it; however, Milton must retain a distance from its pleasures and freedom in order to progress in his poetic career.

Repeating the pattern established earlier in *L'Allegro*, Milton follows his opening with an invocation of the appropriate Muse:

But hail thou Goddess, sage and holy,
Hail divinest Melancholy,
Whose saintly visage is too bright
To hit the Sense of human sight;
And therefore to our weaker view,
O'erlaid with black, staid Wisdom's hue. (ll. 11–16)

Milton here invokes the Muse in the grand style, "Hail divinest Melancholy," thereby implying her higher, spiritual qualities.[23] Moreover, in Milton's invocation, Melancholy assumes the status of a holy mystery, and she is dressed in the black the hue of Wisdom.

After an initial treatment of Melancholy's divine characteristics, *sedes*, powers, and epithets, Milton invokes her a second time to underscore her relationship to the heavens:

Come, but keep thy wonted state,
With e'vn step, and musing gait,
And looks conversing with the skies,
Thy rapt soul sitting in thine eyes:
There held in holy passion still,
Forget thyself to Marble, till
With a sad Leaden downward cast,
Thou fix them on the earth as fast. (ll. 37–44)

In the personification of Melancholy the poet sees an ideal image of himself—indeed, of man in his most perfect condition—in communion with God in a form of *ecstasy*, in which both his thoughts and looks are directed upwards. Yet the movement of the passage, from upward to downward glances, simultaneously reveals the inward—and divine—pull to look always toward God as well as the corresponding pull of mortality that necessarily limits the soul's "rapt" participation in the Holy.[24] Almost as if not to lose contact with his inspiring Muse, the poet calls upon her once again:

> Thee Chauntress oft the Woods among,
> I woo to hear thy Even-Song;
> And missing thee, I walk unseen
> On the dry smooth-shaven Green,
> To behold the wand'ring Moon,
> Riding near her highest noon,
> Like one that had been led astray
> Through the Heav'n's wide pathless way;
> And oft, as if her head she bow'd,
> Stooping through a fleecy cloud. (ll. 63–72)

The poet now sees Melancholy as a "Chauntress," a singer of "Even-Song," who can give direction to one lost in Dante's or Spenser's woods of Error. The poet desires a communion with the goddess under the vault of heaven, and woos her as a lover would woo his beloved—an object of love who requires work and loyalty, unlike those mirthful hussies. But this plea also reveals the fact that the poet is not always successful in his invocations, and shows that he sometimes cannot receive the inspiration he desires. Milton's words, "Missing thee," (l. 65) confirm this possibility of failing at his wooing and interestingly possess a tinge of Melancholy about them—understandable considering that the poet's efforts to woo his goddess had fallen flat.

Nevertheless, the moon at midnight paradoxically provides the greatest light. The poet desiring divine illumination must call upon his source, gazing upward into the heavens. Ideally, then, the goddess will hear his petition and bend down through the clouds to hear him. This relationship of poet to divine source of inspiration and wisdom reaffirms the necessity of prayers and hymns; this is also the relationship that Milton will attempt to establish with the Heav'nly Muse in *Paradise Lost*. Indeed, the heavens are "pathless," and the *vates* requires a favorable heavenly guide to lead him through its mysteries.

Since it is in darkness that the poet finds true light, it is fitting that, as Milton brings *Il Penseroso* to a close, the coming of dawn spurs the poet onto his specific petition:

> And as I wake, sweet music breathe
> Above, about, or underneath

Sent by some spirit to mortals good. (ll. 151–153)

In the mortal world, as Plato would argue, access to the spiritual is limited, and only accessible to those favored by the gods. Here the poet asks literally for inspiration—the goddess' breath of sweet music—to surround and engulf him. Milton also indicates an understanding of what is required of the poet: the Muse grants inspiration only to those who are "good."[25] The poet must purify himself to receive the gift of song; at the same time, he must be chosen by the Muse as deserving of that distinction and responsibility.

Appropriately, therefore, Milton's famous prayer concludes the poem. The first section concerns the poet's chosen path:

But let my due feet never fail
To walk the studious Cloister's pale,
And love the high embowed Roof,
With antic Pillars massy proof,
And storied Windows richly dight,
Casting a dim religious light. (ll. 155–160)

The steps are taken by the poet, but hopefully beneath the eyes of his Muse. He will walk the path of righteousness and studiousness, and will be illuminated by the divine light cast through the stained glass windows, which depict stories from the Bible. Though "richly dight," the windows cast a "dim religious light"; thus will God's light shine through the poet, whose abilities are great but not infinite.[26]

In the second section of the prayer, we find that the poet, once walking his proper path, will be receptive to the "pealing Organ" which sounds with God's truth:

There let the pealing Organ blow
To the full voic'd Choir below,
In Service high and Anthems clear,
As may with sweetness, through mine ear,
Dissolve me into ecstasies,
And bring all Heav'n before mine eyes. (ll. 161–166)

This is a purely Christian moment, with a Christian God and Muse as the addressee. Even the Puritan Milton could appreciate the sublime and aesthetic beauty of the high service of the Church of England and find "sweetness" in the anthems of the choir. The poet now longs to enter into ecstasy so that he can see as God sees. In other words, the poet wants to survey the whole of creation—"all Heav'n"—from the eternal present of God's perspective rather than from the linear and partial view of humanity. It is this divine perspective that Milton will try to achieve through the inspiration of Urania in *Paradise Lost*.

Finally, in the third section of the prayer, Milton concludes by looking forward to his end and aim:

> And may at last my weary age
> Find out the peaceful hermitage,
> The Hairy Gown and Mossy Cell,
> Where I may sit and rightly spell
> Of every Star that Heav'n doth shew,
> And every Herb that sips the dew;
> Till old experience do attain
> To something like Prophetic strain. (ll. 167–174)

Here we have a vision of old age and stasis. But Milton finds peace in a small, sequestered cell; all the poet has to do is wait and write. His vision is more internal than external. He asks his Muse only that he may "sit and rightly spell" God's purpose for all creation. The poet aspires to serve as the middle link, as it were, in the great chain of being, drawing sustenance from both the stars of heaven and the "Herbs that sip the dew." His purpose will be fulfilled at last when he attains "something like Prophetic strain." Then the poet will gain the voice of the *vates*, who seeks and achieves a near contemplation of God. Then the poem ends, as expected, with the summary and conditional statement:

> These pleasures Melancholy give,
> And I with thee will choose to live. (ll. 175–176)

This ending, like that found in *L'Allegro*, neatly caps the argument for Melancholy and leaves the "debate" with Mirth unresolved.

Elaborating upon remarks made by Johnson in his *Lives of the English Poets*, Cleanth Brooks argues that Milton could not afford to exploit the "mere contrast" of mirth and melancholy in *L'Allegro* and *Il Penseroso*. "If he had," Brooks maintains, "the two halves would have been driven poles apart"; they would cease to be "twin halves of one poem, for the sense of unity in variety would have been lost."[27] In short, "by choosing the obvious contrast between mirth and melancholy," Brooks astutely claims, "Milton obligated himself to bring them as close together as possible in their effect on the mind"(53). Indeed, "the tension between the two choices depends upon their presentation as choices that can appeal to the same mind" (53). The mirthful man's days are balanced throughout by those of the melancholy man's, starting with the contrast between light and dark in the invocations of each poem.

Yet Brooks does not settle for a clear dichotomy between light and dark imagery in the companion poems. Brooks remarks that "the spectator moves through what are predominantly cool half-lights . . . as if the half-light were being used in both poems as a sort of symbol of the aesthetic distance which the cheerful man, no less than the pensive man, consistently maintains" (59). This delicate balance ceases, however, at the end of *Il Penseroso*, when the light afforded to the "inward eye" suggests that the life of contemplation is the higher life. This aspect of the contemplative life will continue to figure prominently in Milton's later poetic and prose works, including *Sonnet XIX* ("When I consider . . .), which ends with the poet's belief that "They also serve who only stand and wait." It appears too in *The Reason of Church Government* and in the invocations of *Paradise Lost*. Indeed, Milton's faith in divine, inward illumination seems to grow in strength as the poet advances in his career.[28] Finally, Brooks argues in New Critical fashion that the "dimm religious light" presented in *Il Penseroso* is "paradoxically dim": the light is "dim to the physical eye, though actually the proper light for one who would have the vision too insupportably bright for human sight to receive" (66). The same paradox holds for Milton in *Paradise Lost*, Book IX, when the poet requests an "answerable style" from his Celestial Muse who will enable him to be the vehicle for God's "higher argument . . . sufficient in itself."[29] Both in these early poems and in his later epic, Milton contrasts the insufficient physical light to the all-sufficient light of Truth that resides only in the being and substance of God in order to emphasize the proper relationship between the poet and God necessary for the transmission of higher truths. Thus, the companion poems reveal important insights into Milton's distinction between external and internal sources of poetic inspiration and anticipate his later attempts to take on the mantle of *vates*. To do this, though, he must maintain a balance between self-assertion and self-effacement, offering himself completely to the dictation of his Muse.

In the end, Milton is not merely attempting to present a debate in the manner of *Prolusion I*, which asks "Whether Day or Night is the More Excellent"[30]; instead, Milton is concerned with maintaining a tension between transcendent ideas—timeless and eternal like Platonic forms—which are not necessarily ethical opposites. We must resist the temptation to impose too rigorous a thematic scheme on the companion poems. Milton presents Mirth and Melancholy as self-sufficient principles that, while seemingly mutually exclusive, in fact offer a balanced but split perspective. Leonard Nathanson perceptively observes that "the more interesting tension seems to lie with the question whether these companionate ideals can be possessed and sustained in all the perfection of their pleasures without deteriorating into something the mind must reject."[31] Indeed, if we read *L'Allegro* and *Il Penseroso* as early attempts by Milton to call upon a Muse who will direct him forward towards the greater task of writing epic poetry or even as efforts by Milton to select a pattern of thought and action—either in the service of Mirth or Melancholy—we must conclude that, at this point in his career, the poet is still defining himself and his poetic ambitions. Nevertheless, Milton's invocations in these two poems display the poet's growing technical and intellectual mastery of the classical forms in the service of a balanced presentation of equally appealing perspectives. Though attracted by the liberty of Mirth, however, the serious and ambitious poet Milton seems to favor the quiet communion with God offered by Melancholy. In *Il*

Penseroso, Melancholy seems to function as the ideal neo-Platonic mistress, whose beauty leads to God himself, as in Castiglione's *Il libro del cortegiano* (1528). However, Milton's attraction to both ideals remains constant in both poems, and this tension remains a source of vitality and inspiration to the poet. While Milton neither seeks nor receives a personal poetic voice from his Muse in these poems, he fine-tunes his own in preparation for greater things to come.

Comus, or A Mask: Defining National Virtues

Having left Cambridge for his father's house at Horton, Buckinghamshire, in 1632 to give himself the leisure to reading through the Greek and Latin writers, Milton soon found himself turning from lyric poetry to write his first masque. But *Comus* does not come readily to mind when considering Milton's epic ambitions and his repeated use of invocations. However, *Comus* may in fact have a very important connection to Milton's epic aspirations. First, both the prologue and epilogues serve as quasi-invocations. Second, the Spirit's invocation to Sabrina brings about the release of the Lady from her prison-chair and raises interesting questions about the relationship between chastity and freedom. Third, the masque's political/national theme connecting the masque-world of Ludlow Castle to Britain's legendary origins in the Brutus myth suggests the implicit function of epic.

On Michaelmas Night, 1634, in the Great Hall of Ludlow Castle, Milton presented *Comus*, with the musical assistance of Henry Lawes, before the Right Honorable John, Earl of Bridgewater, upon his installation as Lord President of Wales. Leah S. Marcus notes that Milton's *Comus* was written and performed only a year after King Charles' republication of the *Book of Sports* in 1633 and, though "as thoroughly immersed as any Whitehall entertainment in the festival traditions for its own occasion of Michaelmas," Milton's masque was designed "to win arts and pastimes back from the domination of the court and the Laudian wing of the church."[32] According to Marcus, Milton's *Comus* celebrates the Earl of Bridgewater and his seat at Ludlow Castle as "a locus for political and social reform" that undermines and redefines Stuart politics of Mirth (20). Milton's masque was not a court masque; instead, it was written to honor the Earl of Bridgewater and his family, not the king.

According to Samuel Johnson, *Comus* "is a drama in the epick style, inelegantly splendid, and tediously instructive" (169). Although Johnson's assessment is essentially flawed because he was trying to judge Milton's masque according to contemporary eighteenth-century *dramatic* tastes, his remark about the "epick style" has some value. While not epic in form, *Comus'* occasion was still, as Marcus says, "a public and political one" (179). In this regard, Marcus maintains that "at Ludlow, the integrity of ritual depends on its separation frcm Stuart images of power" (210). Though they are not traditional conventions of the masque, invocations appear in *Comus*. The most important of these are those to Cotytto and Sabrina, which frame the action of the masque and present contrasting world-views, one pagan and disorderly and the other Christian and harmonious. William A. Oram notes that in both invocations a genius or *daimon* calls upon a mysterious female figure to rise and help him. The invocation of Sabrina, writes Oram, "recalls that of Cotytto, but presents a purified and civilized version of what is wild and perverse in the earlier ceremony."[33] Most striking for the purposes of our inquiry is Oram's suggestion that the transition between the two invocations "dramatizes an essential development in the masque, an evolution from what is overtly pagan to what is implicitly Christian, from an opposition of reason and passion to reconciliation" (125).

While Milton's invocations in his masque are not as obvious as in some of his lyric poems, such as the *Nativity Ode* and the companion poems, they are nevertheless crucial to the masque's central concerns with national identity, chastity, freedom, and poetic vocation. By examining the invocations and quasi-invocations in *Comus*, we come to a fuller appreciation of Milton's anti-Laudian position and his optimism for political reform as embodied in the positive function of Mirth in the Earl of Bridgewater's estate. More importantly, we have the opportunity to see if invocations succeed—always, sometimes, or never? We furthermore see a contrast between successful and unsuccessful invocations, which leads to the question of whether the person or thing being invoked hears and responds to the suppliant and how such invocations help to structure a poetic work. Finally we observe the displacement of pagan values for Christian ones of order and harmony by the end of the masque.

Milton sets his masque not in Christian terms but in the universalized terms of Classical allegory.[34] From the beginning of *Comus*, when "the First Scene discovers a wild Wood," Milton presents his audience a world threatened by the disorder implicit in the dark and labyrinthine woods, which resonate with allusions to Dante's dark woods and Spenser's Wood of Errour. It is into this "wild wood" that the Attendant Spirit, played by Lawes, descends to present his Platonic prologue to the audience:

> Before the starry threshold of Jove's court
> My mansion is, where those immortal shapes
> Of bright aerial Spirits live inspher'd
> In regions mild of clam and serene Air,
> Above the smoke and stir of this dim spot,
> Which men call Earth, and with low-thoughted care
> Confin'd and pester'd in this pinfold here,
> Strive to keep up a frail and Feverish being,
> Unmindful of the crown that Virtue gives
> After this mortal change, to her true Servants
> Amongst the enthron'd gods on Sainted seats. (ll. 1–11)

The Attendant Spirit has come into this "pinfold" world from the highest of heavens, the Platonic world of forms, in order to assist those who would serve Virtue. This opening passage contrasts the physical and spiritual worlds by asserting the obscurity of the former with the clarity of the latter. Here, like Plato's cave-dwellers, men are "confin'd" and their vision is hindered by the smoke that obscures clear vision. Whereas the heavenly realm is a region of "calm" and "serenity," on earth men pursue "Feverish" activities, mistaking partial for transcendent and permanent goods. Virtue's "true Servants," who, like Diodati, live in the company of the saints and eternal ideas, must be few, since the path to Virtue is so difficult.

Having planted the idea that Virtue's rewards are ultimately available to selected persons here below, the Spirit describes his own mission in the world and humanity's ultimate end:

> Yet some there be that by due steps aspire
> To lay their just hands on that Golden key
> That opes the Palace of Eternity:
> To such my errand is, and but for such,
> I would not soil these pure Ambrosial weeds
> With the rank vapors of this Sin-worn world. (ll. 12–17)

Although many people are blind to the possibility of the key to Eternity, some—like the Lady and the poet Milton— "by due steps," may hope to gain the "Golden Key." The Spirit's "errand" (l. 15) is to assist the Lady (and Milton) in that aspiration. The Lady, whose journey "lies through the perplex't paths of this drear Wood," must reach her destination, her "Father's residence" (l. 947), where she will join the mirth and celebrations offered to her "Father's state / And new-entrusted Scepter" (ll. 35–36). In this prologue, the Spirit acts as if he were invoked by the author to give direction to the characters of the masque and to lead the audience toward an appreciation for what Ludlow Castle represents. The prologue itself, then, resembles the Muse's reply to the poet who has invoked her.

While the Attendant Spirit's prologue functions, then, as a kind of quasi-invocation, the first formal invocation comes when the masque's antagonist, Comus, appears and invokes darkness. Comus's invocation to darkness and night fulfills the generic expectations of the invocation, but calls upon negative rather than positive powers to respond to his petitions. While in *Il Penseroso* Milton presented evening as the proper time for studiousness—"Or let my lamp at midnight hour, / Be seen in some high lonely Tow'r" (ll. 85–86)—here Comus uses it as a cover for licentious riot. Transformed from its former (and proper) purposes, evening becomes a parody of what was celebrated in *Il Penseroso*.

Comus' dark invocation begins with an address to the goddess in the grand style appropriate to epic poetry:

Hail Goddess of Nocturnal sport,
Dark Veil'd *Cotytto*, t' whom the secret flame
Of midnight Torches burns; mysterious Dame,
That ne'er art call'd but when the Dragon womb
Of Stygian darkness spits her thickest gloom,
And makes one blot of all the air,
Stay thy cloudy Ebon chair
Wherein thou rid'st with *Hecat'*, and befriend
Us thy vow'd priests . . . (ll. 128–136)

Comus' invocation to the "Goddess of Nocturnal sport" contains the conventional epithets and powers, which are used to define the deity in such a way that prepares it for the request. Here they are numerous and often grotesque: Cotytto is associated with darkness, secrecy, and ugliness. She is not called "but when the dragon womb / Of Stygian darkness spits her thickest gloom" (ll. 131–132). The Goddess, moreover, is a "mysterious Dame," suggesting both her dark nature and her perversion of holy mysteries. According to Schindler, this passage is "a full-fledged demonic parody of the interrelation of vocation and invocation."[35] By engaging in these unholy mysteries and offering suitable prayers to the Goddess he invokes, Comus remains the "vow'd priest" of darkness; the images he conjures up stand in stark contrast to images of light and graceful verse normally associated with the world of masque.

Darkness, though threatening, is not all-powerful. In fact, the Lady, walking nearby, refers to Comus' speech—or rather the music and dancing of his followers—as "noise," noting that "methought it was the sound / Of Riot and ill-manag'd Merriment" (ll. 170–171). Comus' Mirth, then, is a perversion of the positive Mirth of Ludlow Castle and ultimately fails to achieve its end. Comus's bacchanalian rite breaks off and Cotytto never responds to his request.

The Lady's speech, on the other hand, functions, as Schindler says, as the "invocatory counterpoint" to Comus's black magic. She invokes her champion, Conscience:

O welcome pure-ey'd Faith, white-handed Hope,
Thou hov'ring Angel girt with golden wings,
And thou unblemish't form of Chastity,
I see ye visibly, and now believe
That he, the Supreme good, t' whom all things ill
Are but as slavish officers of vengeance,
Would send a glist'ring Guardian, if need were,
To keep my life and honor unassail'd. (ll. 213–220)

Faith, hope, and *chastity* become the Lady's three virtues, replacing the Christian ones of faith, hope, and *charity*. Untroubled by Comus's cloudy charms and pagan magic,[36] the Lady's clear mind dismisses the threat of material reality. She "sees visibly" and has full confidence in the Supreme good. Oram notes that Comus's "worship without concern for the God beyond Nature is bound to be perverse in its etymological sense, a turning aside from truth," an observation suggested by Comus's worship "not of Ceres or even Hecate but Cotytto ("The Invocation of Sabrina," 126). The Lady's spiritual fortitude, on the other hand, will protect her honor and will mark her out as one of Virtue's "chosen," who may aspire to the realm of eternity—a path that the poet Milton would also like to take.

Despite her Virtue, though, the Lady remains Comus's prisoner and requires supernatural assistance to regain her freedom. While Comus's invocation to Cotytto had successfully painted a vivid picture of dark, unbridled revelry but resulted in failure, the Attendant Spirit's invocation to Sabrina produces *results*. He also calls upon a female deity associated with water—here the Severn stream—and associated with fertility rites. However, as Oram observes, in Sabrina "the appetites represented by Cotytto receive a beneficially civilized form" (127). The Attendant Spirit describes Sabrina as "a Virgin pure," the "daughter of Locrine," and now "Goddess of the River." "If she be right invok'd in warbled Song," he says, she "will be swift / To aid a Virgin, such as was herself, / In hard-besetting need" (ll. 854–857). Thus the Attendant Spirit invokes Sabrina's aid:

> Sabrina fair
> Listen where thou art sitting
> Under the glassy, cool, translucent wave,
> In twisted braids of Lilies knitting
> The loose train of thy amber-dropping hair;
> Listen for dear honor's sake,
> Goddess of the silver lake,
> Listen and save. (ll. 860–866)

Similar to the implied sexual associations of Cotytto's "nocturnal sport," Sabrina's sensuous "loose train" of "amber-dropping hair" suggests her own sexual freedom. However, we see that Sabrina binds her hair with lilies, traditionally associated with purity, suggesting control and modesty. The Spirit invokes her in the name of "dear honor" to come and save the Lady. Indeed, as the daughter of Locrine, she would have been seen by Milton's audience as a symbol of British and Welsh patriotism. Having been pursued herself by "her enraged stepdam *Guendolen*" and having safely "Commended her fair innocence to the flood / That stay'd her flight with his cross-flowing course" (830–831), Sabrina is receptive to the Spirit's invocation on behalf of the Lady. As Oram suggests, while a reading of Sabrina as "grace" cannot be supported by textual evidence, "the river-goddess does possess a halo of Christian associations"; namely, Sabrina (like the later Lycidas) becomes an example of "Christian patience rewarded with immortality" (129). By trusting in the river to protect her from harm, Sabrina demonstrates her innocent faith in Nature (and in the God who created it) which results in her worthiness to become its guardian spirit and a mediator for the divine. As a result of the Attendant Spirit's invocation, then, Sabrina rises (attended by water-Nymphs), sings a song, and finally states: "I am here."

The Attendant Spirit continues his invocation, a *positive* formal prayer which reaches the ears of the goddess, and petitions Sabrina to free the Lady from the enchanted chair. His appeal closely resembles an invocation to the Muse:

> Goddess dear
> We implore thy powerful hand
> To undo the charmed band
> Of true Virgin here distrest,
> Through the force and through the wile
> Of unblest enchanter vile. (ll. 902–907)

To which petition Sabrina responds:

> Shepherd 'tis my office best
> To help ensnared chastity;
> Brightest Lady look on me,
> Thus I sprinkle on thy breast
> Drops that from my fountain pure
> I have kept of precious cure,
> Thrice upon thy finger's tip,
> Thrice upon thy rubied lip. (ll. 908–915)

Sabrina's reply becomes an antidote to the black magic inflicted upon the Lady, and comes both at the formal request of the Spirit who invoked her and through a recognition of the Lady's worthiness because she is chaste. The power of Sabrina's counter-magic exceeds that of Comus. The situation, in fact, resembles Britomart's rescue of Amoret from the marble pillar in the *Faerie Queene*, Book III,[37] both in its theme of Chastity contained but not ultimately threatened as well as in its presentation of the power of Virtue over evil. When Sabrina descends, therefore, "the Lady rises from her seat." The Spirit responds by praising Sabrina and her lineage.[38] Sabrina's intervention, then, permits and indeed encourages the positive Mirth displayed at Ludlow Castle, first by "All the Swains that there abide, / With jigs and rural dance resort" (ll. 951–952) and then by the refined Mirth of aristocratic dancing.[39]

After witnessing the triumph of "Three branches of your own" (l. 969), the mask ends with an epilogue that resembles an invocation in its depiction of Virtue and once again emphasizes the theme of liberty:

Mortals that would follow me,
Love virtue, she alone is free,
She can teach thee how to climb
Higher than the Sphery chime;
Or if Virtue feeble were,
Heav'n itself would stoop to her. (ll. 1018–1023)

In these final lines of the Spirit's epilogue, Virtue is praised for having given freedom to her follower, the Lady, and is appropriately favored by heaven. Mixing Christian and pagan elements in his picture of Virtue's and Heaven's powers to aid mortals, Milton concludes the masque in the way that it began: quasi-invocations open and close the masque. Milton surely hopes for the same divine favor shown to the Lady in his own path towards his chosen vocation as *vates*.

Although *Comus* does not abound in invocations to the Muse or various hymns to God or to nature deities, it nevertheless contains a prologue that functions as a quasi-invocation in which the Attendant Spirit "invokes" the Platonic world of forms, the "palace of Eternity," where the "true servants" of virtue eventually join the other saints that dwell in the court (ll. 10–14). This world of universals, from whence comes the virtue displayed by the Lady, becomes the source of strength for those who dwell in the temporal world and have to face the temptations and snares of Comus-types. When the Lady is bound to the chair and, though spiritually safe, cannot escape her captor, the Attendant Spirit invokes Sabrina, associated with ancient Welsh folklore, who frees the Lady with her magic. The structure of the exchange—the Attendant Spirit's invocations and Sabrina's reply—resembles that of the *Nativity Ode*, but is less elaborate and serves a more specific purpose. The invocations in *Comus*, though, do suggest the necessity of calling upon a force outside oneself—like a Muse—in order to be able to transcend the limitations of the physical body. *Comus* is epic in how it concerns a national or political theme: the installation of the Earl of Bridgewater by King Charles as the Lord President of Wales and the virtue requisite for the stability and perseverance of that state. In *Comus*, Milton replaces the King with the Earl and his daughter, playing the Lady, as the moral center of the piece. After Sabrina has descended and freed her from the chair, the Attendant Spirit addresses the Lady as "Virgin, daughter of Locrine, / Sprung of old Anchises' line" (ll. 921–922), connecting her directly to the traditional line of Trojan kings of Britain.[40] Milton's provincial masque modifies the tradition by switching the ordering principle from the monarch to one of his newly appointed Lords and attempts to reinvent his listeners' sense of nationalism in his presentation of an altered originary myth about the struggles of this grand-daughter of Brutus.

So, what is the relationship between the poet and his "Muse" in *Comus*? Who is Milton's Muse here? The answer could be Virtue itself, here presented in the actions of the Lady. The Lady's chastity is in keeping with Milton's standards for himself in his preparations for writing his own national epic. As he demonstrates, chastity can withstand temptation and maintain its intrinsic virtue, but it cannot necessarily rise up at its own volition—as the Lady from the chair—into the active, political world. This need for spiritual assistance connects to Milton's ongoing belief in the importance of humanity's free will and the necessity of divine inspiration, even by those chosen by God. As Milton states elsewhere many times, virtue is greater when tested. Virtue as Muse gives the Lady—and, by extension, gives Milton—a hand in resisting temptation; however, she does not assist the poet in the actual task of writing the mask. Here it is very much the author, Milton, who maintains control of the whole production. On the other hand, if we view the Attendant Spirit as Milton's Muse in *Comus*, then we need to ask to what extent he assists the poet in composing the poem or in inspiring his verse. The Attendant Spirit's primary function seems to be assisting Virtue by invoking Sabrina, who releases the Lady from imprisonment. In the end, it is the river goddess Sabrina who confirms the use of invocation and responds to her suppliant.

Chapter III

"But Now my Oat Proceeds": Pastoral Legacy and Epic Beginnings in *Lycidas* and *Epitaphium Damonis*

Epic poets are often made as much by occasion and opportunity as by ambition. If we concede that writing pastoral poetry is a necessary prerequisite to writing epic, as Spenser gleaned from the career of Vergil, then it follows that Milton felt the same pressure and sense of duty in his own career. Walter Schindler notes that for Milton, and Pope after him, aware of the Vergilian progression of pastoral, georgic, and epic, "the pastoral mode is the self-consciously initiatory phase of the serious poet's vocation . . . [and] the test of vocation."[1] Knowing that one's poetic career requires a certain experience in certain genres can limit the success of one's literary productions if they do not display the full abilities and spirit of their author. More important, though, the poet requires the inspiration of his Muse—especially when confronted with mortality. In the case of *Lycidas*, Milton is called to write a pastoral elegy commemorating his fellow collegian and aspiring pastor, Edward King, "before the mellowing year"; in the case of *Epitaphium Damonis*, Milton has mastered the form but chooses to write his elegy to Diodati, his closest friend, in Latin rather than his native English. In both cases, Milton employs the pagan conventions of pastoral in the service, ultimately, of Christian lamentations and consolations. This chapter, which traces Milton's pattern of invocations to the Muse in these two poems, concerns the use of conventions and their relation to personal feeling.

In *The Anxiety of Influence*, Harold Bloom argues that "the greatest pastoral elegies, indeed all major elegies for poets, do not express grief but center upon their composers' own creative anxieties."[2] Moreover, Bloom maintains, "in a poet's lament for his precursor, or more frequently for another poet of his own generation, the poet's deepest anxieties tend to be uncovered" (150). This pattern, he claims, is true of Milton's *Lycidas*, in which the consolation offered is that of the poet's own "ambitions." "Every poem," according to Bloom, "is a misinterpretation of a parent poem. A poem is not an overcoming of anxiety, but is that anxiety" (94). Although I agree that *Lycidas* is concerned with the poet's own "creative anxieties" and that his "deepest anxieties" are "uncovered" in the lament for his fellow shepherd/poet, I find the idea that the poem is not an expression of grief problematic. Indeed, as I shall demonstrate, several outbursts of grief and emotion in *Lycidas* and *Epitaphium Damonis* which appear to be totally artificial, or conventional, paradoxically *do* display real emotion.

I would argue, also, that the "anxiety" experienced by the poet as demonstrated in Milton's *Lycidas* and *Epitaphium Damonis* is that of the survivor who must both make meaning out of loss and accept the legacy of poetic art. In addition to Milton's recognition of the brevity of life—seen in the early death of his fellow Cantabridgean—comes the poet's confrontation with the pastoral traditions, its possibilities and its limitations. Indeed, Milton the poet must write his pastoral elegy before moving on to his higher calling. But the process is not so automatic: Milton must overcome death by *writing through* the loss of Edward King and Charles Diodati. At the same time, however, he must come to terms with his Muse. The tension between pagan and Christian elements in *Lycidas* and *Epitaphium Damonis* sets the stage for Milton's achievement in the invocations of *Paradise Lost* and the poet's divine calling.

Samuel Johnson, in his *Life of Milton*, was one of the first critics to separate *Lycidas* from the poet's mourning experience: "It is not to be considered as the effusion of real passion; for passion runs not after remote allusions and obscure opinions. Passion plucks no berries from the myrtle and ivy, nor calls upon Arethuse and Mincius, nor tells of rough satyrs and fauns with cloven heel. Where there is leisure for fiction there is little grief."[3] Indeed, Johnson's attack on *Lycidas* is as bitter as Milton's diatribe against the corrupt clergy. Questions about Milton's sincerity in *Lycidas* extend from the eighteenth century into the present, since some readers are disturbed by a seeming incongruity between the poem's use of classical conventions—pastoral and elegiac—and the personal feelings it purports to convey. Twentieth-century critics such as Balachandra Rajan emphasize the poem's "total authenticity" as opposed to its sincerity, arguing that the pastoral elements are subsumed by the "deeper assault of experience." For Rajan, *Lycidas* maintains a "passionate sense of genre" while remaining faithful to "experience."[4] Generally, whether conventional aspects of *Lycidas* are viewed positively or negatively, they are posited as the antitheses of the personal or individual. As a result, Johnson's claim—that the incongruity between personal expression of grief and the use of pastoral renders *Lycidas* insincere—has unfortunately influenced subsequent opinions about the "sincerity" of Milton's poem.

Invocations and apostrophes in *Lycidas* confirm the personal and vocational pressures of poetic calling. At the same time, they reveal the uncertain relationship between the poet, Milton, and his Muse in a time of personal crisis. This tension raises certain fundamental questions about the nature of vocation and poetic inspiration. Who is the Muse? Does the Muse exist? Will the Muse respond if called upon? Will the Muse inspire and protect her chosen poet? These questions are resolved to some degree by the end of the poem, though Milton's poetic course and the exact identity of his Muse remain somewhat uncertain. Moreover, this chapter will ask, does a poet's introduction of a pagan figure necessarily involve a rejection of Christianity? I would argue no, if the poet is a syncretist—as the early Milton certainly was—and yes if he is a "Puritan." In both *Lycidas* and *Epitaphium Damonis*, Milton's Muse is both external (a combination of a pagan and a divine source of inspiration) and internal (revealing the hard work and dedication demanded of the poet). In the process of mourning for Lycidas and Damon, Milton demonstrates the ongoing tension between seeking help from without and asserting strength from within.

Indeed, *Lycidas* is a poem about the poet's creative anxieties, heightened when faced with the death of another poet, or at least one who shared similarly high ambitions. It is a poem about the death of one "cut off before his time" that raises questions about the poet's own dedication to his art. While some readers maintain that *Lycidas* does not express grief, either because of its use of pastoral allegory or its preoccupation with the poet's own "anxiety," I would argue that it is actually more authentic because of Milton's very use of the traditions of the pastoral elegy. The poem is not solely about the poet, Milton, and his ambitions (although some have thought so); neither is it about the death of Edward King. Rather, Milton's composition of the poem participates in the process of mourning. The elegiac tradition is the proper medium for expressing grief for the departed as well as for raising the issue of the poet's own mortality. It is the ritual of mourning and writing that must be performed in order for the poet to work through his loss, come to terms with his own mortality, and then accept the responsibility that has been vested in him. In *Lycidas*, the poet Milton inherits both the reed of the shepherd-poet and the office of Poet in a universal sense. Milton's accepted legacy is to mourn his predecessor in order to become the new singer or bard—and eventually to become the inspired Christian poet.

Unlike Bloom and Rajan, however, I see no excessive gap between the personal and the conventional in *Lycidas*. Indeed, in a genre such as elegy, it is most difficult to separate the two. Milton uses the pastoral first to commemorate the death of King and then to probe his own commitment to the poetic art. The artistic process *requires* the mythologizing power of the pastoral, a form seemingly natural to Milton, familiar as he was to the works of Theocritus, Vergil, and Spenser. Thus, in his use of the pastoral elegy, Milton captures the full range of grief, and he pays the highest tribute to his departed colleague by making that grief universal.

In *Western Attitudes Toward Death*, Phillippe Ariès discusses the changing attitudes toward death and writing about death in the seventeenth century. He observes that by the end of the Middle Ages death had become more personalized, and more thought was given to its importance. In fact, thenceforward death would be thought of as a "break," or rather the severance of an individual from life into death, rather than as a collective experience.[5] During the Renaissance, funeral elegies were popular among writers of all ages and abilities; elegies were often assigned to students as rhetorical exercises or as tributes upon the death of notable figures. *Lycidas* was first published in *Iusta Edouardo King*, a volume assembled by the students at Cambridge to commemorate the loss of their learned classmate, Edward King. Unlike many similar volumes of the time, it displays clear signs of organization—each section concluding with a pastoral elegy—as well as some artistic competitiveness among its several contributors.[6]

Conventionality and frequent imitation do not necessarily obliterate the personal element of elegy, since one cannot write about what is mourned without writing about the mourner. In *Table Talk*, Samuel Taylor Coleridge says something compatible to Bloom about the purpose of the elegy. Coleridge maintains that an "Elegy is the form of poetry natural to the reflective mind. It *may* treat of any subject, but it must treat of no subject *for itself*; but always and exclusively with reference to the poet himself" (23 Oct 1833).[7] The headnote to *Lycidas* in the 1645 edition of the *Poems* reflects Milton's concerns with introspection, public statement, and self-examination: "In this Monody the Author bewails a learned Friend, unfortunately drown'd in his passage from Chester on the Irish Seas, 1637. And by occasion foretells the ruin of our corrupted Clergy then in their height." In King, Milton can see that in spite of promise or education, "unfortunate" happenings can curtail individual potential. At this time in Milton's life, his own future career was still uncertain, but it is clear that he would have felt an affinity for King, whose life had been cut short before he could become a pastor, since Milton's calling seemed to be that of a *vates*, or poet-priest.

Not only does Milton struggle with questions about his own vocation and his preparedness for it in *Lycidas*, but he also attacks a corrupt church which had need of good pastors like Edward King (Lycidas). But, since such a pastor has been lost, Milton must step forward prematurely to assume the office of poet:

> Yet once more, O ye Laurels, and once more
> Ye Myrtles brown, with Ivy never sere,
> I come to pluck your Berries harsh and crude,
> And with forc'd fingers rude,
> Shatter your leaves before the mellowing year
> Bitter constraint, and sad occasion dear,
> Compels me to disturb your season due. (ll. 1–7)

In these opening lines, there is a crucial ambiguity about the phrase "before the mellowing year." Milton is essentially saying, "King died prematurely and I am having to write this poem before I am ready." And, indeed, it is "with sad occasion" and great personal grief that the poet writes this monody as a tribute for his fellow poet/scholar; for that reason he cannot separate his own fears concerning his life and literary ambitions from the poem. Peter Sacks observes that the mention of laurels, myrtle, and ivy—all conventional tokens of the poet—as "figures for poetic offerings . . . adds personal urgency" to the question of Milton's ripeness as a poet.[8] By associating King's early death with the possibly unripe verse of the aspiring poet, Milton confronts the possibility that his life and career are as fragile as King's. Yet, this self-reflexiveness does not render *Lycidas* less sincere or less compelling; indeed, that Milton would express such concerns about the loss of a colleague and his own fears about his future in a poem written for King affirms its sincerity and personal nature.

Descended from ancient vegetation rites and their spiritualized successors, the funeral elegy blends the idea of "mourning"—an ambiguous term that can refer to one's emotional state and to the performance of certain rites—with the idea of "inheritance." The elegy itself embodies the process of mourning, in both senses, and the elements of the "contest." For example, the funeral games for Anchises[9] serve to commemorate Aeneas's departed father as well as to establish his son as the rightful heir. In addition, both Theocritus' and Vergil's singing contests lament and honor the dead poet while establishing a poetic heir. In both cases, the participation in the ceremony allows the mourners to transfer their grief into an activity that lauds the virtues of the deceased and enables the participants to work through their grief. According to Peter Sacks, in ancient Greece "the right to mourn was from earliest times legally connected to the right to inherit"; furthermore, ancient Greek and Roman laws often "prevented anyone from inheriting *unless* he mourned."[10] Indeed, since the time of Moschus's lament for Bion, many elegies, like Milton's *Lycidas*, center upon the idea of poetic inheritance, in which the poet/heir must prove his right to the poetic legacy by performing the proper funeral rituals, confirming his close connection to the dead—"For we were nurst upon the self-same hill,/ Fed the same flock, by fountain, shade, and rill" (ll. 23–24)—and demonstrating his worthiness to mourn through song.

While the pastoral was unfashionable as the proper context for funeral elegies at the time that Milton wrote *Lycidas*, it remained for Milton "a convenient medium for the expression of emotion too personal for direct, unrestrained utterance."[11] The pastoral elegy objectified feeling (proving a sense of ritual) while it allowed self-reflexiveness. Milton's use of the conventions, however, seems appropriate and natural as vehicles for expressing grief, especially since King was himself a poet/pastor. Milton undertook the challenge to write in a form, here pastoral elegy, that had declined in favor, and the effort proved to be successful for his being able to join the special community of elegiac poets who had gone before. Indeed, Milton will later breathe new life into the epic form in much the same way, making use of both classical and Christian traditions.

Perhaps the most powerful elements of Milton's elegies, or of the funeral elegy itself, are those that reveal personal feelings for either the person mourned or the poet himself. Perhaps the most explicit expression of those feelings may be found in the pattern of repetition and elegiac questioning. In *Epitaphium Damonis*, Milton's great Latin elegy, for example, the refrain ("Ite domum impasti, domino iam non vacat, agni"), which recalls Vergil's *Eclogue* X, reflects the poet's debilitating grief. The pastor, who should care for his flocks by feeding and watching over them, instead sends his charges away unfed. Moreover, the use of repetition serves as a structural device that changes meaning as the poet progresses through the different stages of mourning.

In her treatment of *Epitaphium Damonis*, Janet L. Knedlik argues that "the poet (and survivor), however, requires both the questioning of fate and the use of elegy's redemptive rituals in order to be able to accept the final consolation. The shunning of responsibility and the feelings of impotency in the face of loss must yield, though not easily, to the responsibilities that the legacy imposes upon the poet."[12] Elegiac questioning is conventionally repetitive and therefore, according to Sacks, "creates a sense of continuity, of an unbroken pattern such as one may oppose to the extreme discontinuity of death."[13] Repetition can also serve to externalize the experience of loss for the mourner and allow him some sort of distance:

> For Lycidas is dead, dead ere his prime,
> Young Lycidas, and hath not left his peer:
> Who would not sing for Lycidas? (ll. 8–10)

Here, the poet not only sings repeatedly for Lycidas by name, but also in the repetition of "dead . . . dead" he forces an acceptance of his loss so that, at the end of the poem, he may say: "Tomorrow to fresh Woods, and Pastures new" (l. 193). The movement from mourning to acceptance presents a real and painful struggle to the poet, whose recognition of the inaudible truth—"death"—requires his repetition of the word and the word's haunting echo. In a sense, the poet must come to hear sound and meaning of his own voice as it commemorates the loss of his colleague and necessitates his own commitment to taking up the poetic mantle.

Sacks suggests that "the survivor leans upon the name, which takes on, by dint of repetition, a kind of substantiality, allowing it not only to refer to but almost to replace the dead."[14] While the repeated name brings momentary comfort to the poet, there are times when strong feelings of grief burst through:

> But O the heavy change, now thou art gone,
> Now thou art gone, and never must return! (ll. 37–38)

Following a portrayal of the idyllic life that Milton and King had enjoyed together as students at Cambridge (ll. 25–36), this phrase (describing the present reality), as is customary in laments, contrasts with their former happiness. The repetitive phrase, "now thou art gone . . . now thou art gone," tolls like a church bell to announce the finality of death, yet resounds with clear memory of the departed. This is a personal utterance, however, and reflects the poet's continuing effort to accept his loss and progress through the ritual of the elegy.

While the opening verse paragraph of *Lycidas*, beginning "Yet once more, O ye Laurels . . .," is clearly invocatory in the sense that the poet charges the lines with the heavy loss and heavy burden of the poet/mourner, the first formal invocation of the poem occurs in the second verse paragraph. This invocation and those that follow work in conjunction with the conventions of the pastoral elegy; this pattern of invocations highlights the poet's need to reach outside himself for inspiration and consolation as well as his dependence upon the Muse for confirmation in his vocation:

> Begin then, Sisters of the sacred well,
> That from beneath the seat of *Jove* doth spring,
> Begin, and somewhat loudly sweep the string. (ll. 15–17)

Milton's first invocation of the Muses in the elegy reveals the poet rousing himself for an arduous task. "Begin *then*," (l. 15) he writes, as if to say, "therefore, since such a song is needed, I step forward to fulfill the task—but not without the aid of the Muses." He asks them to resonate so as to respond to the "parching wind" and sound of lamentations as a result of King's death: "somewhat *loudly* sweep the string" (l. 17).

Milton's naming of the Muses, "Sisters of the sacred well" (l. 15), includes an account of their origin. Milton's source is the beginning of Hesiod's *Theogony*, where the original source of poetic inspiration, Aganippe, on Mount Helicon, featured an altar to Jove, which the Muses frequented. This invocation, which reaches back to the classical origins of poetic inspiration, serves as a response to the opening exordium in which Lycidas' death is acknowledged and the succession of poets confirmed (l. 1–14). The poet has been called upon to offer the departed Lycidas "the meed of some melodious tear" (l. 14). In the manner of Theocritus and Vergil, the poet calls upon his Muses to initiate the dirge and to grant him a voice worthy of the immediate task of lamenting the deceased poet / pastor. However, noticeably absent is Milton's specific naming of the Muses. Here, he calls upon all nine of them, suggesting either that his loss requires the full strength of their combined song or that the poet desires to maintain his distance from the event. Specific Muses, since Roman times, had had specific powers that could be called upon in times of need. But rather than committing himself to one Muse in this pastoral elegy, Milton calls upon all nine. By doing so, Milton connects to the tradition itself, but seemingly renders the poem less personal. I would suggest that Milton's desire for distance suggests a personal struggle that is partially hidden and partially heightened by the use of convention.

What follows is a rejection of worldly inclinations to deny the magnitude of the events and to shrink from the responsibility of confronting one's obligations: "Hence with denial vain, and coy excuse" (l. 18). This line recalls the opening lines of *L'Allegro* and *Il Penseroso*, in which the poet rhetorically dismisses Melancholy and Mirth, respectively, before advancing his current intellectual position. Here, though, the subject is more serious, and one is uncertain whether the poet is addressing the Muse, himself, or both. And there is no time for delay or postponement. Yet rather than launching into a formal monody for Lycidas, the poet turns instead upon his own condition:

So may some gentle Muse
With lucky words favor my destin'd Urn,
And as he passes turn,
And bid fair peace be to my sable shroud. (ll. 19–22)

In this self-reflexive passage, the poet moves from a consideration of his departed Lycidas to an imagined vision of himself in the future. The meditation upon death causes the poet to turn inward and articulate his own desire to be remembered by a future poet, inspired by the Muse, in the same pastoral strain now used to commemorate young Lycidas. The mention of someone *passing* by the poet's "destin'd Urn" reveals an awareness of the swift passing of *Time*, and of all the accomplishments left unfinished and unimagined. Perhaps the poet fears a similar death before his "mellowing year." In the end of the passage, Milton stresses the bonds—expressed in pastoral language—that most closely unite the poet to Lycidas: both were students at Christ College, Cambridge, where they were "nurst upon the self-same hill" (l. 23) and both were devoted to the Muse.

In accordance with the conventions of the pastoral mode and the tone of the poem, it soon follows that the whole of Nature joins the poet in lamenting the death of Lycidas:

Thee Shepherd, thee the Woods, and Desert caves,
With wild Thyme and the gadding Vine o'ergrown,
And all their echoes mourn. (ll. 39–41)

This passage, rather than being so conventional as to approach "insincerity," as Johnson or others might argue, can be better understood through the concept of the "pathetic fallacy." Although Milton consciously uses the pathetic fallacy to universalize his grief, there is a sense in which one could say that his mind is "unhinged by grief" and therefore his imagination does produce (as Milton knows) a "falseness in all our impressions of external things."[15] Laurence Lerner correctly observes that "the artificiality of the style" in this passage is swept aside by "a syntax of exclamation and a rhythm of release of feeling" in the preceding lines ("But O the heavy change . . ."). Lerner argues that Milton captures the "true voice of feeling . . . without ever actually denying the convention."[16]

Similarly, in *Epitaphium Damonis*, since the assurance of immortality for the pure spirit of Damon is recognized from the beginning and reaffirmed throughout the poem, elegiac questioning centers upon the poet's own feelings of loneliness; his questions express the difficulties of overcoming the loss of his closest companion with whom he could share his thoughts and songs: "Quis fando sopire diem cantuque solebit?"[17] The poet does not question Damon's fate, but rather his own: "At mihi quid tandem fiet modo?"[18] The poet's loss is extremely poignant, for Damon was the only one with whom he could confide his heart: "Pectora cui credam?"[19]

In *Lycidas*, the poet's questioning serves not to resolve the question of loneliness but instead, as Sacks says, to "create the illusion that some force or agent might have prevented the death" (that force having been "temporarily absent rather than nonexistent"). Questioning might also help the poet to confront the reality of his grief by "voicing protest" and "deflecting guilt" that could overcome him with melancholy.[20] The poet addresses the Nymphs asking where they were when "the remorseless deep/ Clos'd o'er the head of your lov'd Lycidas?" (ll. 50–51). Milton's apostrophe to the nymphs, which is clearly indebted to the tradition of Theocritus and Vergil, continues the pattern of elegiac questioning. In Theocritus's *Idyll* I, the shepherd Thyrsis is persuaded by a goatheard to sing of Daphnis, an ideal shepherd and friend of the Nymphs and Muses, for a small cup. Calling upon the Muses for song and announcing his past relationship with the goddesses, Thyrsis asks,

> Where were ye, Nymphs, when Daphnis pined?, ye
> Nymphs, O where were ye?
> Was it Peneius' pretty vale, or Pindus' glens? 'twas
> never
> Anapus' flood nor Etna's pike nor Acis' holy river.[21]

As Daphnis, having vowed to remain true to his first love, was pining away for the love of another, the Nymphs were far away and deaf to his cries. Thyrsis's lament captures the common fear of dying alone and without the comfort of one's friends. Daphnis had been beloved by the Muses, indeed loved by all of nature, and yet he died unsung and unwept. Vergil, in *Eclogue* X, takes up the same theme of abandonment in the poet's lament for Gallus, whose mistress had deserted him.

> Quae nemora aut qui vos saltus habuere, puellae
> Naïdes, indigno cum Gallus amore peribat?
> nam neque Parnasi vobis iuga, nam neque Pindi
> ulla moram fecere, neque Aonie Aganippe.[22]

Vergil, like Theocritus, focuses on the particular place where the Naiads may have been while Gallus was wasting away for love. In doing so, both poets attempt to come to terms with death by contemplating what might have been done to save the shepherd and by revealing some hostility towards those whose powers might have prevented such loss. Both Daphnis and Gallus were friends of the grieving poet and beloved of the Muses, as was Milton's friend King, renamed according to the pastoral convention as Lycidas. Also dwelling upon place or geographic location, Milton associates his nymphs with the higher regions of Mona, or Anglesey, traditionally the home of the magical Druids.[23]

The poet suggests that these old pagan/Celtic figures could have intervened to save the dying Lycidas, but soon confronts the futility of such nostalgic speculation: "Ay me, I fondly dream!" (l. 56).

However, after rejecting the possibility of intervention from the Celtic Druids, the poet turns to classical possibilities more closely related to his own temperament. The poet's rhetorical questioning continues in another apostrophe:

> Had ye been there—for what could that have done?
> What could the Muse herself that Orpheus bore,
> The Muse herself, for her enchanting son
> Whom universal nature did lament,
> When by the rout that made the hideous roar,
> His gory visage down the stream was sent,
> Down the swift Hebrus to the Lesbian shore? (ll. 57–63)

Here, there the poet uses repetition to underscore the futility of wishing that things could have been different ("could . . . could; "the Muse herself . . . the Muse herself") as well as elegiac questioning to reveal the powerlessness both of men and of the pagan deities in the face of death ("what could that have done?"). Even the Muse, Calliope, could not save her son Orpheus from death and horrid dismemberment. Milton's use of this allusion to the beloved poet Orpheus[24] reflects his own anxieties about his future relationship to his Muse; it also reveals his fear that even one favored by the Muse may be powerless and vulnerable at times. The poet's tone, at first, expresses his protest against the world's seeming injustice. Arnold Stein remarks that Milton's "varied lament increases 'rage' to a degree unmatched by other elegists opening the recesses of their passions."[25]

The poet's protest, however, abates into a recognition that the nymphs cannot undo that which divine providence has decreed. Even the "Muse herself" could do nothing to save her son, Orpheus; therefore, the poet's own life and works are as fragile as those of Lycidas. William Race observes that these questions raised by the poet "lead to a stronger complaint that calls into question the point of writing poetry at all."[26] The poet then feels compelled to ask, "Alas! What boots it?" (l. 64) in the first complaint when faced with an apparently purposeless world in which the Muse is "thankless" (l. 66) and the hope for fame is severed by a "blind Fury" (l. 75). When the poet despairs of poetry's potential and considers living for pleasure, Apollo reprimands him: "Of so much fame in Heaven expect thy meed" (l. 84).

After Phoebus Apollo's response to the poet, Milton descends from the "higher mood" back to the pastoral when he calls upon Arethuse and Mincius in the elegy's second formal invocation:

> O Fountain *Arethuse*, and thou honor'd flood,
> Smooth-sliding *Mincius*; crown'd with vocal reeds,

That strain I heard was of a higher mood:
But now my Oat proceeds,
And listens to the Herald of the Sea
That came in *Neptune's* plea. (ll. 85–90)

Having learned the difference between fame and reputation from Apollo, that one is heavenly and the other transitory, the poet returns to the pastoral world—now empty because of the loss of Lycidas—with a new perspective. Milton's invocation of Arethuse and Mincius is significant for the types of pastoral represented in the two figures: the former represents Sicilian and the latter Roman pastoral. According to Schindler, Milton's invocation of Arethuse (l. 85), and later of Alpheus (l. 132), is appropriate to the poet's "attempt, through the strength of this very poem, to relocate the homeland of pastoral poetry in England."[27] Schindler goes on to note that Milton invokes Arethuse and Alpheus in times of "transition and transfiguration," and that each of them "appears in the drama of the poem after an intervention by a higher voice: Arethuse, after the voice of Apollo; Alpheus, after the voice of St. Peter."[28] These observations help to illustrate the role invocations to the Muse play in *Lycidas*, especially in terms of moving from divine utterance to poetic utterance. Similar concerns with poetic inspiration will appear later in the more complex invocations in Books 1, 3, 7, and 9 of *Paradise Lost.*

Using the same rhetorical structure in *Epitaphium Damonis* as he does in *Lycidas*, Milton asks what deities he should profess now that Damon has been torn away from him by death—"Hei mihi! quae terris, quae dicam numina caelo,/ Postquam te immiti rapuerunt funere, Damon?"[29]—but the question is prompted by his rampant emotions. Immediately, though, he affirms his faith in one who divides the souls: "ille animas . . . qui dividit."[30] In *Lycidas*, however, it is the Christian consolation at the end that answers the poet's questioning of God's ways; the poem itself is structured upon the unified complexity of the poet's incessant doubt.

A pastoral elegy, *Lycidas* belongs to a long-established tradition characterized by certain stylistic and structural conventions, which normally include the procession of mourners, the laying on of flowers, and the consolation. These generic elements clearly mark the poem as an heir to such works as Moschus's *Lament for Bion*, Theocritus' *Idyll* I, Vergil's *Eclogue* X, and Spenser's *November Eclogue.* Milton seems to call attention to the artificiality of his inherited conventions, but he does not reject that tradition. Indeed, the elements of elegy (especially the laying on of flowers) fulfill the necessary function of consoling the survivors in hopes to "interpose a little ease" (ll. 132–152). Milton undercuts that "ease," for there is no "Laureate Hearse" for Lycidas; his "bones are hurl'd" far away, unable to be given the proper burial rites. What follows, however, is the poet's expression of pure human compassion for the flesh of Lycidas: "Look homeward Angel now, and melt with ruth:/ And, O ye Dolphins, waft the hapless youth" (ll. 163–164), a final cry of grief before the consolation that ends the poem. Perhaps the greatest strength of this "monody" lies in its conscious recognition that pain and sorrow cannot be detached from the experience of death, but that bereavement paradoxically can co-exist with a confidence in divine order.

In many ways, Milton's digression "by occasion" concerning the corrupt clergy is one of the most interesting parts of *Lycidas*, though digressions were not universally praised in such works. Indeed, in an early rhetorical work, Cicero questions Hermagoras's judgment in supporting the inclusion of the digression as a formal part of an oration. Cicero generally disagrees with digressing from the main subject of a discourse, and argues: "Laudes autem et vituperationes non separatim placet tractari, sed in ipsis argumentationibus esse implicatas."[31] Cicero's admiration for unity of structure and dislike of digressions was shared by many writers of the seventeenth century. However, as Race convincingly argues, St. Peter's diatribe is "generically appropriate," for "St. Peter caps the priamel of mourners (ll. 89–109) consisting of Triton, who represents the Graeco-Roman tradition, and Camus, who represents King's humanist education. Furthermore, his speech is essentially an elaboration of the complaint 'the good die, while the unworthy survive.'"[32] The poet recounts St. Peter's response:

> How well could I have spar'd for thee, young swain,
> Enough of such as for their bellies' sake,
> Creep and intrude and climb into the fold?
> Of other care they little reck'ning make,
> Than how to scramble at the shearers' feast,
> And shove away the worthy bidden guest;
> Blind mouths! that scarce themselves know how to hold
> A Sheep-hook, or have learn'd aught else the least
> That to the faithful Herdsman's art belongs! (ll. 112–121)

This complaint against the unworthy "shepherds" who remain in the clergy, according to Race, is "an intensification of its companion at (64–76)"; the two passages together address "the two goals of King's study at Cambridge: poetry and holy orders."[33] According to Samuel Johnson, Milton's phrase, "Blind mouths," is among those "irreverent combinations" that are "always unskilful." Moreover, Johnson believes that Milton's combinations are worse than most: "Here they are indecent, and at least approach impiety, of which, however, I believe the writer not to have been conscious."[34] Later, in his *Life of Dryden*, Johnson points out that in *The Hind and the Panther* "the name Pan is given to the Supreme Being."[35] It is likely, therefore, that Johnson objected to Milton's syncretic reference to God as "all-judging Jove" (l. 82) in *Lycidas*.

While Johnson tends to see Milton's digression upon the corrupt clergy as a "problem" to be regretted, Dennis Kay argues that the digression may be the "heart of the poem, addressing as it does a spiritual crisis in the nation; King's death becomes an omen, an event whose meaning is much larger than the demise of a virtuous individual."[36] Thus, by using the rhetorical digression, the poet vents his grief upon the death of Lycidas, such a grief as to resonate with a force both public and private.

Milton's digression is followed by a third and final formal invocation, this time to Alpheus, suggesting Milton's faith in the restorative power of the waters:

> Return *Alpheus*, the dread voice is past
> That shrunk thy streams; Return Sicilian Muse,
> And call the Vales, and bid them hither cast
> Their Bells and Flowers of a thousand hues.
> Ye valleys low where the mild whispers use
> Of shades and wanton winds and gushing brooks,
> On whose fresh lap the swart Star sparely looks,
> Throw hither all your quaint enamell'd eyes,
> That on the green turf suck the honied showers,
> And purple all the ground with vernal flowers. (ll. 132–141)

In his invocation of Alpheus,[37] Milton reaffirms the life and creativity of Nature. In this passage, the poet appeals to all the senses; there is color, movement, variety, and abundance. With the rain, associated with the tears of the mourners, comes generation, growth, and rebirth. Pagan and Christian themes of death and rebirth, the cycle of nature and the possibility for resurrection, merge together in this description of the flowers. On the ritualistic level, the flowers come together "to strew the laureate hearse where Lycid lies" (l. 151)—but there is no hearse. Milton follows first with a meditation upon the flesh of Lycidas, whose bones become dissolved and integrated into these geographical and mythical areas of the sea, and finally with a consolation, in which Christian transcendence is offered.

The pastoral, indeed, has the power to universalize death and sorrow in ways that no other form can.[38] However, we rarely use the pastoral elegy in the twentieth century because its conventions seem outdated and old-fashioned; shepherds and nymphs seem too far removed from our actual human experience. But these conventions were "old-fashioned" during the seventeenth century (an even as far back as the Hellenistic period and before) as well. The pastoral universalizes because it taps into the natural cycles of birth, death, and regeneration.

Epitaphium Damonis, like *Lycidas*, commemorates a promising young man cut off before his time. But while Milton shared many of the same aspirations and poetic desires as Edward King, his relationship to Diodati was much closer. It is most interesting, therefore, that Milton should choose to write his elegy to Damon in Latin, rather than English. Milton's use of the pastoral mode in an ancient language, then, becomes more intersting when we consider that the Latin elegy was written for his intimate childhood friend.[39] So what does this say about the presence of personal grief in the poem? For one, it suggests that Milton thought the distancing strategy was necessary precisely when the grief was stronger, and seems a total rejection of Johnson's contempt for such strategies. The effect of an expression of grief such as, "Hei mihi! quae terris, quae dicam numina caelo, / Postquam te immiti rapuerunt funere, Damon,"[40] which appears to be an outburst of emotion, but is totally artificial for an English speaker, in this case *is* an outburst of genuine emotion. Perhaps because the loss was so great Milton sought to rewrite Vergil's *Eclogue* VII to commemorate his departed friend. Paradoxically, then, the use of the Latin language and pastoral mode, which seem to offer distance to the speaker because of its pagan conventions and pagan gods, in fact become the appropriate vehicles for grief. Moreover, Thyrsis's rage against the gods who tore Damon away from him becomes a universal rage against death and its power over humanity. By the end of the poem, the gods, or God, will reward Damon with a hybrid Christian-pagan apotheosis. While the Milton of *Paradise Lost* may desire to unmask the pagan Muse to reveal the "meaning, not the name," the Milton of these pastoral elegies remains a comfortable syncretist.

Milton's opening invocation to the Sicilian Muses in *Epitaphium Damonis* again draws attention to the poem's conventionality while at the same time it asserts its necessary relationship to the *truth* of the pastoral tradition of Theocritus and Vergil:

> Himerides nymphae—nam vos et Daphnin et Hylan,
> Et plorata diu meministis fata Bionis—
> Dicite Sicelicum Thamesina per oppida carmen.[41]

Milton heightens Thyrsis's loss of Damon by associating Diodati's death, and Thyrsis's lament, with Thyrsis's lament for Daphnis in Theocritus's *Idyll* I. Here, the speaker calls upon the nymphs to sing their Sicilian song (Diodati died in England while Milton was away in Italy) and to bring the sound of his lament home to England. The inspiring nymphs, moreover, become a *beginning* for the bereaved poet; they sing the song that *is* his grief and the song that *must* be sung. Thyrsis calls upon the Nymphs of Himera to sing the personal moans of Thyrsis: "Quas miser effudit voces, quae murmura Thyrsis."[42] In a sense, the invocation of the Nymphs reveals the poet's need for a voice as well as his need to hear the reality of his own words: Damon is dead and the poet is alone.

The invocation of the Sicilian Muses, though conventional, becomes most personal when we consider that Milton lost his closest friend when the two were geographically separated. Unlike *Lycidas*, which Milton wrote along with other students at Cambridge for inclusion in *Iusta Edouardo King*, a planned memorial volume, *Epitaphium Damonis* was written when Milton felt he was more prepared, in August of 1639—nearly a year after learning of Diodati's death. His preparation apparently involved the deliberate choice of Latin over English and the use of the full array of elegiac conventions.

The emotion of the poem intensifies when Thyrsis contemplates what it means for him to be alone and powerless against death, for death has robbed him of his dearest companion. The following passage illustrates Milton's successful use of pastoral elements, even in a Latin poem, to capture the experience of real loss:

At iam solus agros, iam pascua solus oberro,
Sicubi ramosae densantur vallibus umbrae,
Hic serum expecto; supra caput imber et Eurus
Triste sonant, fractaeque agitata crepuscula silvae.[43]

These lines are certainly among the most poignant, intimate, and tragically moving in all of Milton's verse. Diodati had been Milton's closest friend, with whom the poet had shared all of his life experiences and aspirations. Perhaps it would not have seemed artificial to Diodati for Milton to write a commemorative elegy to him in Latin, or in *Greek* for that matter. After all, the two young men corresponded frequently in these languages and consciously employed conventions and rhetorical patterns of classical writers. However, Milton does achieve some distance by writing a Latin pastoral, but not at the expense of his personal feelings.

Here, as in *Lycidas*, Milton employs repetition (iam solus . . . iam . . . solus) in order to capture the solitude that the poet feels in the present moment, separated from the company of his friend, Diodati. Without Damon, the poet wanders alone through the fields and pastures beneath the shadows and the raging winds, waiting for night, in a world left barren by his friend's death. These verses transcend convention, and *Epitaphium Damonis*, rendered more grievous because the mourned was a fellow shepherd/poet, embodies the poet's deepest grief and fears concerning his own brief span of life. Through the pastoral mode, the poet's grief is mythologized so that his loss becomes universal: Damon's death becomes the death that all men must face and the poet's solitude becomes the solitude that all men must endure.[44]

In *Studies in Seventeenth-Century Poetic*, Ruth Wallerstein argues for the poetic range and potential of the pastoral elegy by underscoring the form's ability to supply the appropriate ritual while connecting the particular loss to the universal problem of death:

> The pastoral gives voice to a universal rhythm of grief in a concentrated way paralleling the statement of it in the ritual and ceremony of funeral: the shock of death, the grief that must be realized, the stilling of that grief. The elegy, in clothing this rhythm in an allegorical convention, makes use of the power of ritual to absorb man into the experience of the race, to detach him from the disproportion of the moment and draw him into that larger experience which he shares with all men. Thus the

> convention is made to reflect and embody a conception of harmony and of the mind's control over feeling.[45]

In *Lycidas* and *Epitaphium Damonis*, Milton weaves his own language of grief amid the conventions of the pastoral elegy; in doing so, he creates works (recalling the boy's carefully crafted cage in Theocritus' *Idyll* I) that establish him as the true heir to his poetic predecessors. By singing this funeral song according to the traditions of the Ancients, Milton establishes his own qualifications as elegiac poet and legitimacy as heir to the poetic mantle. Following the *rota Vergilii*, Milton has now fulfilled the prerequisite task of mastering pastoral before moving on to epic.

More than other forms, Wallerstein argues, the pastoral elegy, in its treatment of and attitude toward death, reveals the seventeenth century desire "to grasp the significance of death and in some form to reconcile us to it" (5). In *Lycidas*, feelings of loss coexist with the confidence in heavenly rewards for the dead. G.W. Pigman remarks that "the mature, even serene, acceptance of the process of mourning at its most disturbing is a major part of the greatness of *Lycidas*." Indeed, Milton's *Lycidas* shows little struggle to diminish or overcome the grief that is dramatically presented, and even "the 'Weep no more' speech does not rebuke the angry questions that precede."[46] The poet, combining Christian and classical elements in the consolation, bestows the highest tribute on Edward King by showing Lycidas not only in the company of "all the saints above" but also present on earth as the "Genius of the shore" (l. 178; l.183). William Race argues that the consolation of earthly fame must yield to a greater consolation: a consolation figured through "a mixture of Greek (Phoebus Apollo), Roman (Jove), and Christian ('Heaven', 84) theology, a combination that reflects Milton's schooling in the Christian-Humanist tradition."[47] Later, in *Epitaphium Damonis*, Milton concludes the poem with a divine vision that also blends the Christian and pagan, but Damon's spirit dwells in pure aether: "purum colit aethera Damon" (l. 203). Whereas in *Lycidas* the poet returns to the sphere of human experience, *Epitaphium Damonis* closes with an ecstatic vision. In both cases, the poet's desire for and need of continuity, embodied in the abiding spirit of Lycidas and the heavenly vision of Diodati, affirms a commitment to his legacy and charges the poems with the passion of personal loss. In *Lycidas*, this acceptance of poetic legacy, both public and private, enables the poet to transcend the conventions inherent in the pastoral elegy.

Milton's *Lycidas* truly affirms the universal quality of poetic inheritance and establishes Milton's place within the line of pastoral poets, from Theocritus to Spenser. As Milton's poety reveals, the poet's office involves the recognition that the value of life is based upon one's commitment to something outside oneself. While that legacy can be challenging, the poet must accept it and endure. Milton proves that the poet's responsibility is to be the new singer, a gift both rewarding and difficult. Milton's bequest, however, is not tradition or custom (and not "anxiety" as Bloom argues), but a responsibility to those singers who have gone before us in the world.[48] It is the responsibility of the new singer to the dead. Quite often, that charge can be overpowering, monumental, and devastating, resulting in doubt and perhaps even protest. But, here, at the grave, the poet must accept his legacy.

Epitaphium Damonis, in taking up the legacy from *Lycidas* as well as the poise and confidence of the inspired poet, becomes Milton's final serious engagement with the pastoral tradition until his depiction of the Garden in *Paradise Lost*. *Epitaphium Damonis* also marks Milton's final participation in Vergilian pastoral, and his last major poem written in Latin. While somewhat more conventional than *Lycidas*, *Epitaphium Damonis* clarifies even further Milton's epic aspirations. Whereas in *Lycidas* Milton, reflecting upon the loss of his fellow collegian, turns to reflect upon the fragility of his own existence, "So may some gentle Muse / With lucky words favor my destin'd Urn" (19–20), only to note that King's fate could be his own, in *Epitaphium Damonis* Milton's projected fate has been further defined and the shortening of his life would be all the more lamentable because his epic plans would not reach their fruition.

Before Damon's final apotheosis, in which his soul transforms into "pure ether," Milton explicitly defines the poetic career that he has imagined for himself after this pastoral elegy. Following the example of *Eclogue X*, in which Vergil states "ipsae rursus concedite silvae,"[49] Milton also bids farewell to the woods, "vos cedite, silvae" (l. 160), in order to take up new pipes. He defines his ambitions as epic and nationalistic:

> Ipse ego Dardanias Rutupina per aequora puppes
> Dicam, et Pandrasidos regnum vetus Inogeniae,
> Brennumque Arviragumque duces, priscumque Belinum,
> Et tandem Armoricos Britonum sub lege colonos.[50]

Already Milton has begun to plan his national epic, which will concern the origins of British people beginning with the wanderings of Brutus and his Trojan followers; the proposed epic quest will result in the founding of Britain and will continue through the Arthurian legends. Therefore, with this elegy to Diodati, Milton wishes to put pastoral poetry behind him, either leaving his pastoral pipe hanging, forgotten, on a tree, or exchanging it for another, on which he may sing an *epic* theme: "aut patriis mutata camenis / Brittonicum strides!"[51]

Milton's resolve to carry out his epic ambitions after properly commemorating his friend, Diodati, in a pastoral elegy may be seen most strikingly in the frontispiece to the 1645 edition of the *Poems*. (See fig. 2.) This frontispiece, which opens the volume of poetry, also marks the end of a stage in Milton's poetic career and the beginning of another. Surrounding the poet we observe four of the classical Muses (*clockwise from the left*): Melpomene, Erato, Clio, and Urania. While the inclusion of the Muses in portraits of poets was commonplace in the seventeenth century, it was not automatic. Milton likely had a hand in deciding which Muses were to surround his portrait and how he

Figure 2. Frontispiece of the 1645 edition of Milton's *Poems*, with four Muses surrounding the poet's portrait. (Courtesy of the Newberry Library, Chicago)

himself would be presented.[52] In this frontispiece, Milton likely wanted to emphasize his movement from the poetry of his early years, pastoral, to the poetry of his mature years, epic. The most important Muses for our discussion, therefore, are Clio, gazing downward towards the earth, and Urania, gazing upward towards the heavens.

E. R. Gregory notes that the pairing of Clio and Urania at the bottom of the frontispiece was not the engraver's invention. According to Gregory, "the Italian musicologist Gafurius had placed the two Muses at opposite ends of the celestial octave depicted in the frontispiece of his own *Practica Musica*," the highest note belonging to Urania and the lowest to Clio; in the sixteenth century, Marcantonio Raimondi also represents the Muses of history and astronomy.[53] Marshall's representation of Urania with her spheres, eyes turned upward toward the heavens, coupled with Clio writing in her book, eyes cast to the ground, Gregory asserts, is not original. Urania's significance, with her eyes turned upward to the heavens, is that of renunciation of earthly things, while Clio's significance is her association with pagan and classical values.[54] Milton the syncretist has been able to balance the values of both Muses, Clio and Urania, in his early poetry; however, Milton the Christian must soon come to renounce the things of the world, adopting the values of Urania, to "tell / Of things invisible to mortal sight" (*PL* 3.54–55). Milton's movement from the pagan Muses to Urania in *Paradise Lost* signifies his movement toward a Christian Muse.

What Gregory does not discuss, however, is the position of the poet in this engraving. Milton, framed by the Muses, is himself seated in front of an open window, which reveals a pastoral landscape, complete with rustics gathered together on a shady hill. Two appear to be dancing to the music of a seated pipe-player. This presentation of Milton clearly suggests that the poet has completed his pastoral phase (the pastoral scene appears *behind* the seated author). Soon Milton will close the curtain behind him and, under the influence of Clio or Urania, will follow his Muses as they lead him *forward* to write historical or religious poetry. Milton has followed the Vergilian and Spenserian career path, culminating his early poetic career first with a pastoral elegy to King—a project thrust upon him prematurely—and finally with this carefully planned Latin elegy to his childhood friend Diodati, which ends the volume.

While it is customary to consider one's own brief span of life and to reaffirm one's own aspirations when writing a funeral elegy, Milton's articulation of his epic ambitions in *Epitaphium Damonis* takes on the spirit of an invocation of the Muse. On a private level, by writing this pastoral elegy, Milton conjures up the memory and meaning of Diodati's life and commemorates the value of their friendship. On a literary level, though, Milton's conversation, or rather monologue, with the departed resembles the poet's struggle with his Muse and with himself. Milton's literary tribute to Diodati ends by offering praise and making a request:

> Quin tu, caeli post iura recepta,

Dexter ades, placidusque fave, quincunque vocaris,
Seu tu noster eris Damon, sive aequior audis
Diodatus, quo te divino nomine cuncti
Caelicolae norint, silvisque vocabere Damon.[55]

Having achieved the status of saint and natural deity alike, Diodati has risen to the status of divinity and can be called upon by those who know his name. Milton develops this idea to some extent here, before mentioning Diodati's purity and virginity as qualities that make him even more worthy of regard. As a spirit, Diodati is not gone, but translated into a higher form; because of his heavenly privileges perhaps he will be able to assist the poet Milton as he progresses to fulfill his poetic ambitions embodied in the figures of Clio and Urania. While those in heaven will call him "Diodati," the only name by which they know him, Milton and those in the forests below can call him by the name associated with pastoral, Damon. Now, Milton clearly plans to write an epic—and even hopes to enjoy the favor of a supportive heavenly spirit—but does not yet know that he will soon discard his national theme for a cosmological one. Through a series of increasingly powerful and self-searching invocations to the Muse in *Paradise Lost*, Milton will reach back, further and further, to tap into the original fount of poetic inspiration—Urania or the Holy Spirit—and to capture in a revitalized epic the origin of humanity as we know it—fallen humanity with the choice to accept or reject the Grace of God.

Milton's early poetry, from his juvenile verse translations of David's *Psalms* to his great pastoral elegies, *Lycidas* and *Epitaphium Damonis*, reveals a steady concern with the notions of poetic calling and responsibility. The primary manifestation of this concern comes in the pattern of invocations that vividly dramatize the poet's maturing relationship with his Muse. Indeed, as Milton begins to see himself as his country's epic poet, both his verse and his prose works abound in references to his desire for inspiration as well as to his own concerns about his worthiness for higher tasks. It is unlikely that Milton planned each poetic project according to its rung on the ladder to the great epic; however, Milton's invocations to the Muse demonstrate the poet's awareness of epic tradition and the burden that it places on those who will seek to write epic. In a sense, then, all of Milton's early poetry assisted in preparing him for his epic calling.

Chapter IV

From Clio to Urania: Milton's Epic Invocations in *The History of Britain* and *Paradise Lost*

> The end then of Learning is to repair the ruines of our first Parents by regaining to know God aright, and out of the knowledge to love him, to imitate him, to be like him, as we may the neerest by possessing our souls of true vertue, which being united to the heavenly grace of faith makes up the highest perfection.
>
> Milton, *Tractate on Education*[1]

Milton's famous definition of learning from his *Tractate on Education to Master Samuel Hartlib* offers readers a useful paradigm for approaching the issue of separation from God and the ultimate goal of reuniting with God. Learning, for Milton, is far more than the accumulation of knowledge or the acquisition of skills which will help one 'get along' in life. According to the Puritan poet, learning means finding one's way back to one's origins. When Milton begins his definition with learning's "end" he means both "aim" and "opposite of beginning." Yet, paradoxically, Milton's conception of learning's end ultimately should bring humanity to its "beginning"—that is, the beginning of us all. Before the Fall, Adam and Eve *did* "know God aright"; they loved him, imitated him, and strove to be perfect images of him. It is only after the Fall, however, that learning (as Milton defines it here) becomes necessary for us; through willful disobedience of God, our first Parents brought about our ruin: essentially our separation from God. But now, through faith and the exercise of "true vertue" as well as through God's grace, we may come as close as possible to repairing that ruin. The story of "Learning" for Milton, then, is the story of the loss of Eden with the possibility of restoration through the mercy of God. Both the prose works and the epics reveal Milton's belief in God's power to fill him with the Holy Spirit and breathe into him new life and inspiration. As God's chosen poet-prophet, Milton must himself first come to "know God aright"—to establish the proper relationship with his source of inspiration—before he can "assert Eternal Providence, / And justify the ways of God to men" (*PL* 1.24-25). Milton establishes this relationship with God and affirms his own ability to convey God's message through his formal invocations to the Muse.

As Milton progresses in his treatise, he would have his reader follow him to an imaginary hillside, where he "will point ye out the right path of a vertuous and noble Education." At "the first ascent," Milton acknowledges, the path is "laborious indeed . . . but else so smooth, so green, so full of goodly prospect, and melodious sounds on every side, that the Harp of *Orpheus* was not more charming."[2] The path to learning bears close similarity to the path to poetic inspiration; in his invocation to Urania in *PL*, Book 7, Milton asks his Muse to "Descend from Heaven" (7.1) so that she may once again lead him up "Into the Heav'n of Heav'ns" (7.12-13).[3] A vision of the Truth, then, requires the poet to ascend from the physical world to a higher world. But he cannot attain the vision without divine assistance; the realm he wishes to perceive affords sounds and sights that exceed even the transcendent music of Orpheus' lyre.

It soon becomes clear that Milton aspires not only to teach, but more specifically to teach through epic poetry, the highest Renaissance genre. Milton notes his sources for learning about the conventions and genres of "that sublime *Art*," Poetry, indicating that they can be found

> . . . in *Aristotle's Poetics*, in *Horace*, and the *Italian* Commentaries of *Castelventro*, *Tasso*, *Mazzoni*, and others, teaches what the laws are of a true *Epic* Poem, what of a *Dramatic*, what of a *Lyric*, what *Decorum* is, which is the grand-masterpiece to observe.[4]

Having listed the literary critics of epic most venerated by Renaissance writers, Milton moves quickly to a critique of contemporary poets who do not observe the important law of *Decorum* in poetry. Taking Milton's sources as a proper reading list for would-be poets and critics of poetry,

> . . . would make them soon perceive what despicable creatures our comm[on] Rimers and Play-writers be, and shew them, what religious, what glorious and magnificent use might be made of Poetry both in divine and humane things.[5]

From this passage we can see that Milton had a low opinion indeed of common writers who do not make use of the great themes. Therefore, any literary productions composed by these writers are merely verse and plays, not *poetry* and *drama*. Well aware of the rhymed couplets of the *Davideis*, Milton was also likely criticizing Cowley and other Cavalier poets for this most un-decorous practice.

Note also that Milton asserts what he believes to be the higher purpose of poetry—that it should be used in "divine and humane things." I take "divine things" to apply to his epic, *Paradise Lost*, and "humane things" possibly to apply to his historical work, the *History of Britain*. Both works are concerned with "learning": they seek to explore our beginnings, whether historical or theological. Moreover, both are concerned with the Truth. *The History of Britain* develops out of Milton's early desire to write an epic on King Arthur (the *Arthuriad*). Because the work contains both formal and informal invocations and presents epic portraits of such notable "founding fathers" as Brutus, Arthur, and Alfred, I shall begin my discussion of epic invocations with Milton's historical work. In some ways, the *History of Britain* may have provided Milton with an opportunity to determine his relationship to the past, and the past's relationship to the present and future that closely resembles parts of *Paradise Lost*. Indeed, Milton's concern with the conflict between myth and history in the *History of Britain* also sheds light on the similar tension between paganism and Christianity in the poet's complex invocations to the Muse in *Paradise Lost*. The tension between epic aims and historical accuracy in *The History of Britain* prepares Milton for the greater challenge of writing *Paradise Lost* and attempting to reach back to humanity's very beginning, the Fall of Man.

Historical Epic Rejected

As seen in the previous chapter, the frontispiece to Milton's *Poems* of 1645 shows the poet in transition between pastoral and epic poetry. With the completion of *Lycidas* and *Epitaphium Damonis*, Milton looks ahead to his calling as epic poet and his relationship with the epic Muse. But Calliope does not appear on the engraving; instead, the poet is surrounded by Melpomene, Erato, Urania, and Clio. With Melpomene and Erato behind him, it is Urania and Clio, then, who vie for influence over Milton as the poet works through his plans for a national epic upon the beginnings of the British people. Rather than writing his *Arthuriad*, Milton channels his national epic urges into his *History of Britain*, which would seem to demand the aid of Clio, not Urania. As it is a prose narrative, Milton's *History of Britain* receives little attention as a work that contributes to the poet's development as epic poet, and virtually no attention as an experimental prose epic.[6] And yet there are some striking similarities between the beginning of *The History of Britain* and the invocations in *Paradise Lost*, as well as similarities between their didactic purposes which warrant close attention before a detailed study of Milton's Christian epic should begin.

Probably written between 1643 and 1648, *The History of Britain* was the sole product of Milton's interest in King Arthur and King Alfred as subjects for epic poetry.[7] Milton planned to write a brief history of his country from its origins to his own time, his purpose being "the good of the *British* Nation." But throughout the work, as Lowenstein notes, Milton "faces the dilemma of the historiographer who simultaneously perceives himself as a poet."[8] Indeed, the opening three paragraphs read like a poetic invocation. Milton opens the work with an acknowledgment of the difficulties of tracing origins: "The Beginning of Nations, those excepted of whom sacred Books have spok'n, is to this day unknown." Noting the reliability of Scripture here, he proceeds to indicate his lack of faith in fables and myths: "Nor only the beginning, but the deeds also of many succeeding Ages, yea periods of Ages, either wholly unknown, or obscur'd and blemisht with Fables."[9] This passage reveals Milton's interest in origins, beginnings, and at the same time attests to his commitment to accuracy in reporting history through a careful examination of original sources. By attending to "authorities" and reducing the use of "controversies and quotations," Milton hoped to "instruct and benefit them that read." Milton concludes the section with both an invocation-like request for inspiration and an assertion of his own authority: "Which, imploring divine assistance, that it [the History] may redound to his glory, and the good of the *British* Nation, I *now begin*" (3). Here, Milton is clearly concerned with beginnings and the conflict between history and fable. And yet, as the work progresses, Milton will make use of fables, finding "something true" even in these "reputed Tales" to "instruct and benefit them that read."

Milton, surprisingly enough, begins his "historical" narrative with an account of the Flood, but moves quickly to a more substantial account of Brutus, which is heavily indebted to Geoffrey of Monmouth's *History of the Kings of Britain.*[10] Although Milton criticizes the historical accuracy of the early chroniclers by referring to the story of the wandering Trojans as "Brutus, and the whole Trojan pretense," and noting their quest for British origins that "gave rise to the lineage," he nevertheless chooses "not to omitt" the legend (6). For Milton, there remains *some truth* in stories, fables, and literature that can transcend the fictional narrative. Lowenstein writes that Milton, aware that most writers of his time had skeptically concluded that the story of Brutus was more poetical than historical, "nevertheless proceeds, as though he were beginning an epic poem, to devote considerable space and detail to this ancient hero's Trojan genealogy and story."[11] I would agree, adding that Milton's poetical leanings manifest themselves even more significantly in his use of epic invocations, both implicit and explicit.

The following verses, translated by Milton from Monmouth's account of Brutus, reveal Milton's continuing concern with national origins as well as the relationship between the poet and his Muse, established through invocation. Having entered a shrine on the forsaken Mediterranean island of Leogecia, Brutus the Trojan appeals to the goddess Diana for her advice and guidance. Milton writes that "*Brutus* . . . with wonted Ceremonies before the inward shrine of the Goddess, in Verse, as it seems the manner was, utters his request, *Diva potens nemorum*, &c." (11) Brutus' prayer and Diana's response then follow:

Goddess of Shades, and Huntress, who at will
Walk'st on the rolling Sphere and through the deep,
On thy third Reigne the Earth look now and tell
What Land, what Seat of rest thou bidst me seek,
What certain Seat, where I may worship thee
For aye, with Temples vow'd, and Virgin quires.

"To whom sleeping before the Altar," says Milton, "Diana in a vision that night thus answer'd;"

> Brutus, far to the West in th' Ocean wide
> Beyond the realm of Gaul a land there lies,
> Sea-girt it lies, where Giants dwelt of old,
> Now void, it fits thy People; thither bend
> Thy course, there shalt thou find a lasting seat,
> There to thy Sons another Troy shall rise,
> And Kings be born of thee, whose dreaded might
> Shall awe the World and Conquer Nations bold. (11-12)

Like Milton's early invocations and those in *Paradise Lost*, this "Hymn to Diana" contains both an *invocation* and *reply*. The exchange between the suppliant, Brutus, and the goddess, Diana, provides a model for the poet who would write of humanity's origins. Like Geoffrey of Monmouth, Milton is interested in the myth of Brutus, the great-grandson of Aeneas, as the legendary founder of the British people. Diana's reply to Brutus' prayer more than fulfills his expectations. She hears his prayer and grants his request; Brutus is "guided now, as he thought, by divine conduct" (12). Diana, goddess of the moon, of country and forest, of the hunt, of springs and brooks, of chastity, and of childbirth, replaces the Muse in this episode as the protectress of the Trojans. Her associations with nature as well as with childbirth suggest that, by invoking her aid, Brutus and his descendants will be welcomed into their new homeland. With the Diana's blessing, the Trojan settlers will multiply and fill the land with their offspring. Milton will write four such prayers or invocations in *Paradise Lost* for inspiration and guidance from his "Heav'nly Muse."

The story of Brutus is closely modeled upon the story of his forebear, Aeneas, arising from a situation of loss and culminating in a situation of rebirth and beginning. Milton writes that "The Iland not yet Britain but Albion, was in a manner desert and inhospitable; kept only by a remnant of Giants" (13). When Brutus and his men arrive, they discover that "excessive Force and Tyranie had consum'd the rest [of the inhabitants of Albion]" (13). Britain is a land "Now void" and waiting to be filled with Brutus and his descendants, with Diana's blessing. With the defeat of Goëgmagog, the greatest of the giants, Brutus can establish his *Troia Nova*—later *Trinovantum*, now London—a city that was granted to him and his people by ancient right. Thus, the end of Brutus' quest becomes the beginning of the British people.

This narrative of Brutus's founding of Britain parallels Milton's general tendency as a poet to fill empty spaces, or to make room for himself where there is seemingly no room to be found. It also suggests that Brutus and his followers are the chosen people destined for the promised land and, by extension, that the poet who prays earnestly to his God will receive his blessing.

While Milton acknowledges his debt to Monmouth, he expresses his distrust of the medieval chronology. Milton places himself as a careful and scholarly historian. Milton says that Monmouth "set out on his way by night, and travail'd through a Region of smoother or idle Dreams," while "our [Milton's own] History now arrives on the Confines, where daylight and truth meet us with a clear dawn, representing to our view, though at a farr distance, true colors and shapes" (31). This is Enlightenment language expressing fascination with light and understanding; Monmouth has paved the way for Milton to blaze ahead with his *true* history of Britain. In a sense, this remark about "light" and "discovery" resembles the poet's experience in *Paradise Lost*; having descended into darkness, the poet, with the nightly visitations of his Muse, is led to divine knowledge of God. But while sources such as Monmouth can provide Milton with only some degree of certainty, Julius Caesar will provide more.

Milton never really seriously considered the Brutus myth as the proper subject matter of a British epic. Instead, he looked to King Arthur. Yet Milton also has real problems with the "historical" figure of Arthur. It is interesting that the poet chose to give more attention to the certainly mythological story of Brutus, with which he essentially opens his history. Milton's reasons for not selecting Arthur as the subject of his epic seem clear enough: "who *Arthur* was, and whether ever any such reign'd in Britain, hath bin doubted heertofore, and may again with good reason" (129). Milton notes that Malmsbury and Monmouth, the chroniclers closest to Arthur, came five hundred to six hundred years after the Battle of Mount Badon, where Arthur defeated the Saxons. The matter of King Arthur is too much the stuff of legends.

> Others of later time have sought to assert him [Arthur] by old legends and Cathedrall regests, . . . he who can accept of Legends for good story, may quickly swell a volume with trash, and had need to be furnish'd with two only necessaries, leisure, and belief, whether it be the writer, or he that shall read. (128)

So while Arthur's deeds make up a good story, they do not offer enough truth for the epic poet, not even one with a powerful Muse.

The same may be said concerning King Alfred, whose interests seem to have struck a familiar chord in Milton. It is clear that Milton admired Alfred, who sought "not only to learn much himself, but to communicate therof what he could to his people."[12] Milton sees Alfred, to some degree, as the philosopher-king in the manner of Marcus Aurelius and as an important link in the English literary tradition because of his translation of major Latin works. King Alfred, though not the proper material for an epic hero, was perhaps an idealized version of what Milton wanted to achieve in his poetic / epic career: Alfred possessed a combined commitment to learning and governing in the service of the truth. That Alfred sought to "communicate" his learning with his people suggests a didactic role, similar in nature to Milton's posture in his *Tractate on Education* and Argument to *Paradise Lost*.

Unfortunately, Milton was prevented from completing his *History of Britain* by the epic history that was happening around him.[13] He soon found himself called upon not to celebrate past kings but to defend the execution of King Charles I. Even so, he managed to complete Book 3 and most of Book 4 before accepting the post of Secretary of Foreign Tongues. Under Cromwell, Milton would not return to the project until the 1650s. Modeled upon Sallust's concise and relatively plain style, Milton's *History of Britain* was intended as a guide for national conduct and values. In the final sentence of the work, Milton admonished his readers to recall past troubles in a more secure age, but to "fear from the Vices without amendment the Revolution of like Calamities" (316). Milton's injunction to recall in peace the lessons learned in war is stressed more explicitly in his Digression on liberty (occurring after his account of the Roman withdrawal from Britain) where he writes, "the gaining or loosing of libertie is the greatest change to better or to worse that may befall a nation under civil government" (114). Nevertheless, as Lowenstein writes, "Milton is aware of the bleakness of much of his historical narrative, which reads too much like a failed national saga, and he thus finds himself confronted with the problem of presenting history unworthy of recording" (86). It is perhaps for this reason that Milton would soon turn to *Paradise Lost* as an appropriate narrative of loss and renewal.[14]

Milton's careful evaluation of primary sources, his concise style, and his dedication to accuracy in his *History of Britain* attest to his belief that an historical narrative still has much truth to offer the modern world. His epic portraits of figures such as Brutus, Arthur, and Alfred, as well as others, serve as *exempla* both to admonish and inspire his contemporary readers.[15] This is the same strategy used by Lucan in *De Bello Civili* and by Cowley in the *Civil War*, but for Milton the Muse seems more nearly present in his work. Milton seems ever to be looking forward to his epic and backwards to our beginnings, observing the parallels between past and present as well as waiting to offer readers the ultimate *exemplum* of God's mercy. Having drawn upon the powers of Clio, though not addressing her by name, Milton will leave the Muse of History to gaze down upon the things of the world while he ascends, gazing upwards by the strength of Urania, to see and tell of "Heav'nly" things.

Milton's "Heav'nly Muse": Epic Invocations in *Paradise Lost*

> Descend from Heav'n *Urania*, by that name
> If rightly thou art call'd, whose Voice divine
> Following, above th' *Olympian* Hill I soar,
> Above the flight of *Pegasean* wing.
> The meaning, not the Name I call . . . (*PL* 7.1-5)

In *Paradise Lost*, Milton reaches farther back than Arthur, Brutus, or even the Flood for his epic material. He does this through the inspiration of his "Heav'nly Muse," Urania, both the classical Muse of Astronomy and Spirit of God. While Milton transforms Urania's identity from a pagan goddess to a Christianized metaphor for divine inspiration, his Muse retains qualities of both her classical and her biblical lineage. Indeed, Milton will "ascend the highest heavens of invention" and surpass the epic themes of Vergil and Homer, but he will do so by participating fully in their tradition. Though he rejects the "Name" of Urania while asserting her "meaning," Milton nevertheless draws upon both aspects of her being as he composes *Paradise Lost*. His repeated invocations of the Muse simultaneously reject the pagan gods in favor of the Christian God while they draw upon the inspiration of their mythology and poetic legacy.

Like Vergil, Milton is similarly concerned with focusing upon a defining moment in human history, in which past glories validate the values and goals of the present. But while Vergil's choice of Aeneas, well-known to literate Romans from Homer's *Iliad* 2.820[16] and 20.158[17] as the heroic son of Anchises and a worthy match for Achilles, seems logical for an heroic poem on the beginnings of Rome, Milton's choice of Adam and Eve and the Son of God as "epic heroes" seems to call those Vergilian heroic values and generic form into question. Milton wishes to transcend human history in his epic—to soar "above th' *Olympian* Hill"—and to affirm epic values rooted in Eternity. However, Milton also rejects epic values by giving Satan the attributes of the epic hero and, in doing so, even building a kind of implicit palinode into the poem.

David Quint argues in *Epic and Empire* that *Paradise Lost*, closer to the "losing" tradition of Lucan than the "winning" tradition of Vergil, "conforms to a general movement of the seventeenth-century epic in the direction of romance, an epic that appears increasingly unwilling or unable to create the absolutist modern state and its centralizing institutions." Quint believes that while Tasso's *Gerusalemne Liberata* subordinates all believers to a "single authority," Milton's *Paradise Lost* insists upon the "autonomy of individual belief and will" (7). However, I find this view problematic, for the narrative of the Fall insists upon humanity's obedience to God. Adam and Eve followed their own individual wills when they chose to eat the forbidden fruit. Moreover, for all of its rejections of the Vergilian tradition—especially in the "heroic" person of Satan, figured as an Aeneas/Achilles/Odysseus type—*Paradise Lost* owes much of its structure to the *Aeneid* as well as its closely paralleled use of epic invocations. In fact, there are few similarities between Milton's epic and Lucan's; if we recall the discussion in Chapter I on Cowley's *Civil War* we can see a much stronger resemblance between his heroic poem and Lucan's. While I would grant Quint's position that individual choice separates Adam and Eve—and all their progeny—from any unified notion of a political state, I would argue that human free will has value only insofar as it helps human beings to reunite with God. Just as Aeneas loses Troy, Adam and Eve lose Eden: both epics are concerned with loss. But also like Aeneas, whose goal is Latium, Adam and Eve are sent out into the world to work towards an origin that is more anciently theirs: through the "one greater Man" and their free choice they may eventually be restored to that "blissful Seat" (*PL* 1.4-5). Quint's reading seems to disregard the doctrine of the *felix culpa* and deny Milton's appropriation of the Vergilian pattern of epic in the service of a greater Christian theme.

Vergil's invocation of the Muse—"Musa, mihi causas memora"[18]—while modeled loosely upon Homer's, takes on a more literary role. In fact, Vergil begins his epic with a complex *propositio* and *invocatio*, and makes use of secondary invocations later to mark transitions in the narrative as well as to request catalogues from the daughter of memory. Homer, on the other hand, begins the *Iliad* with a simple invocation: "Sing, Goddess, the anger of Peleus' son Achilleus / and its devastation" (1.1-2). The invocation implies that what follows the imperative, "Sing, Goddess," is the creation of the Muse, not the poet. The Homeric "I" (if there is such a thing) becomes subordinate to the voice of the Muse, whose words make up the poem that follows. Vergil, on the other hand, begins with *cano*, "I sing," in the first line and delays the invocation of the Muse until the eighth line. In doing so, he expands upon the Homeric model, separating the proposition from the invocation and focusing more attention upon the role of the poet. While Vergil's formal invocations to the Muse are more elaborate rhetorically, Homer's Muse retains her original connection to inspiration and memory. In *Paradise Lost*, Milton reaches back to the origins of the epic genre—blending the Vergilian and Homeric qualities of the Muse along the way—to bring the Muse back to life after years of conventional use and misuse from late Antiquity through the Middle Ages. While Milton's Christianized Muse resembles the Muses of Hesiod and Homer in her *real* power to inspire (she *does* become God), the poet's invocations structurally imitate those of Vergil. As Nuttall argues in *Openings*, Milton's invocation to the Muse in *Paradise Lost*, Book I, is "proudly interventionist, and underlines the decision by doing it twice. At the same time, however, Milton, like Virgil and unlike Homer, continually and strenuously reaches toward a genesis, towards a natural beginning." Indeed, Milton draws upon the strength of Vergil. But while the primacy sought by Vergil is "fundamentally historical," according to Nuttall, in Milton it is "confusedly cosmic. The Virgilian invention of the Great National Subject of epic has become the Great Universal Subject, not just the story of all Romans, but the story of us all" (93).

Although it is a poem of loss, *Paradise Lost* is more importantly a poem of beginnings, figured thematically and generically by Milton within the fabric of his invocations to the Muse. Regina Schwartz has recently argued that *Paradise Lost* is a hymn, and that each instance of prayer, or praise, is an attempt to make the connection with God that was present from the beginning.[19] Milton's invocations to the Muse in *Paradise Lost*, Books I, III, VII, and IX are the best examples of praise to God in the poem (in contrast to Satanic soliloquies and demonic complaints) and underscore Milton's Christian argument. These four proems are personal and self-enclosed lyrics in which the Miltonic *vates* works through his role as poet-priest through his interaction with the Muse, whose identity and influence become central to the poem's meaning and structure.[20]

The Miltonic bard reaches back into pre-Creation biblical history for his inspiration and his very narrative. But for Adam and Eve, as well as the reader who has just completed the poem, there is no *visible* source or beginning—there is only the present. Indeed, I would argue that a tension exists between the poet trying to reach out to his Muse for inspiration or confirmation in the invocations and the characters in "positive" hymns to God and the epic form itself as a search for origins. Even if God's goodness and mercy exist in an eternal present, man lives within Time; the epic must continue reaching back towards a beginning so that we—humanity—can find our final end. Milton's invocations to the "Heav'nly Muse" fulfill the generic demand for locating our homeland and the spiritual demand for our reunion with God, both demands being one and the same. To know our beginning is to know our end.

Milton's early epic aspirations appear in his verse epistle, *Mansus*, written for John Baptista Manso, Marquis of Villa. Having praised Manso for his hospitality towards poets such as Tasso and himself, Milton mentions his desire to write the British epic. Since, according to Renaissance interpretations of Aristotle's *Poetics*, an epic should be grounded in historical fact and should concern the origins of a people, it is natural that Milton would think of the Arthurian legend for his theme: "Si quando indigenas revocabo in carmina reges,/ Arturumque . ." (ll. 80-81). Earlier, when wishing Manso good health, Milton invokes both Clio and the great name of Apollo ("Clius et magni nomine Phoebi," l. 25) and refers to himself as a pilgrim sent from a colder clime, suggesting the extra difficulty northern poets are said to have because of the weather (see *PL* 9). Although Milton does not claim to be a poet-priest at this time, he does follow Tasso's precedent of paying a tribute to Manso. By referring to Clio and Apollo, Milton shows his serious interest in following that author of *Gerusalemne Liberata* in writing an epic.

Another significant poetic reference to Milton's proposed epic comes in his great Latin elegy, *Epitaphium Damonis*, discussed in Chapter III, in which he expands the scope of his epic plans to include the Trojan landing on English shores: "Ipse ego Dardanias Rutupina per aequora puppes / Dicam."[21] Like Vergil, who in *Eclogue* X announces "ipsae rursus concedite silvae" (l. 63), Milton prepares to hang up his pipe unless it can shrill forth a British theme:

> O, mihi tum si vita supersit,
> Tu procul annosa pendebis, fistula, pinu
> Multum oblita mihi, aut patriis mutata camenis
> Brittonicum strides![22]

Having mastered the pastoral elegy and paid tribute to the pastoral tradition, Milton intends to bid farewell to his Latin verse in favor of English, and to dedicate himself to the highest form of Renaissance poetry, the classical epic.

Milton's four invocations to the Muse build upon the poet's previous success in invoking the Muse in his early verse, and are essential to the structure and meaning of the *Paradise Lost.* In these epic invocations, Milton announces his subject and prepares his audience, with the aid of the Muse, for his divine theme. While eighteenth-century writers such as Joseph Addison and Samuel Johnson considered Milton's elaborate invocations to the Muse to be "digressions," elegant but essentially unnecessary to the epic poem, many twentieth-century critics have affirmed their structural and poetic importance, even to the point of arguing for their centrality in the epic.[23] Ann Ferry, for example, focuses upon Milton's "invention" of a distinctive voice capable of narrating and interpreting his "higher Argument" (*PL* 9.1-47). According to Ferry, the passages especially concerned with creating and defining this voice are those found in the proems of Books I, III, VII, and IX, in which the poet "adapts the conventional device of the epic introduction."[24] The epic introductions, or invocations, establish the poet's relationship to his source of inspiration and his connection to his fallen audience, of which he himself is a member. Agreeing with Ferry's argument, Walter Schindler adds that "the invocations are searching meditations on the poetic power and on the powers of the Divine Spirit"; Milton's appeal to this Spirit in the invocations expresses "a theory of poetry that has grown out of his total poetic and religious experience from youth to manhood, but here is specifically applied to the great epic task before him."[25] According to Schindler, Milton's proems constitute "not only a defense of poetry as divine inspiration, but also a defense of Christian epic as 'not less but more heroic' than his predecessors" (46).

While Cowley's unusual invocation to Christ (in which the Muse becomes a redeemed Magdalene) in the *Davideis* faithfully imitates the generic form of Vergil's opening proem and reinforces the religious argument of Du Bartas's *La Muse Chrétienne*, Milton's invocations to the Muse in *Paradise Lost* recapture the vitality of divine illumination found in Homer while drawing upon the strength of Vergilian epic structure. In his invocation and notes, Cowley perhaps tried too hard to be "th' *Apostle*" of "*The Eternal Word*"; Milton, on the other hand, no less committed to his divine purpose, had learned earlier that "They also serve who only stand and wait" (Sonnet XIX). The following discussion of these proems will examine Milton's interest in origins (both classical and biblical) and his blending of pagan and Christian aspects in his epic invocations. Although Milton follows in the footsteps of Tasso, Du Bartas, Spenser, and Cowley in his identification of the Muse with the Godhead, he maintains a balance between the Christian and pagan elements, drawing upon Urania's strength as both the Muse of astronomy and as the Spirit of God.

Milton's proem to Book I (1-26), consisting of a combined invocation and proposition, recalls the Homeric theme of the tragic loss brought about by human error: "Sing, Goddess, the anger of Peleus' son Achilleus / and its devastation, which put pains thousandfold upon the Achaians" (*Il.* 1.1-2). Whereas for Homer Achilleus' wrath brought suffering and death to both the Greeks and the Trojans, for Milton "Man's First Disobedience . . . Brought Death into the World, and all our woe." Milton's Christian epic, however, goes one step further by emphasizing its universal application in the word "all." The Fall and "all our woe" necessitates the coming of "One Greater Man." Unlike Homer, however, Milton delays the invocation of his Muse until the sixth line, recalling the practice of Vergil. Milton first states his theme, invokes the Muse and, then, the Holy Spirit for knowledge of the cosmos before creation, and promises a theme that surpasses all others:

> Of Man's First Disobedience, and the Fruit
> Of that Forbidden Tree, whose mortal taste
> Brought Death into the World, and all our woe,
> With loss of *Eden*, till one greater Man
> Restore us, and regain the blissful Seat,
> Sing Heav'nly Muse . . . (1.1-6)

Milton's bipartite theme of "Man's First Disobedience" and his restoration hinges upon the introduction of the "one greater Man," a pattern also established by Vergil whose hero must undergo exile from his native Troy and suffer on land and sea, "dum conderet urbem / inferretque deos Latio."[26] Adam and Eve, like Aeneas, must leave their Edenic home for a life of struggles and finally death. But just as Aeneas journeys toward a new Troy, which will arise from the line of *pius Aeneas* to become the Augustan Roman Empire from its new beginnings in Latium, Adam and Eve can be restored to God at the end of Time through the sacrifice of the Son. In both cases, the epic movement is toward a clear beginning—for Vergil, a national beginning, and for Adam and Eve, a universal beginning or the story of us all. At the same time, however, Vergil and Milton situate the reader in a time in between the *beginning* and the *end.*

Unlike Vergil, however, who separated the *propositio* (statement of theme) and the *invocatio* (the address to the Muse), Milton follows Homer, who fused the two parts and, in so doing, implied the necessity of divine inspiration for the poet to begin his song. This point is also made by Charles Martindale, who argues that Milton's proem to *Paradise Lost*, Book I, is a "conflation of the openings of the *Iliad*, *Odyssey*, and *Aeneid* (though with many Biblical elements injected)," although Milton keeps closer to the Homeric model, which fused the *propositio* and the *invocatio.* I agree with Martindale that Milton's proem, like Homer's at the opening of the *Iliad*, is "more bardic" than Vergil's because of its reliance upon "such inspiration from outside" before the poet can sing; however, I would suggest that Milton's delayed invocation of the Muse in line 6 suggests that the poet-priest desires a bit more initial time in the lime-light than Martindale would admit.[27] In this practice, Milton seems to be reaching back both to the origins of epic in Homer, whose poetic world was filled with divine presence in all areas of creation, and in the Psalms of David, in which the poet calls upon the name of his God and finds comfort in his response.[28] Although

Milton follows the precedent of Vergil by utilizing multiple invocations throughout the epic, especially in sections that require the change of subject or tone, the invocations to "Urania" or to his "Celestial Patroness" are more elaborate and more personal than Vergil's address to Erato (*Aen.* 7.37), which separates the Odyssean and Iliadic sections of the *Aeneid.*

Although Milton finally calls upon the "Heav'nly Muse," he delays his invocation until the sixth line of the proem.[29] And even when he does call upon her, he does not give her a specific name, only "Heav'nly Muse." While Milton Homerically combines the proposition and the invocation, he reverses their order and gives primacy to his proposition. In this manner he resembles Vergil, but not exactly. Milton's theme and source of inspiration are combined in one long verse paragraph.

Perhaps the designation "Heav'nly" would bring to mind Tasso's Muse,[30] who is not to be found by the "Heliconian spring" but "sittest crowned with stars' immortal rays / In Heaven" (1.9-11). Tasso calls his Muse "heavenly," and asks her:

> Inspire life into my wit, my thoughts upraise,
> My verse ennoble, and forgive the thing,
> If fictions light I mix with truth divine,
> And fill these lines with other praise than thine. (1.13-16)

Having already stated his theme in the proposition, "The sacred armies, and the godly knight, / That the great sepulchre of Christ did free, / I sing . . . (ll. 1-3), Tasso reserves the next verse paragraph for the conventional invocation of the Muse, though here she is clearly Christianized into the "heavenly Muse."

> O heavenly Muse, that not with fading bays
> Deckest thy brow by the Heliconian spring,
> But sitest crowned with stars' immortal rays
> In Heaven . . . (ll. 9-12)

Tasso's Muse is a fully converted into Christian Muse. Renouncing the traditional bays and far away from the Heliconian spring, Tasso's "heavenly Muse" dwells in the heavenly realm of light and Christian truth. Milton's Muse is also transformed from her former pagan identity into a "Heav'nly Muse." Milton asks his. Muse for inspiration to compose his "adventurous song," perhaps an allusion to the romantic qualities of Tasso and Ariosto as well as for the power to ascend into the heavens:

> I thence
> Invoke thy aid to my advent'rous Song,
> That with no middle flight intends to soar
> Above th' *Aonian* Mount, while it pursues

Things unattempted yet in Prose or Rhyme. (1.12-16)

Milton sets himself apart from Tasso, who sought the forgiveness of his Muse in advance in case he should praise the deeds of men too highly. Milton announces his intention "to soar / Above th' *Aonian* Mount" while pursuing "Things unattempted yet in Prose or Rhyme."

Barbara Lewalski writes that through allusions to earlier classical and Renaissance works Milton "indicates that the universal and true story of humankind must necessarily contain, subsume, and endeavor to surpass the greatest poems we know."[31] To do this, however, Milton requires a mighty Muse, the same who inspired Moses on "the secret top / Of *Oreb*, or of *Sinai*" (1.7) giving the law of God to the prophet so that he could teach the "chosen *Seed*, / In the Beginning how the Heav'ns and Earth / Rose out of Chaos" (1.8-10). Identifying himself with Moses, Milton assumes the role of poet-priest; the inspiration that he requests will enable him to return to the beginning of all things—before God created the Heavens and the Earth. In this quest for origins, however, Milton may have more in common with Ovid[32] or Lucretius. In fact, in his invocation to Venus at the beginning of *De Rerum Natura*, Lucretius focuses upon the goddess as both the mother of Aeneas and the principle of love:

Aeneadum genetrix, hominum divomque voluptas,
alma Venus, caeli subter labentia signa
quae mare navigerum, quae terras frugiferentis
concelebras, per te quoniam genus omne animantum
concipitur visitque exortum lumina solis. (1.1-5)[33]

As *Aeneadum genetrix*, Venus symbolizes Rome's origin as a powerful state, and as the "nourishing" mother of nature, she becomes the personification of the Epicurean *summum bonum*, or highest good. As the principle of *voluptas*, she is both the origin of creation and physical reproduction as well as the source of pleasure in poetry; Lucretius invokes her for the benefit of both of these powers. Likewise Milton reaches back to the very origin of matter and inspiration in his invocation to the "Heav'nly Muse."

In line 17 of Book I, however, Milton's Muse changes from the unnamed and perhaps generic "Heav'nly Muse" to the Holy Spirit, who, after all was present with the Father when he created the world; therefore, the Spirit could better instruct the poet in the matter of the creation: "And chiefly Thou O Spirit, that dost prefer / Before all Temples th' upright heart and pure, / Instruct me, for Thou know'st . . ." (1.17-19). While Cowley shows considerable confusion over the identity of his Muse in the invocation to the *Davideis*, shifting from Christ as Muse to "my *Magdalene*," Milton eases subtly from his heavenly Muse to the Holy Spirit, emphasizing that his Muse is not merely a poet's abstraction but rather the creative and instructive principle itself. Cowley offered his *Davideis* as "a *Temple* to thy praise . . . A *Temple*, where if *Thou* vouchsafe to dwell, / It

Solomons and *Herods* shall excel" (*Davideis* 1.33-36), perhaps in an attempt to surpass the poems of Herbert contained in his volume by that name. Milton also uses the image of the temple, but focuses upon the temple of the heart and upon the individual servant of God, whose commitment will be measured by his uprightness and purity rather than upon the temple's architectural stateliness.[34] Despite Milton's poetic ego, his request for instruction here shows the humility that is lacking in Cowley's invocation, where Cowley announces, Hannibal-like in his Notes, that he would be "made an *Apostle* for the for the conversion of *Poetry* to *Christianity*, as *S. Paul* was for the conversion of the *Gentiles*."[35] Having lived to realize the failure of the Commonwealth and having lost his eyesight in the service of his country, Milton likely felt a greater sense of physical powerlessness. Milton's strength, like that of his character Samson, needed to come from God. Milton's invocation to Book 1, therefore, moves from a Homeric/Vergilian invocation to a simple prayer for inward illumination.

Like Lucretius, Milton respects the attributes of generation and priority. Thus, Milton's Muse possesses a significant combination of masculine and feminine qualities, physical might and fertility, found in Lucretius' Venus:

> Thou from the first
> Wast present, and with mighty wings outspread
> Dove-like satst brooding on the vast Abyss
> And mad'st it pregnant. (*PL* 1.19-22)

And in Genesis:

> In the beginning God created the heaven and the earth. And the earth *was* without form, and void; and darkness was upon the face of the deep. And the Spirit of God moved upon the face of the waters. And God said, Let there be light: and there was light. (Gen. 1:1-3)

The Spirit that was able to fill Chaos and void with light and life should be able to fill the Puritan poet with song. Milton's invocation to the Heav'nly Muse and to the Spirit of God, which are not necessarily competing entities, indicates his desire to participate in the Christian epic tradition. His allusions to Tasso and his structural and thematic debt to Homer and Vergil confirm the seriousness of his ambition. To tell this divine story, however, the poet-priest requires more than the conventional instruction and support offered by the Muse.

Indeed the "Heav'nly Muse," or poetic inspiration, is seemingly not sufficient for Milton; the poet requires the Holy Spirit, or divine illumination, to sustain him during the composition of his Christian epic. Following the tradition of ancient hymns, in which the divinity is addressed by various names, Milton's invocation to the "Heav'nly Muse" progresses from the classical grand style to the simple Biblical prayer:

What in me is dark
Illumine, what is low raise and support
That to the height of this great Argument
I may assert Eternal Providence,
And justify the ways of God to men. (1.22-26)

Acknowledging his own need for inner darkness and the power of God's Spirit to surge up within him, providing him with divine knowledge and poetic strength, Milton calls upon his Heav'nly Muse in a prayer-like petition. While Milton asks for Christian illumination in his prayer, his references to his divine ordination as poet-prophet and his invocations to the Muse carefully blend the classical Greek poetic tradition with the Hebraic prophetic tradition. In the *Theogony*, Hesiod's Muses bestow the scepter, laurel shoot, and the breath of divine inspiration upon the poet, bidding him to sing of things that are to come and those things that have been already—specifically, the origins of the gods. Throughout Books I, III, and VII, the poet Milton seeks a similar kind of divine illumination to guide him.[36] However, it is not until Book IX, just before he must relate the Fall of Man, that Milton receives the strength of the Spirit from within and can reveal his fullest confidence as an inspired *vates*.

In *Paradise Lost and the Rhetoric of Literary Forms*, Barbara Lewalski calls attention to the seeming incongruity in Milton's conscious use of literary forms and his presentation of himself in the poem as a prophet-poet, arguing that "there is no contradiction"; rather, "the relationship between conscious art and divine inspiration is a major theme of the Bard's personal proems to Books One, Three, Seven, and Nine" (25). In the invocations in Books I, III, and VII, Lewalski observes, Milton's Bard "implores . . . assured and continuous experience of the Muse's inspiration and of divine illumination" and "engage[es] with his sacred subject by using the terms and the conventions of traditional literary genres and models" for the purpose of "apprehending his subject and his prophetic role, and also of fulfilling that role by accommodating subject to audience, so as to educate that audience in knowing what is true and choosing what is good" (26). While my purpose here is to examine Milton's invocations to the Muse in order to determine her identity and function in the epic, it is also necessary to consider Milton's use of classical rhetorical models in *Paradise Lost*, particularly in his "Hymn to Holy Light" (*PL* 3.1-55). Therefore, I shall first review the history and function of the classical hymn in order to explain its significance in terms of the relationship between the *vates* and the source of personal poetic inspiration.

Most treatments of Milton's "Hymn to Holy Light" place the poem in the category of the invocation. They discuss its innertextual role in demarcating the poet's increasing confidence in his role as *vates*, or else note its structural significance in light of earlier epics. Others, however, discuss the proem to Book III in terms of questions about the identity of Milton's Muse, about light and dark imagery, or about the passage's biographical significance. These critics, however, have not fully considered the generic complexity of the "Hymn to Holy Light" as well as its key relationship to the other proems of *Paradise Lost*. As Barbara Lewalski has argued, Milton was the most genre-conscious of the English poets and *Paradise Lost*, an epic about knowing and choosing, contains the whole genre system, each kind resonating a shared cultural and literary significance between poet and audience." Here, I wish to examine the "invocation" to Book III as a literary hymn, focusing upon its debt to literary history, its function in terms of the invocations in Books I and VII, its generic structure, and its unique poetic / personal function in *Paradise Lost*.[37]

In order to appreciate fully Milton's use of and expansion upon the traditions of the *invocatio* and the hymn, it is necessary to survey the historical grounding for those forms. Philip Rollinson, in "A generic View of Spenser's *Four Hymns*" (1971), says that "it was the neo-Latin revival of the classical hymn which gave direction to the genre in the vernacular literatures of France and England" (292). In fact, he continues, "Michele Marullo's *Hymni Naturales* adopt classical pagan subject matter as well as the classical form," resulting in poetry that is both "philosophically abstruse" like that of Proclus and the Emperor Julian and "rhetorically elaborate" in the manner of Callimachus, whose hymns are known for his erudite use of mythology. In the mid sixteenth century, Marco Girolamo and Julius Caesar Scaliger made further contributions to the genre; both sought to adapt Christian subject matter to classical forms, the former stressing ornate, but mythology-free, rhetoric and the latter demonstrating restraint characteristic of the *Homeric Hymns*, but still displaying the poet's erudition" (293). It was Scaliger's *Poetices Libri Septem* (1561), in fact, that most influenced writers such as Spenser and Milton; in it, Scaliger attacked the poetry of both Marullo and Vida while endorsing his own method of Christian imitation of the classical genres.

However, Scaliger's *Poetices*, in its classification of literary genres, particularly hymns, owes much to the writings of Menander Rhetor (3rd c. A.D.). In his *First Treatise*, Menander treats the subject of epideictic speeches (both of blame and praise), dividing the latter into two divisions: those in relation to gods and those in relation to mortal objects. Those speeches which relate to gods he terms "hymns," and continues to classify them according to the gods concerned.[38] These classifications are later adapted by Roman writers such as Cicero and Quintilian; Menander's writings, then, are compiled by Scaliger and translated into Latin and thus made more available to Renaissance writers.

Scaliger's classification of hymns, based upon Menander, serves as the model for Renaissance writers, including Milton. According to Scaliger, the classical hymn may be divided into six types: 1) the invocatory, such as the hymns of Proclus; 2) the valedictory, such as the Homeric hymns involving divine departures; 3) the physical, celebrating the *numen* of a god or other natural or cosmological force, such as Marullo's neo-Platonic *Hymni Naturales*; 4) the mythical; 5) the genealogical; 6) the inventional, or fictional. In *Treatise I*, Menander Rhetor explains that hymns to the gods can consist of a combination of several of these divisions, but none can be composed outside these patterns.[39] According to Scaliger's system, then, Milton's invocations in *Paradise Lost* might be considered combinations of the invocatory, physical, mythical, genealogical, and inventional. In his "Hymn to Light," however, Milton carefully balances his reliance upon convention with his personal poetic theory of the necessity of divine illumination, made more poignant by reference to his physical blindness.

Early in his career, Milton endorsed a poetic program that approved of using pagan poetics in the service of a Christian culture. In the Preface to Book Two of *The Reason of Church Government* (1642), Milton writes:

> Or if occasion shall lead to imitate those magnific odes and hymns wherein Pindarus and Callimachus are in most things worthy, some others in their frame judicious, in their matter most an end faulty. But those frequent songs throughout the law and prophets beyond all these, not in their divine argument alone, but in the very critical art of composition, may be easily made appear over all the kinds of lyric poesy to be incomparable. These abilities, wheresoever they be found, are the inspired gift of God rarely bestowed.[40]

Milton refers only to the noblest genres in the lyric category—classical hymns and odes, biblical hymns and other songs—and thereby recognizes their special function: to praise God. And, indeed, Milton gives prominence to the hymn in his Christian epic when he structures the movement of *Paradise Lost* with four powerful invocations to his Christianized Muse. The second invocation (in Book III), in fact, serves as a personal offering to the Godhead.

In *Classical Genres and English Poetry*, William Race notes that "Graeco-Roman hymns contain two principal parts: the invocation and the request. The purpose of the invocation is to dispose the god favourably towards the worshipper's request—in short, to secure his *charis* ('favour', 'grace')." In his hymn, Milton addresses his source of inspiration as "Holy Light," an appellation that encompasses multiple connotations of creative power and goodness. "Praise is [the hymn's] dominant mode," continues Race, "as the hymnist mentions the god's powers, *sedes*, genealogy, and amplifies them by means of superlatives, lists and inclusive doublets." Milton remains close to this formulation in his hymn, expanding various portions (according to tradition) by explanations, narratives, and descriptions. Finally, Race notes that the style of the invocation is characterised by "relative clauses, repeated addresses and additive phrasing" (147). Milton uses this bipartite form (invocation and request) to good effect without compromising the power of his prayer to Holy Light; indeed, he manages to maintain a solid balance between the classical form and the Christian message.

Milton's relationship to the "Light" in Book III gives particular significance to his "Hymn to Holy Light," rendered most personal because of its decorum and its revelation of the poet's poetic theory. This hymn holds a special place among the other invocations, for it most nearly conforms to Milton's ideal. He stated in *The Reason of Church Government* that the highest form available to the poet is the hymn; one who is blessed with the divine inspiration of God ought "to celebrate in glorious and lofty hymns the throne and equipage of God's almightiness, and what he works and what he suffers to be wrought with high providence in his church."[41]

In the "Hymn to Light," Milton offers his praise and humbly requests divine illumination. Although the proems to Books I and VII also serve to praise God and to invoke divine aid, their forms are more literary; that is, they serve as formal invocations (based closely upon the classical models of Vergil and Homer) that serve primarily to fulfill the structural demands of the epic form. Indeed, Merritt Hughes correctly calls Milton's "Hymn to Holy Light" "the most personal of his three invocations" and observes that this prayer contains the poet's poetic program which expresses the "Renaissance theory that great poetry . . . can be written only by men who deserve and enjoy divine illumination."[42] Just as Lewalski maintains that "in *Paradise Lost* characters reveal their natures and the values they espouse through the lyrics they devise" (22), the poet aligns himself with the angels who sing lofty hymns to the Father, not with Satan and his cohorts to whom the hymn form is denied.

Unlike Milton the poet-priest, Satan and his fellow fallen angels have access only to the *forms* of praise, such as invocations and hymns. Indeed, Satan perverts the hymn form in his apostrophe to the Sun (*PL* 4.32-113). Looking first upon the pleasant view of Eden and then upwards to Heaven, Satan addresses the Sun in what I would call an anti-hymn or anti-invocation, which employs the features of the classical hymn to blame, rather than praise, the Godhead. Like the poet Milton, Satan invokes Light; however, his invocation reveals his anger and despair:

> O thou that with surpassing Glory crown'd,
> Look'st from thy sole Dominion like the God
> Of this new World . . . To thee I call,
> But with no friendly voice, and add thy name
> O Sun, to tell thee how I hate thy beams." (*PL* 4.32-37)

Satan's remembrance of his previous state only brings him further misery, a commonplace originating in Boethius's *Consolatio Philosophiae*, 2 pr. 4, and passed down through Dante in Francesca's cry, "Nessun maggior dolore / che ricordarsi del tempo felice / ne la miseria" (*Inf.* 5.121-123). By the end of his soliloquy, Satan says farewell to Hope and embraces evil. In a sense, by rejecting the grace of God, Satan confirms himself in his own vocation of evil. Milton, on the other hand, employs the hymn form properly to offer thanks to God and to implore divine assistance in writing of things "invisible to mortal sight." The example of an invocation as hymn is the opening proem to Book III.

Lewalski writes that "the Bard voices numerous apostrophes, hymnic proems, blasons, and an epithalamion. Satan and the fallen angels often fall into laments but cannot sustain them long, and they can only pervert lyrics of praise. The angels celebrate all divine activities with hymnic praises, but they produce their most elaborate and most exalted hymns when divine creativity and divine love are manifested. And pre- and post-lapsarian man and woman exhibit their psychological and spiritual states through a great variety of hymns, odes, love songs, laments, complaints, encomia, and more" (21-22). Thus, while the hymn serves as the appropriate form of praise, it also functions as a rhetorical model that validates the poet's vocation of *vates*. By using the *topoi* of humility and inexpressibility in his hymn, Milton offers his apostrophe to Light as a gift to the Christian Godhead.[43]

In the proem to Book III, Milton not only prepares the reader for the mysterious grandeur of heaven and the beauty of Paradise (as well as all the genres these locations will include), but also offers the praise appropriate to his Christian Muse. To the poet, Light serves as an emblem of divine illumination, the inexpressible force that gives rise to his poetic ability. In order to invoke Holy Light, therefore, the poet must choose the appropriate form of address. That the literary hymn was fitting for such a purpose goes back to the ancient Greek thinkers: Socrates was willing to admit only two genres of poetry into the state: "hymns to the gods and encomia to good men" (*Republic* 10.607a); Aristotle distinguishes as serious those poets who write hymns and encomia (*Poetics* 4). In the manner of Scaliger, therefore, Milton combines the greatest form, the hymn of praise, with the Christian prayer; in so doing, the poet offers the proper reverence to his Creator through praise and honor that recognize his ineffability.

Milton's invocation in Book III (1-50) may be divided into three sections: the apostrophe to Light (1-12), expansions concerning the deity (13-22), and a digression upon the poet's blindness (22-50). The apostrophe to Light includes names, epithets, titles, genealogy, and *sedes* of the deity. Moreover, as is characteristic of Greek hymns, Milton employs direct address call upon his divine Muse and posits the goddess as the source of his hymn.[44]

Hail holy Light, offspring of Heav'n first-born,
Or of th'Eternal Coeternal beam
May I express thee unblam'd? since God is Light,
And never but in unapproached Light
Dwelt from Eternity, dwelt then in thee,
Bright effluence of bright essence increate.
Or hear'st thou rather pure Ethereal stream,
Whose Fountain who shall tell? before the Sun,
Before the Heavens thou wert, and at the voice

Of God, as with a Mantle didst invest
The rising world of waters dark and deep,
Won from the void and formless infinite.

Unlike *Lycidas*, where Milton called upon Apollo, the traditional pagan god of light and leader of the Muses, to relate the divine view of the poet's rewards in heaven, this invocation apostrophizes light itself as both God's first creation and as divine truth. This invocation, as opposed to the address to the Heavenly Muse and to the Holy Spirit in Book I and the address to Urania in Book VII, is both the most personal and the most philosophically and theologically suggestive. The poet's apostrophe to Light is also appropriate for the new subject matter, like Apollonius Rhodius's invocation of Erato in *Argonautica*, Book III,[45] which introduces the new theme of erotic love between Jason and Medea. Most important, however, Milton's invocation to Light celebrates the mystery of God. Having emerged from the depths of hell unscathed unto the light, the poet now has more confidence in his vocation as poet-priest and sufficient strength from his Muse to continue (3.13-23).[46]

This proem, with its emphasis upon descent and re-ascent, bears strong parallels to the journeys into the underworld undertaken by Aeneas with the Sibyl and by Dante with Virgil; it reminds us, too, that the poet cannot make these journeys alone. In keeping with hymnic tradition, Milton's inability to name the deity falls into the inexpressibility *topos*. In this case, I believe that Michael Lieb is correct in arguing that the poet's representation of "the holy" subsumes the literary convention under the Christian notion of the ineffability of God, "in the sense that it completely eludes apprehension in terms of concepts."[47] Indeed, Milton begins with three forms of address ("holy Light," "offspring," and "beam" 1-2) which associate Light with different aspects of the Godhead. He then questions these designations by asking: "Or hear'st thou rather pure ethereal stream" (7). The poet's inability to name the Light, though a classical convention, here befits its Christian topic of God's ineffability, thus affording the proper respect to the deity necessary for the poet who seeks divine illumination.

The second part of the invocation, the expansions upon the deity's powers (13-50), consists of repeated addresses ("Thee I revisit . . . thee I revisit" 13; 21), explanations ("Taught by the heavn'ly Muse . . . 19), *hypomnesis*, and amplification ("sovran vital Lamp" 22):

Thee I revisit now with bolder wing,
Escap't the *Stygian* Pool, though long detain'd
In that obscure sojourn, while in my flight
Through utter and through middle darkness borne
With other notes than to th' *Orphean* Lyre
I sung of *Chaos* and *Eternal Night*,
Taught by the heav'nly Muse to venture down
The dark descent, and up to reascend,

Though hard and rare: thee I revisit safe,
And feel thy sovran vital Lamp. . .

In this section, the poet continues to employ direct address when calling upon the deity ("Thee . . . thee," 13; 21). He recounts his journey through the dark underworld by means of narration and attributes his successful emergence into Light to the power of his Muse. That he was able to descend and to reascend attests to the benevolent intervention of the deity; this reminder of the deity's past interaction with the poet, or *hypomnesis*, serves the rhetorical and personal function of inclining the deity to do the same in the future. Finally, the passage (in the form of a ring-composition) builds toward the controlling theme of Light, the importance of which the poet emphasizes by means of the placement of Light at the beginning and end of the section.

Though the poet has emerged safely from hell to view the "sovran vital Lamp," he digresses into a pathetic complaint concerning the source of his blindness. He hopes that it is not a punishment—Thamyris was blinded for challenging the Muses and Bellerophon fell and was blinded for attempting to scale heaven—but rather a blessing as in the cases of poets and prophets such as Homer, Saint Paul, and Tiresias who were all given supernatural insight. In *Openings*, Nuttall connects what he calls the "slow death of the Muse" with the rise of literacy: "The Muse invoked at the beginning of the *Iliad* and the *Odyssey* is a power experientially familiar to those who compose without pen and paper, who know that at the start of a work which is also a public performance, the lungs must be cleared and then filled with breath, a voice not wholly one's own" (83-84). In a sense, Milton's blindness connects him to Homer, the preliterate father of epic. As Nuttall observes, Milton's blindness does not separate him from the company of poets but rather transforms him into Homer, "the *fons et origo* of all poets" (84).

The third section of the invocation is a digression (in the form of a *lamentatio*) upon the poet's physical blindness (22-50). Its poignancy depends as much upon its juxtaposition with the ascension toward "thy sovran vital Lamp" (22) in the middle of the line as it does upon the biographical implications for the poet. The *lamentatio*, however, is answered by a *consolatio*, for the poet's physical blindness leads him to the specific request for inner, or spiritual, light:

but thou
Revisit'st not these eyes, that roll in vain
To find thy piercing ray, and find no dawn;
So thick a drop serene hath quencht their Orbs,
Or dim suffusion veil'd. Yet not the more
Cease I to wander where the Muses haunt
Clear Spring, or shady Grove, or Sunny Hill,
Smit with the love of sacred song; but chief
Thee *Sion* and the flow'ry Brooks beneath

That wash thy hallow'd feet, and warbling flow,
Nightly I visit: nor sometimes forget
Those other two equall'd with me in Fate,
So were I equall'd with them in renown,
Blind *Thamyris* and blind *Maeonides*,
And *Tiresias* and *Phineas* Prophets old.
Then feed on thoughts, that voluntary move
Harmonious numbers; as the wakeful Bird
Sings darkling, and the shadiest Covert hid
Tunes her nocturnal Note. Thus with the Year
Seasons return, but not to me returns
Day, or the sweet approach of Ev'n or Morn,
Or sight of vernal bloom, or Summer's Rose,
Or flocks, or herds, or human face divine;
But cloud instead, and ever-during dark
Surrounds me, from the cheerful ways of men
Cut off, and for the Book of knowledge fair
Presented with a Universal blank
Of Nature's works to mee expung'd and ras'd,
And wisdom at one entrance quite shut out.

It is interesting to note that the syntax of "but chief / Thee Sion" suggests that Milton is not necessarily rejecting the classical for the Christian tradition, but rather that Sion is one of the possibilities for the frequenter of the Muses.[48] This complaint, however, turns from classical mythology into a personal, Biblical prayer as Milton asks for inward illumination (51-55):

So much the rather thou Celestial Light
Shine inward, and the mind through all her powers
Irradiate, there plant eyes, all mist from thence
Purge and disperse, that I may see and tell
Of things invisible to mortal sight.

According to Race, "when there is a petition at the end of a hymn, it must of course be consonant with the god's power as established in the body of the hymn, and follow naturally from the goodwill established between the god and man."[49] Of course, the deity addressed here is the highest spring of creative power, being the "Pure ethereal stream" (7). The poet, therefore, realizes that his blindness is, in fact, a blessing, for the true Light resides within the soul and is provided by God. According to Nuttall, "blindness has sharpened Milton's sense that his poem has two sources, self and not-self."[50] In his invocation to Light, then, "Albion's bard, who cannot read over what he has written (although he may hear it read) is constrained to a second invocation: this time it is to light, and light becomes God."[51] Milton's invocation and request, then, make use of the classical hymn form but in the service of a Christian prayer for divine illumination.

This request, according to Lewalski, consists of the tripartite structure common to Horace and Callimachus which includes: the *exordium* (invokes God in terms of his many characteristics), *narrative myth* (God's actions/poet's journey), and *peroration* (poet implores divine illumination) (31-32). According to Ferry, the narrative voice, like Man, is a "limited human creature whose vision was dimmed by the Fall"; however, he is also an "inspired seer whose divine illumination transcends the limits of mortal vision" and is able to write of what Man has lost and regained."[52] In fact, the poet learns from his prayer that his blindness is a divine gift that allows for illumination just as the *felix culpa* allows Man to receive Grace from God. Like Homer and Tiresias, Milton, by being blind, can see more clearly into the nature of things.

Milton's third invocation to the Muse occurs in Book VII, before Raphael relates to Adam the story of the Creation, a cosmological beginning that falls in the exact center of *Paradise Lost*. Milton's invocation (1-39) marks a clear transition in the narrative, from the War in Heaven to the account of the Creation of the World. This invocation, like Vergil's invocation to Erato in Book VI of the *Aeneid*, divides the poem in half. More importantly, it is here that Milton finally addresses his Muse by name:

> Descend from Heav'n *Urania*, by that name
> If rightly thou art call'd, whose Voice divine
> Following above th' *Olympian* Hill I soar,
> Above the flight of Pegasean wing.
> The meaning, not the Name I call: for thou
> Nor of the Muses nine, nor on the top
> Of old *Olympus* dwell'st, but Heav'nly born,
> Before the Hills appear'd, or Fountains flow'd
> Thou with Eternal Wisdom didst converse,
> Wisdom thy Sister, and with her didst play
> In presence of th' Almighty Father, pleas'd
> With thy Celestial Song. (7.1-12)

Milton invokes his Muse by name: "Descend from Heav'n Urania, . . . The meaning, Not the Name I call" (1; 5). Urania becomes for Milton, as for Du Bartas in *La Muse Chrétienne* (1574), a symbol for divine poetry based not on the mythological fables of the ancient pagans but on the Judeo-Christian revelation. When calling upon Urania, Milton stresses "The meaning, Not the Name" and dissociates her from the classical model. Instead, she becomes the sister of "Eternal wisdom," having been present from before the creation and therefore able to impart her knowledge of the world's birth to the poet. While he calls her Urania and places her in Heaven, he immediately seems to question her identity: "by that name / If rightly thou art call'd" (1-2). She is clearly "divine," though, and must "descend" to the mortal world to relate her pre-historical account of the Creation. And Milton has followed her "Voice" above the Homeric and Vergilian epic themes, even "above the flight of Pegasean wing" or the height of pagan poetic inspiration.

Urania is clearly more than her classical identity, for Milton calls upon "the meaning, not the Name." In a sense, Milton's invocation to Urania becomes a *recusatio*, in which the poet refuses all previous designations for her: his Urania is not the classical one (or not *merely* the classical one)—that is, one of "the Muses nine"—nor is she necessarily Du Bartas's "Christianized" Urania. On the other hand, paradoxically, she is both, and then some. Milton equates her with the Creation itself (and to creativity). He reaches back to the origin of the universe to find Urania's origin, an origin that apparently precedes the Olympian Gods and even God's creation of the seas and dry land.

Indeed, Milton shifts from the pagan to the Christian by placing her with "Eternal Wisdom." For all of Milton's emphasis upon Urania's priority and her divine attributes, his Muse appears to be a hybrid classical/Christian conception. Hughes notes that in the *Wisdom of Solomon* 7:17-18, Milton found Wisdom gifted with a knowledge of "how the world was made" as well as an understanding of "the operation of the elements." In the Renaissance, he continues, the conception of Wisdom gained prestige from the "half-metaphysical wisdom" of classical philosophy, the wisdom of which, according to Cicero, *De Officiis*, 1.145, is a "knowledge of things divine and human, and in which is contained the relationships and the society of men with gods mutually."[53] Milton presents Urania and Wisdom allegorically as sisters, whose "Celestial Songs" are pleasing to God. While seemingly dismissing Urania's traditional associations, Milton nevertheless invokes a Muse representing Christian wisdom as well as the highest humanistic values. Regarding their song, Milton wishes to emulate the Muse he has just fashioned by writing his own pleasing celestial song for God.

Milton's invocation of Urania also recalls Horace's invocation of the Muse of epic poetry—"Descende caelo . . . Calliope"[54]—and reaffirms the pattern of ascent and descent associated with the epic poet's invocations to the Muse. William M. Porter argues that Milton reworks the themes of *Odes* 3.4, but in "reverse order."[55] While Milton's invocation shares the same themes as Horace's, particularly the poet's calling and his Muse as a source of wisdom and protection, Porter asserts that while Milton's Muse, like Horace's, has kept the poet "safe," (*PL* 3.15, 24), "at the end of the prologue he turns to lament Calliope's failure to save her poet-son Orpheus, as he had done decades earlier in *Lycidas*."[56] Porter sees Milton's reference to Calliope as a "negative exemplum" that would "put the lie to Horace's confident claim to the Muse's patronage.[57] After all, Horace's Calliope, cannot not save her poet-son, Orpheus; Milton's Urania, on the other hand, is as real and powerful as the Old Testament God who answered the Psalmist's prayers for protection.[58] While Milton may have intended an implicit rejection of King Charles II in this invocation, his larger purpose was to assert the power of his Muse over those conventionally employed in classical epic poetry. Porter's claims, however, do enrich our understanding of Milton's purposes in the proem to Book VII.

Indeed, despite Milton's ego, he recognizes that poetic inspiration must come to him from outside himself, and must fill his lungs:

> Up led by thee
> Into the Heav'n of Heav'ns I have presum'd,
> An Earthly Guest, and drawn Empyreal Air,
> Thy temp'ring; with like safety guided down
> Return me to my Native Element:
> Lest from this flying Steed unreign'd, (as once
> *Bellerophon*, though from a lower Clime)
> Dismounted, on th' Aleian Field I fall
> Erroneous there to wander and forlorn. (7.12-20)

An "Earthly Guest," Milton requires Urania's "tempering" in order for him to draw "Empyreal Air" into his lungs and to return him safely to earth to sing his epic. This thought, of flying on Pegasean wing into the farthest reaches of heaven, recalls to the poet's mind the myth of Bellerophon, who attempted to uncover the mysteries of heaven and slew the monster Chimaera, a symbol of falsehood and delusion.[59] Bellerophon's punishment by Zeus was blindness and later, after wandering on the Aleian Plain in Lycia, death. Milton, simultaneously the Puritan and the student of Ovid, could not help identifying with Bellerophon and fearing a similar fate for presuming to tell of heavenly things. Already Milton was blind and his hopes for a permanent English Commonwealth shattered. Some of his enemies had even stated that the poet's blindness was God's punishment for his role in the government and his public defense of executing the king. In terms of his poetry, Milton realized his own ambition, perhaps bordering on arrogance, in attempting to write the Christian epic, and it is likely that he feared failure.

After the digression upon the fate of Bellerophon, Milton suddenly shifts back to an awareness of the demands of his epic structure and the task that awaits him:

> Half yet remains unsung, but narrower bound
> Within the visible Diurnal Sphere;
> Standing on Earth, not rapt above the Pole,
> More safe I Sing with mortal voice, unchang'd
> To hoarse or mute, though fall'n on evil days,
> On evil days though fall'n, and evil tongues;
> In darkness, and with dangers compast round,
> And solitude; yet not alone, while thou
> Visit'st my slumbers Nightly, or when Morn

Purples the East; still govern thou my Song,
Urania, and fit audience find, though few.
But drive far off the barbarous dissonance
Of *Bacchus* and his Revellers, the Race
Of that wild Rout that tore the *Thracian* Bard
In Rhodope, where Woods and Rocks had Ears
To rapture, till the savage clamor drown'd
Both Harp and Voice; nor could the Muse defend
Her Son. So fail not thou, who thee implores:
For thou art Heavn'ly, shee an empty dream. (7.21-39)

Milton's announcement that "half yet remains unsung" (21) mirrors Vergil's statement in the *Aeneid*, Book VII: "maior rerum mihi nascitur ordo, / maius opus moveo."[60] As his new topic will be the Creation, as opposed to the conquest of Latium, Milton's invocation heralds a greater theme, certainly necessitating a new invocation to the Muse for assistance. At first, Milton seems energized: suddenly he has the strength to continue his epic as if his inner doubts have been assuaged by a heavenly voice singing through him. But he soon begins to lament his own personal (and political) struggles in an auto-biographical reflection upon the present "evil days" (emphasized through repetition) that are upon him and the "evil tongues" that would denounce him. No longer active in the government and cut off from physical light and activity because of his blindness, Milton begins to sink into spiritual darkness and despair. However, paradoxically, Milton is not alone.

Milton's prayers have been answered; he can call upon the Muse again by name, although now Urania's "meaning" is more complex. She will govern his song and "fit audience find, though few." His audience may be limited, but as in his own case, few are chosen by God and even fewer follow. But even with the blessing of God, the poet has fears of physical harm. He therefore calls upon the Muse to "drive far off the barbarous dissonance of Bacchus and his Revellers," perhaps referring to political enemies such as the courtiers of Charles II, who would silence and condemn him before he can fulfill his poetic calling. Milton recalls as well the myth of Orpheus, as he had done before in *Lycidas*, and the bard's murder by the drunken Bacchantes. While Orpheus' Muse, Calliope, could not save him, Milton hopes that his Muse, Urania, will not fail him. Milton ends the proem with a prayer for the direct intervention of his "Heavn'ly" Muse: "So fail not thou, who thee implores: / For thou art Heavn'ly, shee an empty dream" (38-39). Here, Milton seems to make a stronger distinction between Orpheus' Muse and his own, metamorphosing his own "Heavn'ly" Muse from the named "Urania" to the unnamed "meaning."

But what does Milton mean by the "meaning" of the Muse? Like Du Bartas and Cowley, Milton seems to posit a Christian, or Christianized Muse as his source of poetic inspiration. But unlike the Muse of the *Davideis*, Milton's Muse possesses a more complex identity than Cowley's reformed Magdalene. Indeed,

Milton's Urania seems closer to her Hellenic models (such as Homer and Hesiod) than to her Christian ones (found in Vida and Du Bartas) in her role as inspirer and protector of her chosen poet. While Milton could have done without the traditional invocation had he wanted to "cleanse" his epic of all previous pagan association, that was not his purpose. As Stella Revard has argued, even as Milton's narrator "denies literal authority to pagan myth, the poet does not hesitate to use the myth freely, side by side with the true account. As he does so, he permits the myth to cast forth its 'poetic' truth . . . Milton's Muse is higher than those that on old Olympus dwelled, Heavenly born, but like them daughter of God and protector and mediator for the poet."[61] I agree with Revard that though Milton "names Urania the heavenly reality and Calliope the empty dream, he deplores neither the idea nor the reputed function of [the] Greek Muse."[62] Indeed, I would argue that Milton's *syncretism* allows him to interpret the classical Muses positively and to blend their attributes successfully with those of the Spirit that inspired Moses and the Old Testament prophets. By rejecting the tradition of Hesiod and Homer, Milton would be rejecting the essential gifts of divine patronage and inspiration.

The fourth and final proem in *Paradise Lost* comes in Book IX. Although not an invocation in the formal sense of the word, it does serve as such in this book and in relation to the proems of Books I, III, and VII. Milton's shift in Book IX (1-47) from the pastoral to the tragic is appropriate for the subject matter that follows—the Fall of Man. The proem is particularly interesting because it introduces the five-act tragedy of the Fall (originally the subject of *Adam Unparadis'd*). The proem like the rest of the narrative seems to take for granted the Muse's continuing role as Milton's source of poetic inspiration. In fact, Milton assumes an ever attentive Muse who does not require further invocations from her poet.

The opening lines of the book, which lack a formal address to the Muse, foreshadow the "breach" to come between God and his beloved creatures:

> No more of talk where God or Angel Guest
> With Man, as with his Friend, familiar us'd
> To sit indulgent, and with him partake
> Rural repast, permitting him the while
> Venial discourse unblam'd: I now must change
> Those Notes to Tragic; foul distrust, and breach
> Disloyal on the part of Man, revolt,
> And Disobedience. . . (9.1-8)

Suddenly the poem shifts from idyllic pastoral and harmony to separation and distrust, brought about by the "revolt" about to occur in this book. "Sin," "Death," and "Misery" (9.12-14), will follow closely upon Adam's and Eve's eating of the forbidden fruit. Man's willful disobedience brings about alienation, "distance and distaste, / Anger and just rebuke, and judgment giv'n" (9.9-10).

God's "just" punishment looms like a shadow over the opening section of this proem; Milton too must live under the constant threat of "Death, and Misery / Death's Harbinger" (9.12-13). With the assistance of his Celestial Patroness, however, Milton hopes to advance an "argument / Not less but more Heroic than the wrath / Of stern Achilles" (9.14-15). Milton's theme will transcend those of Homer and Vergil because it will offer a remedy for all of humanity in the person of the Son of God. Milton's battleground is neither the windy plains of Troy nor the fields of Latium, but rather the whole of creation, on the one hand, and the individual soul on the other.

Milton asserts that his theme transcends human experience; therefore he requires an "answerable style" to match the greatness of his subject. While Milton does not formally invoke the Muse, he does acknowledge her necessity in the completion of his epic poem:

> If answerable style I can obtain
> Of my Celestial Patroness, who deigns
> Her nightly visitation unimplor'd,
> And dictates to me slumb'ring, or inspires
> Easy my unpremeditated Verse. (9.20-24)

While in Milton's previous invocations the poet devoutly implores the Muse for divine assistance, here she remains unimplored. Though given a new name, his Celestial Patroness, Milton's Muse of Book IX is the same as his Heav'nly Muse of Book I and his Urania of Book VII. She has by now sustained him throughout the writing of the poem, and apparently inspires him "unimplor'd." Now *she* calls upon *him*. Milton, therefore, becomes a conduit for the great heavenly argument as well as an inspired bard, equal in stature to Moses and Hesiod. Milton's song, *Paradise Lost*, is God's song; it is an account of the nature of things, as they were and as they will be in the future. Milton's poetic voice comes to him unbidden; it is a gift, a fullness of breath that fills his lungs and provides him with celestial song.[63] With this degree of confidence in himself and his divinely affirmed vocation, Milton steps forward again to refute the epic and romance traditions in order to replace them with his own "Heroic" values:

> Since first this Subject for Heroic Song
> Pleas'd me long choosing, and beginning late;
> Not sedulous by Nature to indite
> Wars, hitherto the only Argument
> Heroic deem'd, chief maistry to dissect
> With long and tedious havoc fabl'd Knights
> In Battles feign'd; the better fortitude
> Of Patience and Heroic Martyrdom
> Unsung . . . (9.25-33)

According to Milton, poets have too long been confined to an inadequate and narrow notion of heroism—one that requires fabulous "Knights / In Battles Feign'd." And he is likely echoing the proem to Ariosto's *Orlando Furioso*, Canto I, which announces these very themes as the subject of his epic. Sir John Harrington's 1607 translation of Ariosto's opening lines reads: "Of Dames, of knights, of arms, of love's delight, / Of courtesies, of high attempts I speak . . ." (1-2).[64] Eschewing the martial valor of Achilles and Aeneas and the chivalric themes of love and courtesy, Milton asserts the spiritual values of "Patience and heroic Martyrdom" found in the Son of God. Milton may also be looking ahead to *Samson Agonistes*, whose heroic martyrdom reflects the poet's own sense of political defeat but spiritual victory after the Restoration. In the lines that follow, Milton further criticizes the heroic values found in works by writers such as Ariosto and Spenser:

> or to describe Races and Games,
> Or tilting Furniture, emblazon'd Shields,
> Impresses quaint, Caparisons and Steeds;
> Bases and tinsel Trappings, gorgeous Knights
> At Joust and Tournament; then marshall'd Feast
> Serv'd up in Hall with Sewers, and Seneschals;
> The skill of Artifice or Office mean,
> Not that which justly gives Heroic name
> To Person or to a Poem (9.33-41)

While Milton attempts to reveal the limitation of epic-romance by focusing upon its ornamentation, he nevertheless demonstrates his mastery of its conventions and color in his catalogue. This passage also demonstrates Milton's familiarity with the works of Ariosto, Tasso, and Spenser; without their influence he could not have written his epic poem nor could he have begun to supplant the classical epic hero and values. Milton's attention returns to himself as Christian epic poet and to the heavenly task before him. What has gone "unsung," Milton proposes to continue singing, strengthened by his Celestial Patroness:

> Mee of these
> Nor skill'd nor studious, higher Argument
> Remains, sufficient in itself to raise
> That name, unless an age too late, or cold
> Climate, or Years damp my intended wing
> Deprest; and much they may, if all be mine,
> Not Hers who brings it nightly to my ear. (9.41-47)

Once again the poet raises concerns about his limitations, his belatedness, and the threat of advancing years—all potential hindrances to the fulfillment of his task and the proper use of his talents. Milton suggests that neither the person nor the poem is heroic, but the Argument "sufficient of itself." Compared to the themes of the previous "pagan" works, Milton asserts that his theme is unparalleled in magnitude and scope, for it treats humanity as a whole. But the passage also reveals some humility and some "paganism" in Milton's reference to Aristotle's *Politics*, in which the philosopher maintains that those dwelling in the northern climates lacked great intelligence. This humanistic reference underscores Milton's belief that inspiration and divine truth come not from within the poet but from God alone. Transcending convention, Milton's invocations reveal the poet's sincere faith in the power of the Holy Spirit to sing through him and through his humanistic mind. By Book IX, the poet has been guided by his Celestial Muse and his prayers have been answered. No longer does he have to seek her aid, for she "dictates to me slumb'ring, or inspires/ Easy my unpremeditated Verse . . . " (20-24). In a sense, the poet becomes the mouthpiece for the divine Muse and gives himself over to her voice. Like the prophets of the Old Testament and the author of the *Iliad* and the *Odyssey*, Milton, or the narrator, assumes the role of *vates*; it is no longer the poet's voice speaking but that of the divine presence.

In *Paradise Lost*, Milton, like Cowley, must confront the Renaissance problem of invoking the pagan Muse, Urania, (though now Christianized) in a generic form such as epic that demanded it while trying to argue a Christian theme. While Cowley fails to make his Muse convincing in his *Davideis* and *Civil War*, Milton gives new life to the Muse by simultaneously drawing upon the strengths of the Vergilian and Homeric epic traditions as well as the Hebraic traditions of the Old Testament in his invocations. While Milton rejects classical heroism in his epic represented by the Aeneas / Achilles / Odysseus figure of Satan, he does not reject the syncretic possibilities of his Muse, unlike Cowley, whose rejection of the pagan gods in his Notes to the *Davideis* consume all of his creative energies.

Milton's invocations and, in particular, his "Hymn to Holy Light," explore the relationship between the *vates* and Light. Part of the difficulty in identifying exactly who the Muse is can be accounted for by Michael Lieb's claim that central to this hymn-proem of Book III and to the other invocations is "the *inexpressibility* of that which is invoked."[65] The light of God is to his poet-prophet the source of wisdom and inspiration, but one that is necessarily unknowable; therefore, the hymn is the proper form of address, for it functions both as a means of praising God as a gift and as an instrument of request for inspiration. I also agree with Race that the difficulty for the hymnist is to maintain a balance between the rhetorical intention to create a hymn pleasing to the god and a formal expression of that intention. The successful hymn, writes Race, is one that can "unite [G]od and man in a reciprocal relationship of *charis*" without becoming a mere rhetorical exercise.[66] According to Joan Malory Webber, "The ability to pay sufficient heed to the past while articulating a new stage of consciousness distinguishes the great or the essential epic from those that are identifiable merely by the traditional stylistic and thematic characteristics."[67] Indeed, in the invocations in *Paradise Lost*, Milton demonstrates his sensitivity and responsiveness to literary history, adopting many of the motifs, topoi, and other conventions of the classical hymn. Although he chooses to write in a classical genre, he does so only to give the proper form to his lofty Christian subject. As in his early *Nativity Ode*, Milton sets out in his "Hymn to Holy Light" to emulate and to surpass his ancient and Renaissance predecessors, achieving, perhaps, the greatest example of its kind in English literature and to affirm his status as a divinely inspired *vates*.

Milton inherits the tradition of the invocation from the ancients. Having used and improved upon it as a poetic convention, he connects himself with the great epic poets of the Western tradition. Not only is Milton audacious in aspiring to create a work of such magnitude that encompassed all of creation, but he does it when, in fact, no other English writer can. Milton, blending the theology of his personal faith with the classical forms of Vergil and Homer, expands the possibilities of his epic verse to metaphysical and cosmic levels. Helen Gardner writes that Milton's Muse is the "poetic embodiment of [his] belief in his vocation."[68] Indeed, Milton's invocations to the Muse in *Paradise Lost* confirm his vocation as *vates*, begun in the *Nativity Ode*, reaffirmed in *Lycidas* and *Epitaphium Damonis*, and finally acknowledged by the "Celestial Patroness" in his Christian epic. The chosen poet fulfills his calling. Milton's Muse is a complex being—at once a pagan daughter of Memory and at the same time Christ or the Holy Spirit; the syncretic blending of pagan and Christian characteristics proves essential to her ongoing and increasing role in the composition of *Paradise Lost*. As Revard argues, "in aiming to justify the ways of God to man, [Milton] had to speak as one to whom God had granted poetic power and authority, in short, as Muse-inspired poet. In claiming the inspiration of the Muse, Milton claims not only to be a poet granted divine voice and assistance, but one who can stand beside those poets of the past who made similar claims."[69] Indeed, Homer, Hesiod, and Pindar made poetry the divine art that Milton wished it to remain, and by drawing upon its poetic "truth," Milton can more successfully assert the real vitality and strength of his own Muse. Milton's poetic invocations in *Paradise Lost* act to chart the development of the poet's faith in his theme and in his vocation while they affirm our true beginning and the source of all inspiration.

Notes

Introduction

1 All citations and translations of the *Inferno* are taken from Dante, *Inferno*, trans. John D. Sinclair (New York: Oxford University Press, 1939).
2 Throughout this study I shall spell the Roman poet's name "Vergil" in accordance with contemporary inscriptions of his name, *Publius Vergilius Maro*, except when quoting from secondary sources that use the traditional form, "Virgil."
3 For an informative discussion of Vergil's fame among the Christians owing to his *Fourth Eclogue*, see Domenico Comparetti, *Vergil in the Middle Ages*, trans. E. F. M. Beneke (Hamden, Connecticut: Archon Books, 1908; repr. 1966), 96–103.
4 See *De Monarchia* 2.3.6: "divinus poeta noster Virgilius."
5 Jean Seznec, *The Survival of the Pagan Gods: The Mythological Tradition and its Place in Renaissance Humanism*, trans. Barbara F. Sessions (New York: Pantheon Books, 1953), 319–320.
6 Laurence Lerner, *The Uses of Nostalgia: Studies in Pastoral Poetry* (London: Chatto and Windus, 1972), 164. Throughout this study I shall employ Lerner's terms, "syncretist" and "Puritan," to distinguish between poets' responses to the problem of paganism in Christian poetry. According to Lerner, the "syncretist" tradition claimed that "the ancient world, though without the benefit of revelation, did through the light of nature find out a good deal of truth. The pagan gods, interpreted allegorically, can then be seen as foreshadowings of Christianity" (163). The "Puritan" tradition, as Lerner defines it, generally criticizes such allegorical readings and rejects "the lying stories of the Greeks" (164). To avoid any confusion, when I refer to "Puritan" in Lerner's sense of the term I shall place it within quotation marks.
7 Guillaume Du Bartas, *His Diuine Weekes and Workes with a Complete Collection of all the Other Most Delight-full Workes*, trans. Iosvah Sylvester (London: Robert Young, 1641), 241–244. Further references to Du Bartas's poem will be cited parenthetically within the text.
8 W. Jackson Bate, *The Burden of the Past and the English Poet* (Cambridge, MA, and London: Harvard University Press, 1970), 134. According to Bate, since the Renaissance, "the remorseless deepening of self-consciousness, before the rich and intimidating legacy of the past, has become the greatest single problem that modern art . . . has had to face, and . . . it will become increasingly so in the future" (4). What Bate argues for "modern" writers, though, also applies to early modern writers such as Spenser, Cowley, and Milton, who were confronted with the task of following in the footsteps of Homer and Vergil and their epic legacy.

9 A. D. Nuttall, *Openings: Narrative Beginnings from the Epic to the Novel* (Oxford: Oxford University Press, 1992).
10 Hesiod, *Theogony and Works and Days*, trans. M. L. West (Oxford and New York: Oxford University Press, 1988), 3–4.
11 Ibid., 4.
12 *The Oxford Classical Dictionary*, 2d ed., s.v., "Muses."
13 *invoco*, *-avi*, *-atum*, to call upon, invoke, especially as a witness or for aid. See Charlton T. Lewis, ed., *A Latin Dictionary* (Oxford: Clarendon Press, 1991). Robert Cawdrey, in *A Table Alphabetical of English Words* (1604), defines *invocation* as "A calling upon any thing with trust in the same." As a literary convention, the *invocatio* was an address to a deity, muse, or patron spirit for aid in poetic creation. For an informative discussion of the invocation as literary formula in the Renaissance, see Marjorie Donker and George M. Muldrow, eds., *Dictionary of Literary-Rhetorical Conventions of the English Renaissance* (Westport, Connecticut and London, England: Greenwood Press, 1982), 131.
14 *Theogony and Works and Days*, 6.
15 "There is a god within us. It is when he stirs us that our bosom warms; it is his impulse that sows the seeds of inspiration. I have a particular right to see the faces of the god, whether because I am a bard, or because I sing of sacred things." Ovid, *Fasti*, 2d ed., trans. Sir James George Frazer, Loeb Classical Library (Cambridge: Harvard University Press, 1989), 318–319.
16 *El VI*, 77–78: "For truly, the bard is sacred to the gods and is their priest. His hidden heart and lips alike breathe out Jove." Translation by Hughes, 52.
17 Homer, *The Iliad*, trans. Richard Lattimore (Chicago and London: University of Chicago Press, 1951), 59.
18 *Aen.*, 1.8, "O Muse, recall to me the cause."
19 *Aen.*, 7.37, "Now act, Erato!"
20 For further parallels between Dante's and Milton's prologues see Irene Samuel, *Dante and Milton: The Commedia and Paradise Lost* (Ithaca: Cornell University Press, 1966), 58–59.
21 "Thou Goddess, do thou prompt thy bard! I will tell of grim wars, will tell of battle array, and princes in their valour rushing upon death—of Tyrrhenian bands, and all Hesperia mustered in arms." Vergil, *Eclogues, Georgics, Aeneid*, 2 vols. trans. H. R. Faircloth, Loeb Classical Library (Cambridge: Harvard University Press, 1986).
22 E. R. Curtius, *European Literature and the Latin Middle Ages*, trans. Willard R. Trask (Princeton: Princeton University Press, 1953), 232.
23 1 p 1, lines 32–34: "Hae sunt enim quae infructuosis affectum spinis uberem fructibus rationis segetem necant hominumque mentes assuefaciunt morbo, non liberant." See Boethius, *Tractates, The Consolation of Philosophy*, trans. H. F. Stewart, E. K. Rand, and S. J. Tester, Loeb Classical Library (Cambridge: Harvard University Press, 1973).

24 Ibid., lines 39–41: "Get out, you Sirens, beguiling men straight to their destruction! Leave him to *my* Muses to care for and restore to health." Loeb. translation.

25 Lady Philosophy argues for the privileged position of philosophy over poetry, although she employs poetry throughout the *Consolation*. Indeed, Lady Philosophy's prayer (3 m 9) is a classical hymn. The *Consolation*'s prosimetron style further suggests that Boethius valued the Muses.

26 Renaissance critics who substantiate Milton in his use of poetic invocations include: Ludovico Castelvetro, *Poetica D'Aristotele* (Basilea, 1576); Alessandro Lionardi, *Dialogi* (Venetia, 1554); Antoni Minturno, *De Poeta* (Venetus, 1559) and *L'Arte Poetica* (1563); Gio. Battista Pigna, *Gli Heroici* (Vinegia, 1569); Julius Caesar Scaliger, *Poetices Libri Septem* (Commeliano, 1617); and Marco Girolamo Vidă, *The Art of Poetry*, trans. Pitt, ed. A. S. Cook (Boston: Ginn and Co., 1889). For texts and translations of passages of Renaissance criticism of the epic (including epic invocations), see Ivar Lou Myhr, "The Evolution and Practice of Milton's Epic Theory" (Ph.D. diss. Vanderbilt University, 1940), Appendix to Chapters I–V, i–cxxiv.

27 See *Monsieur Bossu's Treatise of the Epick Poem*, Trans. M.J. (London, 1695), Book III, Chapter IV, 124.

28 See Le Bossu, *Traité du Poëme Epick* (Paris, 1675). Le Bossu concludes his discussion of the invocation and proposition by writing: "que l'invocation peut être mêlée avec la Proposition, & qu'elle en peut être séparée: Qu'elle est toûjours une partie nécessaire du Poëme Epique; & qu'elle est une priere addressée au Genie allêgorique de la Poësie, sous le nom de Muse, ou de quelque autre, dont le Poëte demande d'être inspiré, soit dans tout ce qu'il a entrepris de raconter, soit seulement en quelque partie" (Livre Troisième, Chapitre IV, 313–314).

29 *Openings*, 204.

30 Horace, *Satires, Epistles, and Ars Poetica*, trans. H. Rushton Faircloth, Loeb Classical Library (Cambridge: Harvard University Press, 1978), 462.

31 "the middle is not discordant with the beginning, nor the end with the middle," 463.

32 Alvin Snider, *Origin and Authority in Seventeenth-Century England: Bacon, Milton, Butler* (Toronto: Toronto University Press, 1994), 88.

33 David Quint, *Epic and Empire: Politics and Generic Form from Virgil to Milton* (Princeton: Princeton University Press, 1993).

34 Margaret Anne Doody, *The Daring Muse: Augustan Poetry Reconsidered* (Cambridge: Cambridge University Press, 1985).

Chapter I

1 See Cowley, *The Motto*, in *The Poems of Abraham Cowley*, A. R. Waller, ed. (Cambridge: Cambridge University Press, 1905), 15. Unless otherwise

indicated, subsequent references to Cowley's poetry will come from this edition and will be indicated parenthetically by page number in the text.

2 See Cowley, *Davideis*, Book I, 325.

3 Thomas Sprat, "An Account of the Life of Mr. Abraham Cowley," In *The Works of Mr. Abraham Cowley* (London: Henry Herringman, 1669). Concerning Cowley's "translation" or "imitation" of Pindar's *Odes*, Sprat writes: "This way of leaving Verbal Translations, and chiefly regarding the Sense and Genius of the Author, was scarce heard of in England, before this present Age. I will not presume to say, that Mr. Cowley was the absolute Inventor of it. Nay, I know that others had the good luck to recommend it first in Print. Yet I appeal to you Sir, whether he did not conceive it, and discourse of it, and practice it as soon as any Man."

4 Samuel Johnson, "Life of Cowley," *Lives of the English Poets*, George Birkbeck, ed. (New York: Octagon Books, 1967), vol. 1, 56.

5 Well known and respected in his own time, Cowley has been virtually ignored in this century, with some few exceptions. See especially the full-length studies of Arthur H. Nethercott, Abraham Cowley: *The Muse's Hannibal* (New York: Russell and Russell, 1931; 1967; Jean Loiseau, *Abraham Cowley: sa vie, son oeuvre* (Paris: Henri Didier, 1931); Robert B. Hinman, *Abraham Cowley's World of Order* (Cambridge: Harvard University Press, 1960); and David Trotter, *The Poetry of Abraham Cowley* (Totowa: Rowman and Littlefield, 1979).

6 See Sprat, Account.

7 *The Survival of the Pagan Gods*, 319–320.

8 Torquato Tasso, *Discourses on the Heroic Poem*, trans. Mariella Cavalchini and Irene Samuel (Oxford: Clarendon Press, 1973), Book 1, 11.

9 *Discourses*, Book 4, 111. Tasso continues, remarking that writers may also invoke divine aid "occasionally in the middle or at the end, and whenever they come to something that apparently requires it" (111). Du Bartas clearly takes Tasso at his word, invoking God as his Muse at almost every opening and every juncture in the *Divine Weekes and Workes*. Although Cowley had ample precedent in Vergil for invoking the Muse at the beginning and at important turns in an epic, his emphasis upon the Muse as Christian, and specifically Protestant, owes more to Du Bartas.

10 Du Bartas, *His Diuine Weekes and Workes*, Trans. Joshua Sylvester (London: Humphray Lownes, 1621). All citations will be taken from this edition.

11 In the *Aeneid*, Vergil first gives the proposition ("Arma virumque cano") and then the invocation ("Musa, mihi causas memora"), a pattern accepted and employed by subsequent epic poets from late antiquity through the Renaissance. For example, see Spenser's invocation to *The Faerie Queene*, Book I.

12 Abraham Cowley, *The Works of Mr. Abraham Cowley*, 2d ed. (London: Henry Herringman, 1669).

13 From *The Norton Anthology of English Literature*, 4th ed., vol. 1, M. H. Abrams, et al., ed. (New York and London: W. W. Norton, 1986), 1640–1642. Further references to this edition will be cited parenthetically within the text.

14 Petitions are commonplace in classical and Christian hymns, and this poem has two: one for divine assistance in fighting the forces of Satan in the world and another for the poetic ability to achieve that end in verse. In "Aspects of Rhetoric and Form in Greek Hymns," *Greek, Roman, and Byzantine Studies* 23 (1982), 10, William H. Race writes that a petition at the end of a hymn should "be consonant with the god's powers as established in the body of the hymn, and follow naturally from the goodwill established between the god and man." What applies to the pagan gods applies to the deified Crashaw as well; Cowley is consciously employing a Christian (or papist) form for a poetic end. By acknowledging Crashaw's poetic service to God and recalling his friendship with the departed poet, Cowley fulfills the demands of the form.

15 See 2 Kings 2:1–15.

16 By focusing upon the prophetic inheritance of Elisha, Cowley may also be making an allusion to Sylvester's role in translating *Du Bartas' His Diuine Weekes and Workes*. Invoking God for assistance in translating the poem and disseminating heavenly "knowledge to the Ignorant," Sylvester writes:

> Grant me first judgement, Grace, and Eloquence,
> So correspondent to that Excellence,
> That in some measure, I may seeme t'inherit
> (Elisha-like) my deare Elias spirit. (1.23–26)

Note the verbal similarity in the phrase "Elisha-like." More generally, however, both passages capture the poetic anxiety felt by one who would take up the mantle of another poet, and both appeal to God for confirmation in the role of poet-priest.

17 Celeste Marguerite Schenck, *Mourning and Panegyric: The Poetics of Pastoral Ceremony* (University Park and London: The Pennsylvania State University Press, 1988), 2.

18 Developing his ongoing theme of Cowley's precocity, Thomas Sprat records the time and circumstances of the epic's creation: according to Sprat, the *Davideis* "was written in so young an age; that is we shall reflect on the vastness of the Argument, and his manner of handling it, he may seem like one of the Miracles, that he there adorns, like a Boy attempting Goliath . . . he had finish'd the greatest part of it, while he was yet a young student at Cambridge." Sprat goes on to make some qualifications, conceding "some youthfulness, and redundance of Fancy, than [Cowley's] riper judgment would have allowed." See Sprat's *Account*.

19 Douglas Bush, *English Literature in the Earlier Seventeenth Century, 1600–1660* (New York: Oxford University Press, 1945), 357.

20 In his note on *The Verse of Paradise* Lost, Milton calls rhyming in epic poetry "the Invention of a Barbarous Age, to set off wretched matter and

lame meter," arguing that it is "no necessary Adjunct or true Ornament of Poem or good verse, in longer Works especially." Milton follows Homer and Vergil in his neglect of rhyme and maintains that rather than being "taken as a defect, as it may seem so perhaps to vulgar readers," it should be regarded as "an example set, the first in English, of ancient liberty recover'd to Heroic Poem from the troublesome and modern bondage of Riming." See Hughes, 210.

21 Arthur H. Nethercott, *Abraham Cowley, the Muse's Hannibal* (Oxford: Oxford University Press, 1931), 49.

22 David Trotter, *The Poetry of Abraham Cowley* (Totowa, New Jersey: Rowman and Littlefield, 1979), 100.

23 David Trotter notes that David's fitness for the role of God's champion was particularly "reinforced" by the poet-king's "pious interest in song, a point made by St. Augustine in *The City of God*," Ibid., 99.

24 Compare David's heroic qualities with those of Alexander the Great, which were praised by Aristotle in the *Politics*. For an interesting and useful discussion *areté* as reflected in Alexander, see Peter Green, *Alexander of Macedon, 356–323 B. C.: A Historical Biography* (Berkeley: University of California Press, 1991), 57–58.

25 Cowley calls attention to God's priority and his creative role, citing John 8.58: "Jesus said unto them, Verily, verily, I say unto you, Before Abraham was, I am." Also, Cowley seems to compare David with Jesus and even to God. The scriptural passage also underscores the difference between Time and Eternity, as seen in Cowley's note upon Boethius's *De Consolatione Philosophiae*, Book 5. By appealing to God's priority, Cowley appeals to that which exists beyond time—that which is eternal and unchanging—the *summum bonum*.

26 Cowley, *Preface*, 12–13.

27 Richard Crashaw, *The Poems: English, Latin, and Greek*, L. C. Martin, ed. (Oxford: Clarendon Press, 1927), 307–314. Further references to Crashaw's text will be indicated parenthetically by stanza number.

28 Robert T. Peterson, *The Art of Ecstasy: Teresa, Bernini, and Crashaw* (New York: Athenaeum, 1970), 118.

29 See Exodus 13:21.

30 A. D. Nuttall also notes Cowley's "odd logic" in dedicating his Muse, Christ, to Christ. See *Openings*, 98.

31 Ibid., 99. Nuttall continues by saying that the Muse as a metaphor for poetry, though a "pregnant" one as "a redeemable whore, a Magdalene who may be brought to the feet of Christ," lacks the "Miltonic strengthening-from-within, the Muse becoming God himself, living as the Holy Spirit in the throat, lungs, and brain of the singer" found in the invocation of *Paradise Lost*, Book 3.

32 See Crashaw, *Poems: English, Latin, and Greek*, 239–245.

33 *Openings*, 104.

34 Cowley, Ibid., 267.

35 Cowley's Latin version (*Davideios*, Liber Primus, lines 42–48) reads: "Sed tu me, Verbum æternum, tu voce vocâsti, / Et novus insolito percussus lumine Paulus, / Prodeo Musarum immensos convertere Mundos, / Et Cœlum series ignotum aperire Poëtis; / Ut juvat, ô, purgare suis sacra flumina monstris! / Ut vili purgare algâ, cænoque profundo, / Et liquidi ingenuos Fontes inducere Veri!" Cowley extends his narrative to dwell upon the unusual light that struck Paul and to assert his own divine calling to convert the pagan world to God's truth.

36 Ibid., 253.

37 Cowley, Ibid., 14.

38 Sprat, *Account*.

39 Cowley, Ibid., 14.

40 In his *Preface* to the 1656 edition of his *Poems*, Cowley stated that he had written a poem in three books on the Civil War, which he left unfinished when the tide turned against the Royalist cause after the Battle of Newbury. And indeed Cowley gave the impression that he had destroyed all copies of it (Sprat does not mention the poem in his Life of the author). In 1679, twelve years after Cowley's death, an incomplete version of the poem was published with the title, *A Poem on the Late Civil War*. It was assumed that the remainder of the poem was irrevocably lost until the recent discovery of two manuscript copies of the whole poem among the Cowper family papers in the Panhanger MSS at the Hertford County Record Office. See Abraham Cowley, *The Civil War*, Allan Pritchard, ed. (Toronto: University of Toronto Press, 1973), for the authoritative version of books 1–3 of the *Civil War*. Since my focus is upon epic beginnings (and the textual variations are slight) and since the earlier version was the only one available to audiences of the Seventeenth Century, I shall cite the 1679 edition, *A Poem on the Late Civil War*, in my discussion.

41 See Pritchard, 11–18.

42 Abraham Cowley, *A Poem on the Late Civil War* (London, 1679). As there are no line numbers in this edition, I shall provide page numbers for quoted passages.

43 Gerald M. MacLean, *Time's Witness: Historical Representation in English Poetry, 1603–1660* (Madison: University of Wisconsin Press, 1990), 180.

44 D. M. Rosenberg, "Epic Warfare in Cowley and Milton," *Clio* 22:1 (1992): 70–71. Rosenberg continues by making a distinction between the kind of praise offered by Cowley and Milton. According to Rosenberg, "Milton, in his narration of warfare, does not exalt man, but glorifies God" (71). For this reason, I would argue, Milton's epic can transcend human history in a way that Cowley's cannot. While Cowley's adaptation of poetic invocations to the need for praising military men fits with the theme of his work, it fails to rise above the level of literary convention—that it, Cowley's panegyrics lack the inspiration of Milton's invocations to the Muse.

45 Ibid., 72.

46 Ibid., 76.

47 *Discourses*, Book 1, 11.

48 Those familiar with sixteenth- and seventeenth-century grave markers throughout England and the northeastern United States will recognize the similarities between the winged cherubs or winged skeletons and the figure used in this text. In both cases, the passerby is called upon to contemplate death.

49 *Time's Witness*, 180.

50 Ibid., 180–181.

51 Indeed, in its allegorical power, Cowley's proposition prefigures his presentation of the death of the King in his *Plantarum* and the ills of the body of England so prevalent in that poem.

52 MacLean also notes the unconventional opening of the poem and suggests that Cowley was consciously experimenting with generic form by omitting the invocation to the Muse and substituting a question mark after "What rage." MacLean justly notes the absence of the opening proposition and formal invocation to the Muse—found earlier in Daniel's *Civil Wars*—but perhaps overstates his point by suggesting that invocations are entirely "missing" from the poem. See *Time's Witness*, 184. I would suggest that instead of invocations Cowley gives us rhetorical questions and references to the Muse, which constitute attempts to call upon a Muse who is already engaged in the serious business of the war.

53 *Aen.* 1.11: "Can resentment so fierce dwell in heavenly breasts?"

54 *Luc.*, 1.1-17: "Of war I sing, war worse than civil, waged over the plains of Emathia, and of legality conferred on crime; I tell how an imperial people turned their victorious right hands against their own vitals; how kindred fought against kindred; how, when the compact of tyranny was shattered, all the forces of the shaken world contended to make mankind guilty; how standards confronted hostile standards, eagles were matched against each other, and pilum threatened pilum." All citations and translations of *The Civil War* are taken from Lucan, *The Civil War*, trans. J. D. Duff, Loeb Classical Library (Cambridge: Harvard UP, 1988).

55 See *Luc.*, 1.8: "What madness was this, my countrymen, what fierce orgy of slaughter?" Loeb translation.

56 See *Luc.*, 1.33–34. Having described at great length the bloodshed and dire costs of the civil war, Lucan writes, "Quod si non aliam venturo fata Neroni / Invenere viam . . . ," as if to say that even such violence and gore would be worth it, after all, if it meant that in the end the Roman people could see Nero rise to power.

57 *A Poem on the Late Civil War*, 4–5. While blood and death predominate both the current state of affairs and those wars of the past, immortality and honor are given to those who fought on the side of what was "right." Turned against ourselves (and against our King) in civil war, Cowley would argue, "we alive are dead." This serves as a grim contrast to Henry's promise of honor and immortality to his men before the battle of Agincourt: "For he

today that sheds his blood with me / Shall be my brother" (*Henry V* 4.3.61–62).

58 Refusing to mention them, but nevertheless doing so, Cowley provides another catalogue of heroes: " . . . and next thy Name / Should Berkly, Stanning, Digby press to Fame. / Godolphin thee, thee Greenvil I'd rehearse . . .", Ibid., 25.

59 Ibid., 30.

60 Cowley himself remained with the King's court at Oxford while these men saw battle; he therefore shows respect towards men such as Hopton, Greenvil, and Cavendish by stepping aside so that they may receive the rewards of the Muse.

61 Pritchard provides the completed text, books 1–3, which contains additional portraits that draw inspiration from the Muse; book 3 concludes with an elegy to Falkland.

62 In the longer version of the poem, Cowley makes a final reference to the Muse, here in association with the death of Lord Falkland (3.545–548):

A Muse stood by mee, and just then I writ
My Kings great acts in Verses not unfit.
The trowbled Muse fell shapeless into aire,
Instead of Inck dropt from my Pen a Teare.

As in all previous references to the Muse, this one too reveals the author's acknowledgment of the dire consequences of war. Here, the lament becomes more personal and the reflection upon the war's outcome more pronounced. Cowley goes on to write that even "Had all the Puritan Name that day bin lost" (552), Falkland's death would have "Cost us as much in Teares as them in Blood" (554). The Muse can provide no relief to the Parliamentarians, and the unfinished poem ends with this lament for Falkland and a prayer to God, calling for forgiveness and for revenge: "Thinke on our sufferings, and sheath then againe; / Our Sinnes are great, but Falkland too is slaine" (647–648). See Pritchard, 121–124.

63 See the anonymous seventeenth-century translation of Book Six of Cowley's *Plantarum* (London, 1680), which concerns the "late Rebellion, the Happy Restoration of His Sacred Majesty, and the Dutch War Ensuing." Cowley clearly drew from his earlier material on the Civil War and blended Lucanian and Vergilian traditions in to the work in order to achieve what he had failed to achieve earlier in his *Civil War*. Cowley provides the same kinds of heroic portraits in this later work and has more distance from his subject matter. His writing has more confidence, but he remains concerned with origins and new beginnings.

Chapter II

1 *Vates*, according to Richard Helgerson, was the term Vergil used to distinguish himself from the mere *poetae* of his age, and it clearly affected

Spenser's and Milton's conception of their role while it excluded Jonson, who had no "prophetic" ambitions. However, even as the new writers of the English Renaissance proclaimed their "ancient lineage," Helgerson maintains that they were also contributing to the manifestation of "a literary system that had no precise counterpart in antiquity." According to Helgerson, the efforts of writers such as Spenser, Jonson, and Milton, as well as others like Sidney, Puttenham, and Webb, to establish a single term that would "unequivocally denote the function they strove to exercise ended in failure. The necessary distinction could thus be made only with the circumlocution of self-presentational gesture." While Helgerson selects the term "laureate" to designate the poets in his study, I shall frequently use the term "*vates*," or "poet-priest," since its implied prophetic connotations are central to my reading of Milton and Cowley as epic poets. See *Self-Crowned Laureates: Spenser, Jonson, Milton, and the Literary System* (Berkeley: University of California Press, 1983), 3–4.

2 For a more detailed discussion of Milton's influences, see Merritt Y. Hughes, ed., *John Milton: Complete Poems and Major Prose*, notes, 3–5.

3 "Believe me, when the ivory key is played and the festive throng dances through the perfumed halls to the sound of the lute, you will feel the silent approach of Phoebus in your breast like a sudden heat that permeates to the marrow; and through a maiden's eyes and music-making fingers Thalia will glide into full possession of your breast." Translation by Hughes, 51.

4 See Leah S. Marcus, *The Politics of Mirth: Jonson, Herrick, Milton, Marvell and the Defense of Old Holiday Pastimes* (Chicago and London: University of Chicago Press, 1986). Marcus maintains that Milton's *Comus* "replicates the stringent Jonsonian tactic of offering trenchant criticism under the protective veil of holiday license [but] . . . Milton's art of festival pushes toward a much more radical social and political transformation" (20). Moreover, Marcus argues that Milton's defense of festive mirth, like other Renaissance defenses of holiday pastimes, "both acknowledges and transcends the pathos of the occasional. It is . . . bittersweet, accepting its fragility along with the ephemeral existence of the holiday it celebrates" (22).

5 " . . . his youth must be innocent of crime and chaste, his conduct irreproachable and his hands stainless. His character should be like yours, O Priest, when, glorious with sacred vestments and lustral water, you arise to go into the presence of the angry deities." Translation by Hughes, 52.

6 See, for example: Robert Southwell, *The Burning Babe*; Henry Vaughan, *Christ's Nativity*; Thomas Traherne, *On Christmas Day*; Robert Herrick, *An Ode on the Birth of Our Saviour*; Richard Crashaw, *On the Holy Nativity of Our Lord.*

7 For an instructive introduction to Pindar, his poetic career, and the thematic and generic qualities of his *Odes*, see William H. Race, "Introduction," *Pindar*, 2 vols., Loeb Classical Library (Cambridge: Harvard University Press, 1997), 1–41. Discussing Pindar's often difficult Victory odes, Race

notes that "Pindar's art, like Bach's, presents a constant tension between the constraints of form and the freedom of innovation; it too exhibits tremendous energy, great variety within its genres, and reveals ever-new depths upon repeated hearings" (2). The same tension, complexity, and resonance may also be attributed to Milton's *Nativity Ode*.

8 *CG*, 669.

9 Ibid., 669.

10 Italics mine. According to Plato in *Timaeus* 27c, a hymn or prayer to God is necessary before beginning a great task. Hymns and *encomia* to the gods are the only forms worthy of divinity. This is reaffirmed by Lady Philosophy in Boethius' *De Consolatione Philosophiae*, III prose 9.

11 See *George Herbert and the Seventeenth-Century Religious Poets*, ed. Mario A. di Cesare (New York and London: Norton Critical Edition, 1978), 46–47.

12 See A. D. Nuttall, *Overheard by God: Fiction and Prayer in Herbert, Milton, Dante and St John* (London and New York: Methuen, 1980), 2–3.

13 Ibid., 8.

14 See *John* 1.1: "In the beginning was the Word, and the Word was with God, and the Word was God." See also *John* 1.14: "And the Word was made flesh, and dwelt among us, (and we beheld his glory, the glory as of the only begotten of the Father,) full of grace and truth.

15 E. R. Curtius notes that even Hesiod, the originator of didactic poetry, feels bound to the Muses; in him and in Pindar the invocation of the Muses "must serve to prove the poet's pedagogical vocation." (*European Literature*, 229).

16 See *Pindar*, trans. William H. Race, 2 vol., Loeb Classical Library (Cambridge: Harvard University Press, 1997).

17 *L'All*, lines 151–152; *IlPen*, lines 175–176.

18 Walter Schindler, *Voice and Crisis: Invocation in Milton's Poetry* (Hamden, Conn.: Archon Books, 1984), 28. Schindler continues: "The natural evolution of the poems' scenes out of the character of the Muse each invokes makes it clear that the pressure of choice in inherent in the invoking moment and that every important invocation defines an approach to experience." Ibid., 28.

19 Ibid., 28.

20 *L'All*, 17; 19; 24.

21 *L'All*, 25–26; 34–36.

22 See Hughes, *Prolusion* VII, 621ff.

23 In *L'All*, Milton invokes Mirth differently: "But come thou, Goddess fair and free, / In Heav'n y'clept *Euphrosyne*, / And by me, heart-easing Mirth" (lines 11–13). Mirth has both a formal, Classical name as well as a common one. Moreover, Milton deliberately uses a Spenserian archaism "y-clept" here—part of his playfulness as a poet. In *IlPen*, on the other hand, he uses clear, but grand-style Anglo-Saxon—and not overly Latinate—language. In

IlPen, finally, Milton gives the Muse only one name, which is Melancholy, and associates her with heavenly light.

24 This notion of being pulled back from the highest state of spiritual connection to God extends back into Antiquity, and serves as a potent trope in the Middle Ages. The narrator's thwarted desire at the conclusion of *The Pearl* to cross the river to join his daughter, now one of the Brides of Christ, is just one example.

25 See also *PL* 1.16–18: "And chiefly Thou O Spirit, that dost prefer, / Before all Temples th' upright heart and pure, / Instruct me . . ."

26 The poet may attempt to write of heavenly things, though without the possibility of creating a one-to-one correspondence between word and thing. Mortals are necessarily limited in their perceptions of spiritual things by virtue of their mortality; however, like the authors of the scriptures, Milton would argue, the poet may relate heavenly matters in human language, according to the doctrine of accommodation.

27 Cleanth Brooks, "Light Symbolism in 'L'Allegro-Il Penseroso,'" in *The Well Wrought Urn: Studies in the Structure of Poetry* (San Diego, New York, and London: HBJ, 1947), 53.

28 Brooks also adds that *Il Penseroso* is twenty-four lines longer than *L'Allegro*, indicating that Milton perhaps valued the contemplative over the mirthful life. Ibid, 66.

29 *PL*, IX. 20; 42–43.

30 See Hughes, 595ff.

31 William B. Hunter, et al., eds., *A Milton Encyclopedia* (Lewisburg: Bucknell University Press, 1978), vol. 4, s.v. "*L'Allegro* and *Il Penseroso*," by Leonard Nathanson, 198.

32 Marcus, *Politics of Mirth*, 20.

33 See William A. Oram, "The Invocation of Sabrina" *SEL* 24 (1984), 124–125.

34 This is not to say, of course, that Milton is not indebted to Christian allegory as well. Milton's ongoing debt to Spenser's *Fairie Queene* is evident throughout the masque.

35 Schindler, *Voice and Crisis*, 33.

36 Milton mixes local English traditions and classical pagan rites in his depiction of Comus as darkness's chief priest. The Wales of *Comus*, as in *Lycidas*, is strongly connected to its Celtic past, which includes a tradition of Druid bards and magicians.

37 See *FQ*, III, xii, 29–45. Having emerged from viewing a masque, bold Britomart discovers and rescues Amoret, bound to a pillar by the "vile Enchaunter" Busyrane. The description reads:

Ne liuing wight she saw in all that roome,
Saue that same woefull Ladie, both whose hands
Were bounden fast, that di her ill become,
And her small wast girt round with yron bands,
Vnto a brasen pillour, by which she stands. (Canto XXX)

The same elements of chastity threatened by male potency abound in Spenser's scene as they do here in *Comus*. In the end, Britomart destroys the pillar, restoring Amoret, complete and undamaged, to Scudamore.

38 Note Sabrina's connection to the line of Anchises and Brutus, as well as her place in Welsh folklore.

39 The Shepherds and their innocent mirth must soon make way for the higher form of aristocratic dancing. See *Comus*, lines 957–975.

40 According to Geoffrey of Monmouth's *History of the Kings of Britain*, the legendary Trojan kings of Britain descended from Anchises, father of Aeneas, and the line from Anchises to Locrine followed thus: Anchises, Aeneas, Ascanius or Iulus, Silvius, Brutus, and Locrine. By placing the Lady in this line, Milton seems to be suggesting the need for a new order in Britain, founded upon the virtue displayed in this mask by the Earl of Bridgewater's daughter.

Chapter III

1 *Voice and Crisis*, 36.

2 Harold Bloom, *The Anxiety of Influence: A Theory of Poetry* (London, Oxford, and New York: Oxford University Press, 1973), 151.

3 Samuel Johnson, "Life of Milton," *Lives of the English Poets*, George Birkbeck Hill, ed., 3 vols. (New York: Octagon Books, 1967), Vol. 1, 163.

4 Balachandra Rajan, *The Lofty Rhyme* (London: Routledge and Kegan Paul, 1970), 55.

5 Phillippe Ariès, *Western Attitudes Toward Death: From the Middle Ages to the Present*, trans. Patricia M. Ranum (Baltimore: Johns Hopkins University Press, 1978), 57–58.

6 See Dennis Kay, *Melodious Tears: The English Funeral Elegy from Spenser to Milton* (Oxford: Clarendon Press, 1990), 222.

7 Samuel Taylor Coleridge, *Specimens of the Table Talk of Samuel Taylor Coleridge*, H. N. Coleridge, ed., 2 vol. (London, 1835).

8 Peter Sacks. *The English Elegy: Studies in the Genre from Spenser to Yeats* (Baltimore: Johns Hopkins University Press, 1985), 95.

9 See *Aen.*, Book V.

10 *The English Elegy*, 37.

11 William Riley Parker, *Milton: A Biography*, 2 vols. (Oxford: Clarendon Press, 1968), volume 1, 157.

12 Janet Leslie Knedlik, "High Pastoral Art in *Epitaphium Damonis*," *Milton Studies* XIX, Ed. James A. Freeman and Anthony Low (Pittsburgh: University of Pittsburgh Press, 1984), 161.

13 *The English Elegy*, 22–23.

14 *The English Elegy*, 26.

15 For the origin of the expression "pathetic fallacy," see John Ruskin, *Modern Painters*, vol. 3, part IV, chap. xii. While we owe the expression to Ruskin,

I disagree with his use of the term. In *Modern Painters*, Ruskin suggests that the use of the "pathetic fallacy" is a bad thing, and seems to believe that the poet himself believes that fallacy. However, the whole point is that readers are meant to realize that it is fallacious.

16 *The Uses of Nostalgia*, 31.

17 *Damon*, line 43: "Who now is to beguile my days with conversation and song?" Translation by Hughes, 133.

18 *Damon*, line 37: "But what at last is to become of me?" Translation by Hughes, 133.

19 *Damon*, line 45: "To whom shall I confide my heart?" Translation by Hughes, 133.

20 Sacks, *The English Elegy*, 22–23.

21 J. M. Edwards, trans., *The Greek Bucolic Poets*, Loeb Classical Library (Cambridge: Harvard University Press, 1960), 14–15.

22 *Ecl.* 10.9–12: "What groves, what glades were your abode, ye virgin Naiads, when Gallus was pining with a love unrequited? For no heights of Parnassus or of Pindus, no Aonian Aganippe may you tarry." See Vergil, *Eclogues, Georgics, Aeneid, 1–6*, trans. H. Rushton Faircloth, Loeb Classical Library (Cambridge: Harvard University Press, 1986), 72–73.

23 See Drayton's *Polyolbion* 9.415–429, 436.

24 Milton's likely sources for the Orpheus myth are Ovid's *Met.* 9. 1–55 and Vergil's *Georg.* 4. 454–527.

25 *House of Death*, 153.

26 William Race, *Classical Genres and English Poetry* (London: Croom Helm, 1988), 105.

27 *Voice and Crisis*, 40.

28 Ibid., 40.

29 *Damon*, lines 19–20: "Ah me! What deities shall I profess in earth or heaven, now that they have torn you mercilessly away in death, O Damon?" Translation by Hughes, 133.

30 *Damon*, line 23: "But he who divides the souls . . ." Translation by Hughes, 133.

31 Cicero, *De Inventione* 1. 97: "Moreover, I am of the opinion that praise and vituperation should not be made a separate part, but should be closely interwoven with the argumentation itself." From Cicero, *De Inventione, De Optimo Genere Oratorum, Topica*, H. M. Hubbell, trans., Loeb Classical Library (Cambridge: Harvard University Press, 1993), 146–147.

32 *Classical Genres*, 107.

33 Ibid.

34 Johnson, *Lives of the English Poets*, 165.

35 Ibid., 295.

36 *Melodious Tears*, 226.

37 See also *Arcades*, 30–31: "Divine *Alpheus*, who by secret sluice, / Stole under Seas to meet his *Arethuse*."

38 Samuel Johnson, of course, does not agree. In fact, he maintains that "Nothing can less display Knowledge, or less exercise invention, than to tell how a shepherd has lost his companion, and must now feed his flocks alone . . . He who thus grieves will excite no sympathy; he who thus praises will confer no honour." *Lives of the English Poets*, 164.

39 In his *Argumentum* to *Epitaphium Damonis*, Milton states that he and Diodati (presented respectively as Thyrsis and Damon) were more than shepherds from the same field but from childhood had shared the same intellectual interests and were intimate friends: "Thyrsis et Damonis, eiusdem viciniae Pastores, eadem studia sequuti a pueritia amici erant, ut qui plurimum. Thyrsis animi causa profectus peregre de obitu Damonis nuntium accepit." Hughes, 132.

40 *Damon*, lines 19–20: "Ah me! what deities shall I profess in earth or heaven, now that they have torn you mercilessly away in death, O Damon?" Translation by Hughes.

41 *Damon*, lines 1–3: "Nymphs of Himera—for you remember Daphnis and Hylas and the long-lamented destiny of Bion—utter your Sicilian song through the cities of the Thames." Translation by Hughes.

42 *Damon*, line 4: "Sing the moans and sighs that the wretched Thyrsis poured out." Translation by Hughes.

43 *Damon*, lines 58–61: "Alone now I stray through the fields, alone through the pastures, wherever the branches make dense shadows in the valleys, there I wait for the evening. Over my head the rain and the southeast wind make their sad sound in the restless twilight of the wind-swept trees." Translation by Hughes, 134.

44 The stoic commonplace to endure misfortunes, *dure . . . dure*, frequently appears in the poetic works of Horace. See, for example, Horace's *Odes* 1.24, addressed to Vergil on the death of his friend and critic, Quintilius Varus. The poem concludes with a stoic consolation: "durum: sed levius fit patientia, / quicquid corrigere est nefas" (19–20). The word *durum*, "hard," sums up the painful helplessness of the grieving Vergil; the consolation offered by the speaker of the poem is *patientia*, "endurance." Milton was surely familiar with this stoic ideal and would have been aware of its connection to the funeral elegy.

45 Ruth Wallerstein, *Studies in Seventeenth-Century Poetic* (Madison: University of Wisconsin Press, 1950), 120.

46 G. W. Pigman, *Grief and English Renaissance Elegy* (Cambridge: Cambridge University Press, 1985), 5.

47 *Classical Genres*, 107.

48 It may also resemble the Medieval trope of the *ubi sunt qui ante nos*, which differs by not expressing the same sense of responsibility.

49 *Ecl.*, line 63.

50 *Damon*, lines 162–165. "I, for my part, am resolved to tell the story of the Trojan ships in the Rutupian sea and of the ancient kingdom of Inogene, the daughter of Pandrasus, and of the chiefs, Brennus and Arviragus, and of old

Belinus, and of the Armorican settlers who came at last under British law." Translation by Hughes, 137.

51 *Damon*, lines 170–171. "Or else, quite changed, you shall shrill forth a British theme."

52 Milton's inscription in Greek, *In Effigiei Eius Sculptorem* (On the Engraver of His Likeness), directed at the sculptor for producing such a poor likeness of him, reads: "Looking at the form of its original, you might say, mayhap, that this likeness had been drawn by a tyro's hand; but, friends, since you do not recognize what is modelled here, have a good laugh at a caricature by a good-for-nothing artist." Translation by Hughes, 142. Despite Milton's apparent levity toward the engraver in this episode, the iconographic representation of the young author in the frontispiece of the 1645 edition of the *Poems* offers some interesting insights into the poet's early epic ambitions and his relationship to his Muses, especially Clio and Urania.

53 E. R. Gregory, *Milton and the Muses* (Tuscaloosa and London: University of Alabama Press, 1989), 112–114.

54 Ibid.

55 *Damon*, lines 207–211. "And now, since you have received the privileges of heaven, assist and gently favor me, however you may be called; whether you are to be known as our Damon or would rather be Diodati, by which divine name the inhabitants of heaven will know you, while in the forests you will keep the name of Damon." Translation by Hughes, 139.

Chapter IV

1 In John Milton, *Poems, &c. Upon Several Occasions* (London, 1673), 97–98.

2 Ibid., 101–102.

3 The idea of descending and re-ascending occurs also in *PL*, Book III, when Milton, after having described Satan and the fallen angels, addresses Holy Light in a hymn: "Taught by the heav'nly Muse to venture down / The dark descent, and up to reascend, / Though hard and rare" (*PL* 3.19–21). Milton's goal is to uncover the mysteries of God and, in both cases, the poet requires the assistance of the "heav'nly Muse."

4 Ibid., 110.

5 Ibid.

6 A noteworthy exception is David Lowenstein's *Milton and the Drama of History: Historical Vision, Iconoclasm, and Literary Imagination* (Cambridge: Cambridge University Press, 1990), 81–88. Lowenstein argues that Milton's aborted *History of Britain* reveals a more pronounced tension between invention and truth-telling in historical narrative, as Milton explores the dark, convoluted course of his nation's past up until the Norman conquest . . . this massive enterprise of charting his nation's distant past—a full-scale history in its own right—raised for Milton the problem of

an imaginative and creative process response to the historical process, a problem he chose to struggle with directly in his work" (81–82). Lowenstein suggests that Milton's *History of Britain* reveals its author "divided between presenting an objective, factual response to history and presenting a more literary and mythopoetic one" (82).

7 In *PL* 9.25–47, Milton writes that he was "long choosing" his epic theme. He rejects "Wars, hitherto the only Argument / Heroic deem'd" in favor "Of Patience and Heroic Martyrdom / Unsung." In the face of the failure of the Commonwealth, Milton reaches back before human wars and glory to the very creation and the Fall of Man for fit subjects for his "higher Argument." The *History of Britain* (which might have become the *Arthuriad*) containing heroes such as Brutus, Arthur, and Alfred cannot rival *Paradise Lost* and its "hero," the Son of God.

8 *Milton and the Drama of History*, 84.

9 John Milton, *The History of Britain*, ed. George Philip Krapp, in *The Works of John Milton*, Vol. 10 (New York: Columbia University Press, 1932), 1.

10 Alexander Pope, following in the footsteps of Milton, also sought to compose a national epic poem on the origins of the British people. Pope's *Brutus* was to have been a blank-verse epic upon the legendary founding of the British people by the Trojan Brutus, great-grandson of Aeneas. Blending the historical and mythical aspects of Geoffrey of Monmouth's account and the literary aspects of Vergil's *Aeneid*, Pope's epic would have dealt with the journey of Brutus and his followers to the island of Britain, where they would found the ideal commonwealth based upon such enlightenment ideals as Benevolence, Freedom, and Justice. Pope's working notes for the unfinished poem exist as Egerton MS. 1950 in the British Library.

11 *Milton and the Drama of History*, 85.

12 Ibid., 221. Alfred, when he was not engaged in military campaigns and the affairs of his kingdom, translated Orosius, Boethius, and Bede out of the Latin into English, and "permitted none unlearn'd to bear Office, either in Court or Common-wealth." Milton was certainly sympathetic to these practices.

13 Intending to write a history of Britain from its historical/mythological beginnings starting with the Great Flood and the coming of Brutus to his own times, Milton instead ended the work with the Norman Conquest.

14 Lowenstein notes in the conclusion of his discussion of *The History of Britain* that "by breaking off suddenly at the Norman Conquest, Milton leaves us with a haunting sense of incompleteness. Nothing more poignantly highlights the sense of artistic strain and exhaustion of this massive enterprise. Its incompleteness, perhaps more than any other detail, expresses the unresolved dilemma of Milton as mythopoetic historiographer — divided between the urge to shape the process of history through imaginative and rhetorical discourse and the commitment to represent its

'truth naked,' with its 'bare and reasonless actions.'" See *Milton and the Drama of History*, 87–88.

15 Rowland L. Collins and Sarah H. Collins make a similar point, observing that "throughout his work Milton was deeply aware of the parallels between past events and problems of contemporary England," especially considering the collapse of British society after the fall of the Roman Empire. See William B. Hunter, et al., eds., *A Milton Encyclopedia* (Lewisburg: Bucknell University Press, 1978) vol. 3, s.v. "The History of Britain," 194.

16 See *Iliad* 2.819–821: "The strong son of Anchises was leader of the Dardanians, / Aineias, whom divine Aphrodite bore to Anchises / in the folds of Ida, a goddess lying in love with a mortal." Translation by Richard Lattimore.

17 See *Iliad* 20.158–160; 160ff.: "Two men far greater than all the others / were coming to encounter, furious to fight with each other, / Aineias, the son of Anchises, and brilliant Achilleus. Translation by Richard Lattimore.

18 *Aen.* 1.8: "O Muse, relate to me the cause." Loeb translation.

19 Regina M. Schwartz, *Remembering and Repeating: On Milton's Theology and Poetics* (Chicago and London: University of Chicago Press, 1988), 83. Schwartz writes, "As pastoral aspires to prophesy in *Lycidas*, so in *Paradise Lost*, the epic would swell into a hymn . . . Milton would distinguish himself from the Satan who refuses to praise and who 'remember'st not' his making."

20 For another treatment of Milton's claim to prophetic inspiration as displayed in the epic invocations in *Paradise Lost*, see William Kerrigan, *The Prophetic Milton* (Charlottesville: University Press of Virginia, 1974), 126–143.

21 Lines 162–163: "I, for my part, am resolved to tell the story of the Trojan ships in the Rutupian sea." Translation by Hughes.

22 Lines 168–171: "And then, O my pipe, if life is granted me, you shall be left dangling on some old pine far away and quite forgotten by me; or else, quite changed, you shall shrill forth a British theme to your native Muses!" Translation by Hughes.

23 For treatments of Milton's invocations in *Paradise Lost* see Lee M. Johnson, "Milton's Epic Style: The Invocations in *Paradise Lost*," in *The Cambridge Companion to Milton*, Ed. Dennis Danielson (Cambridge: Cambridge University Press, 1989), 65–78; Anne Ferry, *Milton's Epic Voice: The Narrator in Paradise Lost* (Chicago and London: University of Chicago Press, 1963), 20–43; Barbara Lewalski, *Paradise Lost and the Rhetoric of Literary Forms* (Princeton: Princeton University Press, 1985), 25–54; Mary Ann Radzinowicz, *Milton's Epics and the Book of Psalms* (Princeton: Princeton University Press, 1989), 138–148; Irene Samuel, *Dante and Milton: The Commedia and Paradise Lost* (Ithaca: Cornell University Press, 1966), 47–66, 292–294; Walter Schindler, *Voice and Crisis: Invocation in Milton's Poetry* (Hamden, Connecticut: Archon Books, 1984), 45–62; and John M. Steadman, "Urania," in *A Milton*

Encyclopedia (London and Toronto: Associated University Presses, 1980) 8:106–113.

24 *Milton's Epic Voice*, 21.

25 *Voice and Crisis*, 46.

26 *Aen.* 1.5–6: "till he should build a city and bring his gods to Latium." Loeb translation.

27 See *John Milton and the Transformation of Ancient Epic* (London and Sydney: Croom Helm, 1986), 71–72.

28 See Radzinowicz, *Milton's Epic and the Book of Psalms*, who argues that Milton "found in David the model for the kind of personal utterance he also saw in the prophets. The proems would not take their distinctive shape without Milton's awareness of Vergil, Ariosto, and Dante as predecessors in the mode; neither would they have their distinctive form without inspiration from the Book of Psalms" (140).

29 Other critics have noted Milton's delayed beginning, including Regina Schwartz, who writes that "in the opening invocation of *Paradise Lost*, where Milton is so concerned with first things, he has deferred the first words of the Bible. Instead of beginning, 'In the beginning . . . ,' he begins with the fall and only then does he proceed to the account of the creation." She goes on to argue that this "inversion of the apparent Biblical order of creation and fall" continues throughout the poem. Once we become aware of the redemptive character of the Biblical creation, Schwartz maintains, "it becomes clear that Milton's order only seems to depart from the Bible; instead, he is a most attentive reader, for in the Bible, a recurring pattern of chaos/order (fall/creation) describes an ongoing process of re-creation," a notion central to Schwartz's reading of *Paradise Lost*. See *Remembering and Repeating*, 2–3.

30 See Torquato Tasso, *Jerusalem Delivered* (1600), trans. Edward Fairfax, Ed. Henry Morley (New York: Colonial Press, 1901). All references to the poem will be taken from this edition and will be indicated by line number in the text.

31 See *Paradise Lost and the Rhetoric of Literary Forms*, 28.

32 See the opening exordium in Ovid, *Metamorphoses*, Book I.

33 "Mother of Aeneas and his race, darling of men and gods, nurturing Venus, who beneath smooth-moving heavenly signs fill with yourself the sea full-laden with ships, the earth that bears the crops, since through you every living thing is conceived and rising up looks on the light of the sun." Loeb translation.

34 In Note 4 on the *Davideis*, Book 1, Cowley calls attention to the significance of his use of "Temple," suggesting that with the inspiration and divine presence of God his *Davideis* will excel all other epic poems in grandeur and longevity: "Though there have been three *Temples* at *Jerusalem*, the first built by *Solomon*, the second by *Zorobabel*, and the third by *Herod* (for it appears by *Josephus* that *Herod* pluckt down the old *Temple* and built a new one) yet I mention only the first and last, which

were very much superior to that of *Zorobabel* in riches and magnificence, though that was forty-six years a building, whereas *Herods* was but eight, and *Solomons* seven; of all three the last was the most stately; and in that, and not *Zorobabels* Temple, was fulfilled the prophesie of *Hagai*, that the glory of the last House should be greater than of the first."

35 See *Note* 4, 267.

36 Milton's multiple invocations find a strong precedent in Dante's *Commedia.* According to Irene Samuel, Dante "renews invocations at various critical moments in his narrative when he consciously changes style, turning to address his readers in his own person as narrator when it suits him, and commenting at need on the stage at which his poem has arrived . . . [Dante's invocations] point to an elaborately conceived architecture. And in this they furnish a structural precedent for Milton." *Dante and Milton*, 55. For a detailed listing of the proems of *Paradise Lost* and the *Commedia*, see Appendix D in Ibid., 292–293.

37 Until the Romantics, the classification of poems according to literary genre was an important means of understanding poetic works. In "A Generic View of Spenser's *Four Hymns*" *SP* (1971): 292–304, Philip Rollinson argues that the intrinsically related concepts of decorum and genre provided Milton and most Renaissance poets, "given as they were to imitation and emulation, with their fundamental standard for measuring artistic achievement." In *Resources of Kind: Genre-Theory in the Renaissance* (Berkeley: University of California Press, 1973), Rosalie L. Colie argues "that literary invention—both 'finding' and 'making'—in the Renaissance was largely generic, and that transfer of ancient values was largely in generic terms" (17). That Milton was aware of and consciously using ancient models in the composition of his great works cannot be questioned; just as he determined to write his *Nativity Ode* in the form of a hymn, so did he choose to address the fount of his poetic inspiration in *Paradise Lost*, first, in the epic invocations and, second, in his personal hymn to Light.

38 See D. A. Russell and N. G. Wilson, eds., *Menander Rhetor* (Oxford: Clarendon Press, 1981), 3.

39 Ibid., 7.

40 Hughes, 669.

41 Hughes, 669–670.

42 Hughes, Note 56, 199.

43 See also Milton's *Nativity Ode* and *Elegia Sexta.*

44 Race, "Aspects of Rhetoric and Form in Greek Hymns," 5–6.

45 See *Argonautica* 3.1–5: "Come now, Erato, stand by my side, and say next how Jason brought back the fleece to Iolcus aided by the love of Medea. For thou sharest the power of Cypris, and by thy love–cares dost charm unwedded maidens; wherefore to thee too is attached a name that tells of love." Loeb translation. This invocation perhaps reveals Vergil's debt to Apollonius Rhodius, who used such additional invocations to demarcate stages in his epic; the passage also reveals the poet's dedication to the

Hellenistic interest in personal love relationships in literature. Erato, then, becomes a metaphor for erotic love.

46 The passage also suggests the influence of neo-Platonic and Zoroastrian thought.

47 Michael Lieb, *Poetics of the Holy: A Reading of Paradise Lost* (Chapel Hill: University of North Carolina Press, 1981), 185.

48 The OED contains no usage of "chief" or "chiefly" with the sense of "instead of."

49 Race, "Aspects of Rhetoric and Form in Greek Hymns," 10.

50 *Openings*, 85.

51 Ibid., 85.

52 See *Milton's Epic Voice*, 28–29.

53 See Hughes, *Note* 9, 345.

54 Horace, *Odes* 3.4: "Descend from heaven . . . Calliope." Loeb translation.

55 See William M. Porter, *Reading the Classics and Paradise Lost* (Lincoln and London: University of Nebraska Press, 1993), 71.

56 Ibid., 71–72.

57 Ibid., 72. Porter continues by noting that "the final line of the prologue, 'For thou art heavenly, she an empty dream' (39), looks back to line 1 to undercut Horace's prayer, 'descende caelo,' by exposing Horace's 'heaven' as nothing more than the 'Olympian hill' above which Milton soars."

58 In the end, however, Porter reminds us that Milton's dismissal of Calliope is part of the "anti-pagan bravado" of *Paradise Lost* (73). Indeed, Porter asserts that Milton's own position toward the classical Muses was "ambivalent" and his "staged rejections of the classics . . . a backhanded recommendation" (74). According to Porter, Milton, like Horace, was as concerned with politics here as he was with theology. Porter writes: "By politicizing his Muse, Horace politicizes himself. He is inspired by the civic Muse, at least in the Roman Odes. By rejecting Calliope, Milton implies his rejection of the restored King Charles II and simultaneously signifies his refusal of the classical poet's role as spokesperson on behalf of the civic community" (74).

59 See Hughes, 346.

60 *Aen.* 7.44–45: "Greater is the story that opens before me; greater is the task I essay." Loeb translation.

61 For an insightful and authoritative treatment of Milton's Muse, and his debt to Hesiod, see Stella P. Revard, "Milton's Muse and the Daughters of Memory." *English Literary Renaissance* 9 (1979): 432–441.

62 Ibid., 438.

63 In *A Preface to Paradise Lost* (Oxford: Oxford University Press, 1942), C. S. Lewis writes that "from its early association with the heroic court there comes into Epic Poetry a quality that survives, with strange transformations and enrichments, into Milton's own time" (16). It is a quality which moderns may find hard to understand, Lewis maintains, but one which would make an unmistakable impression upon us—he speaks here of the

quality of receiving inspiration *from within.* Lewis says that "if we had *seen* the poet . . . seated and honored with wine and spontaneously beginning his tragic lay at the inner prompting of a goddess, we should never forget it" (14–15). I would argue, moreover, that Milton's proems, which initially employ Vergilian-style invocations, move toward the spontaneous type of inspiration found in Homer by the beginning of Book IX. Lewis's vivid recreation of the oral bard comes very close indeed to the notion of inspiration toward which Milton aspires in *Paradise Lost.*

64 See Ariosto, *Orlando Furioso*, trans. Sir John Harrington, Rudolf Gottfried, ed. (Bloomington and London: Indiana University Press, 1963).

65 See Michael Lieb, *Poetics of the Holy: A Reading of Paradise Lost* (Chapel Hill: University of North Carolina Press, 1981), 186.

66 See "Aspects of Rhetoric and Form in Greek Hymns," 14.

67 See Joan Malory Webber, *Milton and His Epic Tradition* (Seattle and London: University of Washington Press, 1979), 8.

68 Gardner, Helen, *A Reading of Paradise Lost* (Oxford: Clarendon Press, 1965), 18–20.

69 "Milton's Muse and the Daughters of Memory," 441.

Bibliography

I. Primary Sources

Apollonius Rhodius. *The Argonautica*. trans. R. C. Seaton. Loeb Classical Library. London: William Heinemann Ltd., 1921.

Ariosto, Ludovico. *Orlando Furioso*. trans. Sir John Herrington. Rudolf Gottfried, ed. Bloomington and London: Indiana University Press, 1963.

Aristotle. *The Poetics*. trans. W. Hamilton Fyfe. Loeb Classical Library. Cambridge: Harvard University Press, 1927.

———. *Art of Rhetoric*. trans. J. H. Freese. Loeb Classical Library. Cambridge: Harvard University Press, 1926.

Blackmore, Sir Richard. *Creation, A Philosophical Poem*. London, 1722.

Boethius. *Tractates, The Consolation of Philosophy*. trans. H. F. Stewart, E. K. Rand, and S. J. Tester. Loeb Classical Library. Cambridge: Harvard University Press, 1973.

Cicero. *De Inventione, De Optimo Genere Oratorum, Topica*. trans. H. M. Hubbell. Loeb Classical Library. Cambridge: Harvard University Press, 1993.

———. *De Natura Deorum, Academica*. trans. H. Rackham. Loeb Classical Library. London: William Heinemann Ltd., 1933.

Cowley, Abraham. *Collected Works of Abraham Cowley*. 6 vols. Thomas O. Calhoun, Laurence Heyworth, and Allan Pritchard, eds. Newark: University of Delaware Press, 1989.

———. *Complete Works in Verse and Prose* (Edinburgh, 1881). Alexander B. Grosart, ed. 2 vols. New York: AMS Press, 1967.

———. *A Poem on the Late Civil War*. London, 1679.

———. *Poems: Miscellanies, The Mistress, Pindarique Odes, Davideis, Verses Written on Several Occasions*. A. R. Waller, ed. Cambridge: Cambridge University Press, 1905.

———. *A Translation of the Sixth Book of Mr. Cowley's Plantarum. Being a Poem upon the late Rebellion, the Happy Restoration of His Sacred Majesty, and the Dutch War Ensuing*. London, 1680.

———. *The Works of Mr. Abraham Cowley*. 2d ed. London: Henry Herringman, 1669.

Crashaw, Richard. *The Poems: English, Latin, and Greek*. L. C. Martin, ed. Oxford: Clarendon Press, 1927.

Daniel, Samuel. *The Civil Wars* (1609). Laurence Michel, ed. New Haven: Yale University Press, 1958.

Dante. *Inferno*. trans. John D. Sinclair. New York: Oxford University Press, 1939; repr. 1961.

Di Cesare, Mario A., ed. *George Herbert and the Seventeenth-Century Religious Poets*. New York and London: W. W. Norton, 1978.

Du Bartas, Guillaume. *Divine Weeks and Workes*. trans. Joshua Sylvester. London, 1621.

Eliot, T. S. *The Complete Poems and Plays, 1909–1950*. San Diego, New York, and London: HBJ, 1980.

———. *The Varieties of Metaphysical Poetry*. Ronald Schuchard, ed. New York: Harcourt Brace and Co., 1994, c1993.

Hesiod. *Theogony and Works and Days*. trans. M. L. West. Oxford and New York: Oxford University Press, 1988.

The Holy Bible. Authorized King James Version. Cambridge: Cambridge University Press, 1878.

Homer. *The Iliad*. trans. Richard Lattimore. Chicago and London: University of Chicago Press, 1951.

Horace. *Odes and Epodes*. trans. C. E. Bennett. Loeb Classical Library. Cambridge: Harvard University Press, 1988.

———. *Satires, Epistles, and Ars Poetica*. trans. H. R. Faircloth. Loeb Classical Library. Cambridge: Harvard University Press, 1978.

Johnson, Samuel. *The Lives of the English Poets*. 3 vols. George Birkbeck Hill, ed. Oxford: Clarendon Press, 1905.

Lucan. *The Civil War*. trans. J. D. Duff. Loeb Classical Library. Cambridge: Harvard University Press, 1928.

Lucretius. *De Rerum Natura*. 2d ed. trans. W. H. D. Rouse and Martin Ferguson Smith. Loeb Classical Library. Cambridge: Harvard University Press, 1982.

Menander. *Menander Rhetor*. D. A. Russell and N. G. Wilson, ed. Oxford: Clarendon Press, 1981.

Milton, John. *Complete Poems and Major Prose*. Merritt Y. Hughes, ed. New York: Macmillan, 1957.

———. *History of Britain*. London, 1670.

———. *Poems*. London: Humphrey Mosley, 1645.

———. *Poems, &c. Upon Several Occasions*. London, 1673.

Monmouth, Geoffrey of. *The History of the Kings of Britain*. trans. Lewis Thorpe. New York: Penguin, 1966.

Ovid. *Fasti*. 2d ed. trans. Sir James George Frazier. Loeb Classical Library. Cambridge: Harvard University Press, 1989.

Pindar. *Pindar*. 2 vols. trans. William H. Race. Loeb Classical Library. Cambridge: Harvard University Press, 1997.

Pope, Alexander. *The Poems of Alexander Pope*. A one-volume edition of the Twickenham text. John Butt, ed. New Haven: Yale University Press, 1963.

Puttenham, George. *The Arte of English Poesie*. London, 1589.

Quintilian. *Institutio Oratoria*. 4 vols. trans. H. E. Butler. Loeb Classical Library. Cambridge: Harvard University Press, 1968.

Scaliger, Julius Caesar. *Poetices Libri Septem* (1561). Stuttgart-Bad Cannstatt, 1964.

Shakespeare, William. *King Henry V*. Andrew Gurr, ed. Cambridge: Cambridge University Press, 1992.

Spenser, Edmund. *The Faerie Queene*. Thomas P. Roche, Jr., ed. New York: Penguin, 1978.

———. *The Yale Edition of the Shorter Poems of Edmund Spenser*. William A. Oram, et al., eds. New Haven and London: Yale University Press, 1989.

Sprat, Thomas. "An Account of the Life of Mr. Abraham Cowley." In *The Works of Abraham Cowley*. 2d ed. London: Henry Herringman, 1669.

Statius. *Silvae, Thebaid, Achilleid*. 2 vols. trans. J. H. Mozley. Loeb Classical Library. London: William Heinemann Ltd., 1928.

Tasso, Torquato. *Discorsi Del Poema Heroico*. Naples, 1594.

———. *Discourses on the Heroic Poem*. trans. Mariella Cavalchini and Irene Samuel. Oxford: Clarendon Press, 1973.

———. *Jerusalem Delivered*. trans. Edward Fairfax. Henry Morley, ed. New York: Colonial Press, 1901.

Theocritus. *The Greek Bucolic Poets*. trans. J. M. Edwards. Loeb Classical Library. Cambridge: Harvard University Press, 1960.

Vergil. *Eclogues, Georgics, Aeneid*. 2 vols. trans. H. R. Faircloth. Loeb Classical Library. Cambridge: Harvard University Press, 1986.

II. Secondary Sources

Ariès, Phillippe. *Western Attitudes Toward Death: From the Middle Ages to the Present*. trans. Patricia M. Ranum. Baltimore: Johns Hopkins University Press, 1974.

Astell, Ann W. *Job, Boethius, and Epic Truth*. Ithaca and London: Cornell University Press, 1994.

Bate, W. Jackson. *The Burden of the Past and English Poetry*. Cambridge: Harvard University Press, 1970.

Beye, Charles Rowan. *Ancient Epic Poetry: Homer, Apollonius, Virgil*. Ithaca: Cornell University Press, 1993.

Blessington, Francis C. *Paradise Lost and the Classical Epic*. London: Routledge and Kegan Paul, 1979.

———. "'That Undisturbed Song of Pure Concent': *Paradise Lost* and the Epic-Hymn." In *Renaissance Genres: Essays on Theory, History, and Interpretation.* Barbara K. Lewalski, ed. Cambridge: Harvard University Press, 1986.

Bloom, Harold. *The Anxiety of Influence: A Theory of Poetry.* New York: Oxford University Press, 1973.

Broadbent, J. B. *Some Graver Subject: An Essay on Paradise Lost.* London: Chatto and Windus, 1960.

Bush, Douglas. *English Literature in the Early Seventeenth Century, 1600–1660.* New York: Oxford University Press, 1945.

Cairns, Francis. *Generic Composition in Greek and Roman Poetry.* Edinburgh: Edinburgh University Press, 1972.

Colie, Rosalie L. *The Resources of Kind: Genre-Theory in the Renaissance.* Berkeley: University of California Press, 1973.

Comparetti, Domenico. *Vergil in the Middle Ages.* trans. E. F. M. Beneke. Hamden, Connecticut: Archon Books, 1908; repr. 1966.

Coolidge, John S. "Great Things and Small: The Vergilian Progression." *Comparative Literature* 17 (1965): 1–23.

Curtius, Ernst Robert. *European Literature and the Latin Middle Ages.* trans. Willard R. Trask. Princeton: Princeton University Press, 1953.

Daiches, David. *God and the Poets.* Oxford: Clarendon Press, 1984.

———. "The Opening of *Paradise Lost.*" *The Living Milton.* Frank Kermode, ed. London: Routledge & Kegan Paul, 1960.

Doody, Margaret Anne. *The Daring Muse: Augustan Poetry Reconsidered.* Cambridge: Cambridge University Press, 1985.

Donker, Marjorie and George M. Muldrow. *Dictionary of Literary-Rhetorical Conventions of the English Renaissance.* Westport: Greenwood Press, 1982.

Dykstal, Timothy. "The Epic Reticence of Abraham Cowley." *SEL: Studies in English Literature, 1500–1900.* 31 (1991 Winter): 95–115.

Ferry, Anne. *Milton's Epic Voice: The Narrator in Paradise Lost*. Chicago: University of Chicago Press, 1963.

Gardner, Helen. *A Reading of Paradise Lost*. Oxford: Clarendon Press, 1965.

Green, Peter. *Alexander of Macedon, 356–323 B. C.: A Historical Biography*. Berkeley: University of California Press, 1991.

Gregory, E. R. *Milton and the Muses*. Tuscaloosa and London: University of Alabama Press, 1989.

Griffin, Dustin. *Regaining Paradise: Milton and the Eighteenth Century*. Cambridge: Cambridge University Press, 1986.

Guillory, John. *Poetic Authority: Spenser, Milton, and Literary History*. New York: Columbia University Press, 1983.

Hainsworth, J. B. *The Idea of Epic*. Berkeley: University of California Press, 1991.

Hammond, N. G. L., and H. H. Scullard, eds. *The Oxford Classical Dictionary*. 2d ed. Oxford: Clarendon Press, 1970.

Hardie, Philip. *The Epic Successors of Virgil: A Study in the Dynamics of a Tradition*. Cambridge: Cambridge University Press, 1993.

Helgerson, Richard. *Forms of Nationhood: The Elizabethan Writing of England*. Chicago and London: University of Chicago Press, 1992.

———. *Self-Crowned Laureates: Spenser, Jonson, Milton and the Literary System*. Berkeley, Los Angeles, and London: University of California Press, 1983.

Highet, Gilbert. *The Classical Tradition: Greek and Roman Influences on Western Literature*. London, Oxford, and New York: Oxford University Press, 1949.

Hill, Christopher. *The Century of Revolution, 1603–1714*. New York: W. W. Norton, 1961.

Hill, John Spencer. *John Milton: Poet, Priest, and Prophet*. London, 1979.

Hinman, Robert B. *Abraham Cowley's World of Order*. Cambridge: Harvard University Press, 1960.

Hunter, William B. *The Descent of Urania: Studies in Milton, 1946–1988*. Lewisburg: Bucknell University Press, 1989.

———., et al., eds. *A Milton Encyclopedia*. 9 vols. Lewisburg: Bucknell University Press, 1978.

———., and Stevie Davies. "Milton's Urania: "The Meaning, Not the Name I Call." In *The Descent of Urania, Studies in Milton, 1946–1988*. William B. Hunter, ed. Lewisburg: Bucknell University Press, 1989.

Johnson, Lee M. "Milton's Epic Style: The Invocation in *Paradise Lost*." In *The Cambridge Companion to Milton*. Dennis Danielson, ed. Cambridge: Cambridge University Press, 1989.

Kay, Dennis. *Melodious Tears: The English Funeral Elegy from Spenser to Milton*. Oxford: Clarendon Press, 1990.

Kerrigan, William. *The Prophetic Milton*. Charlottesville: University Press of Virginia, 1974.

Kirk, G. S. *The Iliad: A Commentary*. Vol. 1. Cambridge: Cambridge University Press, 1985.

Knedlik, Janet Leslie. "High Pastoral Art in *Epitaphium Damonis*." *Milton Studies* XIX. James A. Freeman and Anthony Low, eds. Pittsburgh: University of Pittsburgh Press, 1984.

Leranbaum, Miriam. *Alexander Pope's 'Opus Magnum,' 1729–1744*. Oxford: Clarendon Press, 1977.

Lerner, Laurence. *The Uses of Nostalgia: Studies in Pastoral Poetry*. London: Chatto and Windus, 1972.

Lewalski, Barbara. *Paradise Lost and the Rhetoric of Literary Forms*. Princeton: Princeton University Press, 1985.

Lewis, C. S. *A Preface to Paradise Lost*. London: Oxford University Press, 1942.

Lieb, Michael. *The Dialectics of Creation: Patterns of Birth and Regeneration in Paradise Lost*. University of Massachusetts Press: 1970.

———. *Poetics of the Holy: A Reading of Paradise Lost*. Chapel Hill: University of North Carolina Press, 1981.

Loiseau, Jean. *Abraham Cowley: sa vie, son oevre*. Paris: Henri Didier, 1931.

Lord, George DeForest. *Classical Presences in Seventeenth-Century Poetry*. New Haven and London: Yale University Press, 1987.

Lowenstein, David. *Milton and the Drama of History: Historical Vision, Iconoclasm, and the Literary Imagination*. Cambridge: Cambridge University Press, 1990.

Martindale, Charles. "The Epic of Ideas: Lucan's *De bello civili* and *Paradise Lost*." *Comparative Criticism: A Yearbook* 3 (1981): 133–156.

———. *John Milton and the Transformation of Ancient Epic*. London and Sydney: Croom Helm, 1986.

Martz, Louis L. *Poet of Exile: A Study of Milton's Poetry*. New Haven and London: Yale University Press, 1980.

McLean, Gerald M. *Time's Witness: Historical Representation in English Poetry, 1603–1660*. Madison: University of Wisconsin Press, 1990.

Miner, Earl. *The Restoration Mode from Milton to Dryden*. Princeton: Princeton University Press, 1974.

Murrin, Michael. *History and Warfare in Renaissance Epic*. Chicago and London: University of Chicago Press, 1994.

Myhr, Ivar Lou. "The Evolution and Practice of Milton's Epic Theory." Ph.D. diss., Vanderbilt University, 1940.

Nethercott, Arthur H. *Abraham Cowley: The Muse's Hannibal*. New York: Russell and Russell, 1931; 1967.

Newlyn, Lucy. *Paradise Lost and the Romantic Reader*. Oxford: Oxford University Press, 1993.

Nuttall, A. D. *A New Mimesis: Shakespeare and the Representation of Reality*. London and New York: Methuen, 1983.

———. *Openings: Narrative Beginnings from the Epic to the Novel*. Oxford: Clarendon Press, 1992.

———. *Overheard by God: Fiction and Prayer in Herbert, Milton, Dante and St. John*. London and New York: Methuen, 1980.

Ong, Walter J. *The Presence of the Word.* New Haven: Yale University Press, 1967.

Oram, William A. "The Invocation of Sabrina." *Studies in English Literature* 24 (1984): 121–139.

Parker, William Riley. *Milton: A Biography.* 2 vol. Oxford: Clarendon Press, 1968.

Patterson, Annabel. *Pastoral and Ideology: Virgil to Valéry.* Berkeley and Los Angeles, University of California Press, 1988.

Perkin, M. R. *Abraham Cowley: A Bibliography.* Folkstone, Kent: Dawson, 1977.

Peterson, Robert T. *The Art of Ecstasy: Teresa, Bernini, and Crashaw.* New York: Athenaeum, 1970.

Pigman, G. W. *Grief and English Renaissance Elegy.* Cambridge: Cambridge University Press, 1985.

Porter, William M. *Reading the Classics and Paradise Lost.* Lincoln and London: University of Nebraska Press, 1993.

Quint, David. *Epic and Empire: Politics and Generic Form from Virgil to Milton.* Princeton: Princeton University Press, 1993.

———. *Origin and Originality in Renaissance Literature: Versions of the Source.* New Haven and London: Yale University Press, 1983.

Race, William H. "Aspects of Rhetoric and Form in Greek Hymns." *Greek, Roman, and Byzantine Studies* 23.1 (Spring 1982): 5–14.

———. *Classical Genres and English Poetry.* London: Croom Helm, 1988.

Radzinowicz, Mary Ann. *Milton's Epics and the Book of Psalms.* Princeton: Princeton University Press, 1989.

———. "The Politics of *Paradise Lost.*" In *Politics of Discourse: The Literature and History of Seventeenth-Century England.* Kevin Sharpe and Steven N. Zwincker, eds. Berkeley: University of California Press, 1987.

Rajan, Balachandra. *The Lofty Rhyme.* London: Routledge and Kegan Paul, 1970.

Revard, Stella P. "Milton's Muse and the Daughters of Memory." *English Literary Renaissance* 9 (1979): 432–441.

Rollinson, Philip. "A Generic View of Spenser's *Four Hymns*." *SP* 68 (1971): 292–304.

———. "Milton's Nativity Poem and the Decorum of Genre." In *"Eyes Fast Fix't" Current Perspectives in Milton Methodology. Milton Studies* VII. Albert C. Labriola and Michael Lieb, eds. Pittsburgh: University of Pittsburgh Press, 1975.

Rosenberg, D. M. "Epic Warfare in Cowley and Milton." *Clio: A Journal of Literature, History, and the Philosophy of History*. 22 (Fall 1992): 67–80.

Sacks, Peter M. *The English Elegy: Studies in the Genre from Spenser to Yeats*. Baltimore and London: Johns Hopkins University Press, 1985.

Said, Edward W. *Beginnings: Intention and Method.* New York: Basic Books, 1975.

Samuel, Irene. *Dante and Milton: The Commedia and Paradise Lost.* Ithaca: Cornell University Press, 1966.

Schenck, Celeste Marguerite. *Mourning and Panegyric: The Poetics of Pastoral Poetry*. University Park and London: Pennsylvania State University Press, 1988.

Schindler, Walter. *Voice and Crisis: Invocation in Milton's Poetry*. Hamden, Connecticut: Archon Books, 1984.

Schwartz, Regina. *Remembering and Repeating: On Milton's Theology and Poetics*. Chicago: Chicago University Press, 1988; repr. 1993.

Seznec, Jean. *The Survival of the Pagan Gods: The Mythological Tradition and its Place in Renaissance Humanism and Art*. trans. Barbara F. Sessions. New York: Harper, 1961, c1953.

Shawcross, John T. *John Milton: The Self and the World.* Lexington: University Press of Kentucky, 1993.

Smith, Nigel. *Literature and Revolution in England, 1640–1660*. New Haven and London: Yale University Press, 1994.

Snider, Alvin. *Origin and Authority in Seventeenth-Century England: Bacon, Milton, Butler*. Toronto: University of Toronto Press, 1994.

Steadman, John M. *Milton's Biblical and Classical Imagery*. Pittsburgh: Duquesne University Press, 1984.

Stein, Arnold. *The Art of Presence: The Poet and Paradise Lost*. Berkeley, Los Angeles, and London: University of California Press, 1977.

———. *The House of Death: Messages from the English Renaissance*. Baltimore: Johns Hopkins University Press, 1986.

Summers, Joseph H. *The Muse's Method*. Cambridge: Harvard University Press, 1962.

Taaffe, James G. *Abraham Cowley*. New York: Twayne Publishers, 1972.

Trotter, David. *The Poetry of Abraham Cowley*. Totowa: Rowman and Littlefield, 1979.

Wallerstein, Ruth. *Studies in Seventeenth-Century Poetic*. Madison: University of Wisconsin Press, 1950.

Webber, Joan Malory. *The Eloquent "I": Style and Self in Seventeenth-Century Prose*. Madison: University of Wisconsin Press, 1950.

———. *Milton and His Epic Tradition*. Seattle and London: University of Washington Press, 1979.

Index

RENAISSANCE AND BAROQUE
STUDIES AND TEXTS

This series deals with various aspects of the European Renaissance and Baroque. Studies on the history, literature, philosophy, and the visual arts of these periods are welcome. The series also will consider translations of important works, especially from Latin into English. These translations should, however, include a substantial introduction and notes. Books in the series will include original monographs as well as revised or reconceived dissertations. The series editor is:

Eckhard Bernstein
Department of Modern Languages
and Literatures
College of the Holy Cross
Worcester, MA 01610

To order other books in this series, please contact our Customer Service Department:

800-770-LANG (within the U.S.)
212-647-7706 (outside the U.S.)
212-647-7707 FAX

Or browse online by series at:

www.peterlang.com